ELK GROVE VILLAGE PUBLIC LIBRARY

3 1250 00

SEP 2 3 2004

Discarded By Elk Grove
Village Public Library

P9-BAT-773

ELK GROVE VILLAGE PUBLIC LIBRARY
1001 WELLINGTON AVE.
ELK GROVE VILLAGE, IL 60007
(847) 439-0447

A NEW GENERATION OF ROCK WRITERS RECONSIDERS THE CLASSICS

kill your idols

YA 781.66 KIL
DeRogatis, Jim.
Kill your idols : a new
generation of rock writers

EDITED BY
JIM DeROGATIS
AND
CARMÉL CARRILLO

BARRICADE BOOKS

Fort Lee, New Jersey

Published by Barricade Books Inc.
185 Bridge Plaza North
Suite 308-A
Fort Lee, NJ 07024

www.barricadebooks.com

Copyright © 2004 by Jim DeRogatis and Carmél Carrillo
All Rights Reserved.

No part of this book may be reproduced, stored in a retrieval system, or transmit-
ted in any form, by any means, including mechanical, electronic, photocopying,
recording, or otherwise, without the prior written permission of the publisher,
except by a reviewer who wishes to quote brief passages in connection with a
review written for inclusion in a magazine, newspaper, or broadcast.

Library of Congress Cataloging-in-Publication Data

Kill your idols : a new generation of rock writers reconsiders the classics / edited
    by Jim DeRogatis and Carmél Carrillo.
        p. cm.
    "A collection of thirty-four essays in which each writer addresses an allegedly
    'great' album that he or she despises"--Foreword.
    ISBN 1-56980-276-9 (pbk.)
    1. Rock music--History and criticism. I. DeRogatis, Jim. II. Carrillo, Carmél.

ML3534.K53 2004
781.66--dc22

                                                                2004047637

First Printing
Manufactured in Canada

CONTENTS

Contents

Contents

FOREWORD
Canon? We Don't Need No Steenkin' Canon!

By Jim DeRogatis

Twenty-five years ago, Greil Marcus, the self-appointed Dean of the Rock-Critic Academy (West Coast), signed off on the editor's note that opened the first edition of *Stranded: Rock and Roll for a Desert Island*, originally published by Alfred A. Knopf. That anthology rounded up twenty members of the pioneering first generation of rock critics—the folks having all of that fun in *Almost Famous*—and each weighed in with an essay praising the one album they'd choose for company if marooned on a desert island.

Despite that unforgivably goofy premise, many of these essays—Nick Tosches on the career of the Rolling Stones, Lester Bangs on Van Morrison's *Astral Weeks*, Ellen Willis on *The Velvet Underground*, Dave Marsh on *Onan's Greatest Hits* (an invented compilation of great rock songs about masturbation)—remain essential reading for anyone interested in good writing about great rock 'n' roll. Some of the others are equally unforgettable, but for different reasons; these include such classics as John Rockwell championing Linda Ronstadt's *Living in the U.S.A.* and Grace Lichtenstein cheering for the Eagles' *Desperado*.

Stranded was reprinted by the fine folks at Da Capo Press in 1996, and in the introduction to that edition, Robert Christgau, the self-appointed Dean of the Rock-Critic Academy (East Coast), expressed his hope that a new generation of rock writers—the one that came of age in the late '80s and early '90s, and which has now largely replaced

1

the pioneers of the '60s and '70s in the paying gigs—will produce a *Stranded* of its own.

This is not that book.

In the words of the Velvet Underground's "Sweet Jane," these are different times, and the central notion of *Stranded* seems cornier than ever in an era when a peculiarly narrow vision of rock history is enshrined and hermetically sealed in a pyramid-shaped Hall of Fame on the banks of Lake Erie, following an annual five-hundred-dollars-a-plate, tuxedo-clad induction ceremony at New York's Waldorf-Astoria. The time is indeed ripe for an anthology that displays the aesthetics and voices of some of the best new music writers, but this is a group that is more diverse, cynical, sarcastic, curious, and irreverent than the one that preceded it, and any anthology of its work should capture its contentious alternative spirit, as well as its contrarian vision of rock history.

Welcome to *Kill Your Idols: A New Generation of Rock Writers Reconsiders the Classics,* a collection of thirty-four essays in which each writer addresses an allegedly "great" album that he or she despises. If we want to be high-minded about it, we can call it a spirited assault on a pantheon that has been foisted upon us, or a defiant rejection of the hegemonic view of rock history espoused by the critics who preceded us. If we want to use the vernacular, let's just say it's a loud, angry, but hopefully amusing "Fuck you."

I first conceived of this collection in 1995, during my mercifully brief tenure at *Rolling Stone*—which isn't surprising, given that magazine's obsessive devotion to charting a rock 'n' roll canon. (More about that silly business in a moment.) In the years that followed, I pitched this book to several publishers, all of whom responded with a look of shocked indignation and some variation of the authoritative dismissal that, "No one wants to read a book of all negative reviews." Jeff Nordstedt was the first editor who enthusiastically responded in the affirmative—which, again, isn't surprising, given that he works for Barricade Books, a house founded by the octogenarian publishing legend and First Amendment absolutist, Lyle Stuart, a punk-rock soul if ever I encountered one.

Jeff agreed with me that it is often more fun to read a really bad review than it is to read a really good one. A savage but well-considered critique of a piece of art that you love gets your blood flowing. The point isn't necessarily to change your thinking about a work that you adore, but to prod you to consider anew why you admire that work. As such, the pan can be much more stimulating (and useful) than the paean. The most illuminating reviews I've read of *On the Road*—a book I consider a sacred text—are not the many fawning praises, but the brutal trashings (Kerouac wasn't writing, he was typing), because they make me reexamine what I love about the novel. Of course, it can be a jolly good time indulging in the public flogging of a sacred cow, and why should rock criticism be any more polite or restrained than the nightly debate at the corner sports bar or the spirited back-and-forth of politics? Why should anything be accepted as dogma in an art form (the devil's music, no less!) that, at its best, is about questioning *everything*?

A lot of people don't think this way; a lot of people don't like to think, period. Baby Boomers, the largest generation in American history, some seventy-six million strong, are particularly prone to safeguarding works whose value they adopted as articles of faith in their youth, even though said youth is now several decades behind them.

Nostalgia is still a relatively new concept, and many scholars view it as a by-product of fears about industrialization and modernization. With Greek roots meaning "to return home" ("*nostos*") and "pain" ("*algos*"), the word was coined in 1688 in a medical treatise by a nineteen-year-old Swiss physician looking to describe a severe and sometimes lethal form of homesickness as he studied soldiers suffering from a mysterious malaise while serving far away from their mountain homes. In the Victorian era, the word came to signify a spiritual sickness rather than a genuine illness; in 1874, the poet Arthur O'Shaughnessy called nostalgia "the disease of the soul." More recently, scholar Susan Stewart dubbed it "a social disease" and defined it as "the repetition that mourns the inauthenticity of all repetition." Parse the academic-speak, and Stewart is basically saying that it's foolish to live in the past—especially a glorified, rose-tinted past that is largely a fictitious recreation. Or, as political pundit Art Buchwald quipped, "Nothing is more responsible for the good old days than a bad memory."

It is particularly sad to see people who are nostalgic for a past they never even experienced. As I write this, the downstairs neighbor in my Chicago three-flat—one of the seventy-two million members of Generation Y, the second-largest generation in American history, and the Baby Boomers' snot-nosed progeny—is once again playing *The Freewheelin' Bob Dylan* at ear-shattering, floor-rattling volume. He does this two or three times a day, every day, and has ever since I moved in six months ago. Granted, it could be much, much worse— he could be blasting Dave Matthews or the Grateful Dead—but while I once loved this album, I am now at the point where I never want to hear it again. When I asked this fellow about his fascination with this disc, he responded with the question, "What *else* is there to listen to?" He can't fathom the idea that there's ever been another album worthy of his time, or that there's been any worthwhile music made at all since 1962, which is approximately two decades before he was born. He's an extreme case, and I pity him: He's in his early twenties, and his life is already over. In fact, it never even began, at least not in terms of experiencing great art made in the moment—his moment, instead of his parents'.

Now, about that canon business: In the early '90s, the hallowed halls of the academy were rudely awakened from their soporific slumbers by the sound and fury of the so-called "culture wars." Here was a rabid backlash against what conservatives perceived as the insidious plague of "political correctness" on our college campuses, spread by the voices of diversity who'd been trying since the mid-'60s to broaden the literary curriculum away from "dead white European males"—you know, guys like Shakespeare, Milton, Dryden, and Pope—in order to include folks who weren't … well, quite so dead, white, European, or male.

The heavy hitters of literary conservatism and canon defense were, ironically, two unrelated men named Bloom. Allan Bloom, the late sociology professor and philosopher, published *The Closing of the American Mind* in 1987, and Harold Bloom, a professor of humanities at Yale, gave us *The Western Canon* in 1994. Here were the cornerstones of the defensive wall erected in the war against P.C., and the battle still rages today. Do a quick Web search on key words such as "Western" and "canon," and you'll find not only reams of blatherous articles, pro and con, but countless syllabi for courses with titles such as "Canon Revision: History, Theory, Practice" that attempt to answer pressing queries like, "Why does society need a canon?" and "Why does the just-in-time society of 'postindustrialism' need revisionary canons?"

Good questions, but I would like to think that the dynamic, impolite, and ever-evolving art form of rock 'n' roll has better things to be concerned about. Hell, Allan Bloom said as much in *The Closing of the American Mind*. "Rock music has one appeal, a barbaric appeal, to sexual desire not love, but sexual desire undeveloped and untutored," he wrote. "It acknowledges the first emanations of children's emerging sensuality and addresses them seriously, eliciting them and legitimizing them." He meant that as a slam—rock is too juvenile to ever be considered as "Art" by Bloom's kind—but I take it as a compliment. At its best, rock music is focused on living in the present, celebrating the wonder in the intense discovery of the world around you, just as a child does. It would seem by definition to be opposed to the very notion of fixing in stone a canon. Yet the rock media is obsessed with doing exactly that.

In recent years, we've seen countless unimaginative efforts to enumerate and rank rock's icons in just about every mainstream rock rag, as well as on radio, MTV, VH1, and in that ludicrous glass pyramid in Cleveland that I mentioned earlier. But the institution most dedicated to charting the sounds we need to venerate is the granddaddy of 'em all, *Rolling Stone*. I'll confess that in the midst of editing this collection, I had a brief crisis of conscience when I wondered if this book was too much of a childish exercise—the rock-critic equivalent of the bratty kid wiping his snot on the blackboard in feeble protestation of the injustices of third-grade life—but that very day, *Rolling Stone* No. 937 arrived, a "Special Collectors Issue" all-knowingly titled "The 500 Greatest Albums of All Time," and *Kill Your Idols* once again seemed not only valid, but absolutely necessary.

Set aside for a moment consideration of whether the album as we know it—a collection of songs recorded at a particular point in time and arranged in a particular order in the attempt to capture an elusive moment, like snapshots in a photo album—is still a valid concept in the age of downloading, when the fan has as much power to define the listening experience as the artist, if not more. Anachronism or no, I still love the album as a measure of artistic value, and so do all of the contributors to this book. But even if we play by *Rolling Stone*'s old-fashioned rules, there are still serious problems with this business of dictating "the best albums of all time."

For one thing, there's the issue of consistency. *Rolling Stone* now tells us that the ten best albums ever are, in order: *Sgt. Pepper's Lonely Hearts Club Band* (which isn't even the best Beatles album!), *Pet Sounds, Revolver, Highway 61 Revisited, Rubber Soul, What's Going On, Exile on Main St., London Calling, Blonde on Blonde,* and *The Beatles* (a.k.a. "The White Album"). But back in the summer of 1987, the mag's twentieth anniversary issue was dedicated to listing "The 100 Best Albums of the Last Twenty Years." At that point, rabid Beatlemaniac Jann Wenner and his sycophantic underlings announced that the top ten albums were, once again in order: *Sgt. Pepper's Lonely Hearts Club Band, Never Mind the Bollocks ... Here's the Sex Pistols, Exile on Main St., Plastic Ono Band, Are You Experienced?, The Rise and Fall of Ziggy Stardust and the Spiders from Mars, Astral Weeks, Born to Run,* "The White Album," and *What's Going On.*

Given that the top picks in both cases span the same time frame, what happened to Bowie, the Boss, Van Morrison, and the Plastic Ono Band that made them fall out of grace in the intervening years? Did those albums somehow grow "less great," while the additional Beatles efforts and *Pet Sounds* got better? And how could *Rolling Stone*

possibly be *more* conservative fifteen years later, knocking the Sex Pistols all the way down to No. 41, and remaining as blissfully dismissive of hip-hop as it was before the genre started its decade-plus run as the dominant sound in popular music? (Rap's first appearance on the new list is at No. 48, with *It Takes a Nation of Millions to Hold Us Back*.)

What we're really seeing here is a panicked, turtle-like, Blooms-style defense by a still absurdly Boomer-centric publication against the notion not of P.C., but of "critical correctness"—a more expansive, postmodern view of the history of "rock" (and I've used that term all-inclusively throughout this introduction) which dares to acknowledge that, say, in the eyes of legions of today's punks, the Ramones are infinitely more important than the Rolling Stones; that to countless hip-hoppers, Run-DMC is more revered than Jimi Hendrix, and that the entire electronic music and dance underground views Kraftwerk as boundlessly more influential than the Beatles.

Primarily members of Generations X and Y (with a few strays who are, technically speaking, demographic Baby Boomers, though they identify philosophically as X'ers), the men and women who've written for this book resent the notion that they missed out on everything just because they weren't at Woodstock. They've seen the movie and it sucked, and many of them have been to raves in warehouses and muddy fields that had much cooler soundtracks, not to mention better drugs. How much of the "classic rock" of the last fifty years is defended by the lame notion that, "You really had to be there"? Shouldn't a great album speak to you even if you weren't?

Postmodernism has taught us that history is fluid, and it can be considered from many different perspectives. An event like Custer's Last Stand can be examined from the points of view of the conscripts, the officers, the headstrong general, the Native-American warriors, the chiefs, the wives, the white politicians, the settlers, or the forces of capitalist expansion, among many others. In the rock world, the reason that alternative views are so frightening to conservative critics is that they require these cultural arbiters to keep listening and grant that maybe, just maybe, the best sounds ever are still to come, instead of being forever embalmed in the amber of the past. The only valid response that any true rock fan should have to some pompous, omniscient windbag standing at the front of the class prattling on about "the true masterpieces" and "the good old days" is to make the loudest farting noise possible.

When I asked my fellow flatulent troublemakers to include a list of their top ten albums along with their biographies—a task that, iconoclasts one and all, many groused about, and a few never did fulfill—I wasn't trying to illustrate some revisionist canon that would "correct" all of these problems. In addition to giving the reader some insight into what albums each of these critics value (after you've just read about one they believe is offensive, overrated, over-hyped, or just plain lousy), I fully expected that many of them would laud one or more discs that their peers have just demolished. They didn't let me down: It happened no less than thirty-six times. This is to say that many of these writers will be as angry with each other as you might be with them, if they just pissed on your particular tree. For the record, I myself think that no fewer than sixteen of them are just dead wrong. And all of this is as it should be.

We ought to just abandon the whole stupid idea of having a single rock canon, and instead stand ready to question and re-examine our values and assumptions at any time, while communicating with people who share our passions, thereby coming to a greater understanding not only of differing viewpoints, but of ourselves. Most of all, we should revel in whatever joyful noises each and every one of us decides is "the greatest" for ourselves in the here and now.

In closing, I have to say that I am a fan of all of the writers I approached to contribute an original essay to this book, and I'm happy to note that all but a few of them—folks who were otherwise occupied with lame obligations such as crushing deadlines or the recent birth of a child—happily obliged. In fact, they were all chomping at the bit to have at one reputed classic or another, generally harboring a long list of pent-up grievances that have been mounting since their teens. Given that they were, essentially, working for free (there is a down side to Lyle Stuart being a First Amendment absolutist), these were labors of love—which may seem like a strange thing to say, because they were writing about albums that they hate. But there was a sadomasochistic element to this entire endeavor: In agreeing to deconstruct a work they intensely disliked, by necessity, they had to spend much more time with that album than they were able to spend with the countless others that they love. I'm veering off into some very murky waters of the psyche here, but I'll venture that deep down, at some level, some part of you must admire an album—or at least the genre it comes from and what it is *supposed* to represent—in order to adequately explain why you find it thoroughly repugnant.

Kill your idols, indeed.

In addition to the writers, I have to thank Jeff Nordstedt, Lyle Stuart, Carole Stuart, Jennifer Itskevich, and everyone at Barricade Books; my bandmate, Chris Martiniano, for his outstanding cover design; my intern, Robin Linn; my agents, Chris Calhoun and Kassie Evashevski; my beautiful and brilliant co-editor, co-conspirator, collaborator, and wife, Carmél Carrillo; and most of all, you, the reader. I hope that you enjoy reading this book as much as we enjoyed putting it together—or at the very least, that you love hating it.

THE BEATLES
Sgt. Pepper's Lonely Hearts Club Band
Capitol, 1967
By Jim DeRogatis

For nigh on thirty-six years now (give or take, depending on when my capacity to understand language kicked in), I have been hearing about that crazy-quilt mosaic of social, political, and cultural upheaval called *The Sixties*, which, as we all know from history class, our parents, and VH1, was the time of Beatlemania, Bob Dylan, long hair, LSD, Tim Leary, Ken Kesey, Jimi Hendrix, Janis Joplin, Andy Warhol, Ho Chi Minh, burning bras, free love, riots in the streets, hell no (we won't go), tune in, turn on, freak out, and by the time we got to Woodstock, we were half a million strong.

Sounds like a hell of a party, but I wasn't there, and what's more, I refuse to feel sorry about missing it, because I have here the album generally considered the Numero Uno soundtrack of the time—yep, *Sgt. Pepper's Lonely Hearts Club Band*—and you know what? It sucks dogs royally.

We all know that music is a mighty strong signifier. In fact, there's nothing better than the sound of a particular song to send you rushing back in time to the point when you first heard it. Scientists say it's rivaled only by our olfactory capacities. But with all due respect to Proust's madelines, while the smell of a certain cologne or the whiff of mom's fresh-baked bread (yeah, right, whose mom still bakes?) can be sweet nostalgia indeed, other odors are best left unrecalled, including a high-school gym locker, a baby's diaper, and Michael Arcell after two weeks at summer camp without a shower.

On the other hand, whenever I hear "Walking On the Moon" by the Police, in the dentist's office or on Lite-FM, I'm transported back to freshman year at Hudson Catholic Regional High School for Boys in Jersey City, New Jersey, and I vividly relive my very first Friday-night make-out session with Eileen Cribbins (short blonde hair, cute librarian specs, braces) in her friend's parents' basement rec room. I viscerally recall walking her home afterward—a true gentleman, I was, despite my adolescent frustrations—with a light snow starting to fall, and I can feel it crunching underfoot, me with rubbery legs, and our two hands awkwardly entwined. When I got home, I turned on WNEW-FM, and there was that former English teacher affecting a Jamaican accent while crooning, "Walking back from your house / Walking on the moon," and I'll be damned if that wasn't *exactly* how I'd felt on that stroll home.

At the time, it seemed like the most profound sentiment I'd ever heard expressed in a pop song. Now, of course, I recognize that the tune—like much of "Stink's" output—is pure Velveeta, but the point is, *the music takes me back*, and it's a swell place to revisit, indeed.

There is clearly something similar going on with *Sgt. Pepper's Lonely Hearts Club Band*, a bloated and baroque failed concept album that takes a generation of Baby Boomers back to the best shindig of their lives, a time when they were young and free and full of possibilities, yadda yadda yadda, *you just had to be there*. But all of that has little or nothing to do with the actual sounds on the album.

When the album was released, there was very little "serious" rock criticism in the mainstream press; it's illuminating to note that the most famous examination of *Sgt. Pepper's Lonely Hearts Club Band* in its day was a brutal evisceration by pioneering rock-crit Richard Goldstein in *The New York Times*. ("Like an over-attended child, this album is spoiled ... It reeks of horns and harps, harmonica quartets, assorted animal noises, and a forty-one-piece orchestra.") But the many, many chin-strokers who weighed in on it during the years that followed cheerfully played right into the grand con.

Writing in *The Rolling Stone Illustrated History of Rock & Roll*,

Langdon Winner declared that, "The closest Western Civilization has come to unity since the Congress of Vienna in 1815 was the week *Sgt. Pepper's* was released" (and I've always wondered how on earth he could claim to know that). In *A Day in the Life,* rabid Beatleologist Mark Hertsgaard contends that, "with its seemingly effortless articulation of the Flower Power ethos of freedom, fun, and creative possibility," *Sgt. Pepper's* is virtually the '60s incarnate. Adds Ian MacDonald in his otherwise clear-eyed *Revolution in the Head*: "Anyone unlucky enough not to have been aged between fourteen and thirty during 1966-67 will never know the excitement of those years in popular culture."

I was only three years old in 1967, so I can't say for sure, but I'll grant these boys the fact that *everybody* was listening to this album. Big deal, so what: *What were they hearing?* The boilerplate analysis holds that it is a great technical accomplishment and a testament to the power of multi-track recording, as well as the first flowering of rock 'n' roll as Art, and a work that perfectly captures the spirit of a generation throwing open the doors of perception and breaking on through to the other side in a frenzy of exploration—psychedelic, political, sexual, you name it.

Well, that first bit is easily dismissed. The Beach Boys had already pulled off a more impressive technical feat in the studio in 1966 with *Pet Sounds,* and the Beatles themselves had shown their mastery of the tape machine (with a little help from their friend, George Martin) that same year with *Revolver,* as well as singles such as "Rain" and "Paperback Writer." Released the month the group ended its last tour and retired from the stage, *Revolver* had already called attention to the fact that it was a studio creation with tastefully employed orchestral arrangements on "Eleanor Rigby" and "For No One," Eastern experimentation on George Harrison's "Love You To," and creative psychedelic effects on the rollicking "She Said She Said." And of course it all ended with the mind-bending tour de force, "Tomorrow Never Knows," in which John Lennon used all the tricks the gang at Abbey Road could think of (compressed drums, backwards guitars, voices fed through a rotating Leslie speaker, double-speed guitar, tape loops, and percussive sounds played on wine glasses among them) to recreate his personal journey toward the white light.

So much for innovation, and who besides muso gearheads really cares about that techie stuff, anyway? It's the other two claims—the rock-as-Art and the spirit-of-a-generation raps—that still resonate in the popular imagination, and those are what keep *Sgt. Pepper's Lonely Hearts Club Band* in the spotlight going on four decades later. To get to the bottom of these, we need to go to the audio tape. So let's listen, shall we?

The conceptual conceit is laid out on Pop artist Peter Blake's famous funereal cover and in the album's opening track. The Beatles are portraying an old-time Salvation Army-type band of the sort that their grandparents heard in the gazebos on Sunday afternoons. (No doors to the future opening here.) It's been said that the Fabs adopted the role of a different group to free themselves from the expectations of making "Beatles music," but why they chose such a sentimental, old-fashioned, out-of-date ensemble remains a mystery. It certainly wasn't to parody Sgt. Pepper's combo, because the title track is a warm and loving homage in the form of a plodding rocker completely lacking in subtlety. The crowd greets the group enthusiastically—they can be heard cheering and laughing at what's presumably some onstage shtick during the trumpet solo—and the emcee (Paul McCartney) and bandleader (Lennon) kiss the listeners' asses, fawning over them and telling them they're that "such a lovely audience" before introducing the singer, the one and only Billy Shears.

The opening theme seamlessly segues into "With a Little Help from My Friends" as the album takes the unique approach of getting the now-obligatory Ringo Starr showcase out of the way early on. Previous efforts such as the cover of "Matchbox" or the children's sing-along "Yellow Submarine" at least allowed Ringo to display a certain winsome charm, but "With a Little Help from My Friends" is something of a slap in the face to the guy, implying that he certainly can't get by on his own—not with *his* looks, *his* drumming chops, or,

Lord knows, *his* singing voice—so he needs the assistance of his much cooler pals to accomplish anything. He sounds rather pathetic as he plays the Everyman pleading for someone to love, and his bandmates are condescending as they add their two cents via the backing vocals. (*They* have no problem getting laid, *ha ha ha*.) All in all, it's a judgmental little tune that makes fun of the fool on the hill rather than celebrating him, which is rather un-peace-and-love-like. On top of all that, the *dah-dah-dah, dah-dah-dah* melody and mid-tempo groove are banal and boring.

A harpsichord—the very symbol of the baroque and Victorian!—ushers in "Lucy in the Sky with Diamonds," a catchy but slight piece of psychedelic escapism. Lennon had already done this sort of thing better three months earlier on the single, "Strawberry Fields Forever," in which he painted a stylized picture of returning to a scene from his youth. (McCartney offered *his* variation on this theme with "Penny Lane," which is also better than most of the tunes on *Sgt. Pepper's Lonely Hearts Club Band*, and Martin has said that the biggest mistake of his career was keeping those two tracks off the album.) Though Lennon contended that it was purely coincidence that the initials of the song spell "L-S-D," you *know* that's what inspired his vision of tangerine trees and marmalade skies, and he drives the point home with the terrible pun about flowers that "grow so in-*cred*-i-bly high." It must not have been a great trip—it was certainly nowhere near the violent spiritual rebirth described in "Tomorrow Never Knows"—because the music is definitely earthbound, tripping on the clunky three-beat transitions between verses and choruses, and mired in the weird, metallic, springy sound of the mix, which suggests that somebody was overdosing not on hallucinogens, but on Abbey Road's plate reverb.

Now it's McCartney's turn for a more-or-less solo bow. Mr. Optimism declares that he's perfectly content with his life—he must have been the only person in the '60s who was—and while he used to be mad at his school (wotta rebel!), it's "Getting Better" all the time because, oh boy, he's in *l-u-v.* Hold on, though, there's something creepy going on just below the placid facade of romantic middle-class contentment: Lennon's backing vocals are singing, "It can't get no worse," and now McCartney is telling us he used to be mean to his woman, he beat her and kept her apart from the things that she loved. This guy's a freaking misogynist scumbag, and I don't buy for a minute that he's "changing his scene." Like Travis Bickle, he's just waiting for an excuse to explode. That insistent piano is like a nervous facial tick, the waltz-like tempo is barely keeping him restrained, and it's time to run and lock the door when the tune dissolves into a psychedelic breakdown with droning sitar and echoed tabla. Hey, the Hell's Angels took LSD, but they didn't automatically start loving everyone. Remember Altamont?

Scary shit, and perhaps I'd best stop free-associating. What a coincidence: Paul suggests the same thing on the very next tune. "I'm fixing a hole where the rain gets in / And stops my mind from wandering / Where it will go." Wait a minute: I thought free-ranging intellectual exploration was the psychedelic ideal? Why is Macca trying to plug the leak and shut it down? The tune—*another* mid-tempo, lame-ass ballad with heavy overtones of Vaudeville and the music hall—gives us the answer: "It really doesn't matter / If I'm wrong I'm right / Where I belong I'm right." This is the very definition of Baby Boomer myopia: "I'm the center of the universe, bub. *I'm* in charge now, and even when I'm *wrong,* I'm *right!*" Hey, I worked for the über-Boomer himself, Jann Wenner, the spoiled rich kid who started *Rolling Stone* magazine the same year *Sgt. Pepper's Lonely Hearts Club Band* was released, and I heard him sing that tune *a lot.*

Lest the Beatles be accused of showing too much spine, the next number bears a conciliatory gesture to their parents' generation in the form of the saccharine, strings-drenched melodrama, "She's Leaving Home." It's an interminable step-by-step account of a chick leaving the nest in search of—what great '60s Holy Grail? Political and social justice? Sexual equality? Spiritual enlightenment?—nope, it's "fun, the one thing that money can't buy." Oh, well, at least she's finally setting out on her own. But get this: The Beatles ally themselves with the girl's folks, handing them a tissue, consoling them, and patting them on the back as they wring their hands and wonder what they did to drive her away. Some rock 'n' roll spirit there, guys! The Rolling Stones gave us the impression that they'd spit in mom and dad's faces to trumpet their little girl's deflowering. Now *that's* rock 'n' roll!

As Beat survivor-turned-hippie guru Allen Ginsberg noted, the Beatles were interested in closing the generation gap, not exploiting it for purposes of spurring on the Cultural Revolution. At least that's the net effect of *Sgt. Pepper's Lonely Hearts Club Band*, where Lennon is pretty much curled up into himself instead of raging at the world (my favorite of his several modes), and his bandmates are all present with their worst traits at the forefront. Ringo is maudlin and self-pitying, McCartney is bourgeois and nostalgic, Harrison is hippie-dippy. You could argue that John is sneering at the circus that the Beatles have become in "Being For the Benefit of Mr. Kite!," the song that ends side one of the old vinyl LP, and that would be sort of admirable. But I think he's really just coasting, offering us more easy nostalgia—the lyrics are lifted directly from an old poster that he found in a café—set against a cheesy fairground melody and an elaborate but ultimately hollow production that takes the theme way too literally, injecting spliced-and-diced tape loops of circus calliopes.

Yawn, and yawn again for the opener on side two, Harrison's Indian trifle, "Within You Without You," which you probably can't recall, even though you've heard it a million times. This is with good reason. It has no melody—no rhythm, either—and the lyrics are stupid stoner babble: "When you've seen beyond yourself then you may find peace of mind is waiting there." Wake me when ya figure it all out, George.

Next, McCartney gives another big hug to grandma and grandpa—what a *good* boy he is, and clean, too!—with "When I'm Sixty-Four," doing a little of the ol' soft-shoe in the process. If we wanted this mock-ragtime crap, we'd have played the New Vaudeville Band. Picturing himself as a pensioner, he asks his hip young lover if she'll stick by his side when he starts to break down and reach for the

Depends and Viagra. We can only hope she comes to her senses and runs the other way, because in addition to the old coot being a drooling mess, he's one of those doddering geezers who insists on living in the past ("Let me tell you, in *my* day, sonny, I could be handy mending a fuse!"), and he was almost certainly as big a bore at twenty-four as he is at sixty-four. Why would any hot babe want to waste her waning years on a lifeless old gimp like this? Unless it's an Anna Nicole Smith–J. Howard Marshall affair.

Similarly, it's hard to imagine a less cool topic for a rock song in the '60s or at any other time than professing your love for a cop. McCartney was no Ice-T or N.W.A, though, and he does exactly that in "Lovely Rita." This song finally rocks a bit, but it's dragged down by the cheesy piano and mundane lyrics—unless of course I'm missing the homoerotic subtext. The song's protagonist is attracted to traffic warden Rita because, in the cap and with the bag across her shoulder, she looks "a little like a military *man*." Then they go on a date and Rita pays. *Hmmm.* Too bad her sisters are home to prevent young Paul from getting handcuffed to the bed and finding out *Crying Game*-style what sorta six-shooter Rita is really packing.

Meanwhile, am I the only one, or have you also lost the narrative thread in this alleged concept album? Actually, the Beatles got tired of that idea back with Billy Shears, and Ringo has admitted that the attempt to tell a coherent story with *Sgt. Pepper's Lonely Hearts Club Band* "went out the window" early on. Lennon said his own songs "had absolutely nothing to do with the idea of Sgt. Pepper and his band, but it works 'cause we *said* it worked." When I'm *wrong*, I'm *right*!

Continuing to plow through side two, I've always heard "Good Morning, Good Morning" as Lennon's inferior sequel to McCartney's exuberant "Good Day Sunshine" from *Revolver*. Harrison's lead guitar is a welcome burst of energy, but those damn horns ruin the tune, the barnyard animal sound effects are ripped off from *Pet Sounds*, and there's more annoying nostalgia in the lyrics: "Then you decide to take a walk by the old school." These guys simply refuse to live in the present.

Next thing you know, they're rushing to put a lid on things, and we're into a reprise of the title track—a more rocking version this time, maybe so you'll wake up, get your butt out of the chair, and go home. As fawning and obsequious at the end of the show as they were at the beginning, the members of Sgt. Pepper's Lonely Hearts Club Band thank us once again and press a business card into our palm, making sure the transaction goes down swiftly so we don't linger to complain or ask for our money back. If you're happy, they're available for bar mitzvahs and weddings.

But wait, it's not over just yet: In blithe disregard for the concept—the show being over and Sgt. Pepper's boys cleaning the spit from their horns before going home to slurp their porridge—the Beatles tack on another tune. Surprise! It's the album's finest moment.

The sequencing of "A Day in the Life" mirrors the placement of "Tomorrow Never Knows" at the end of *Revolver,* and it suggests that Lennon and McCartney knew that the song was head and shoulders above the rest of the lot here. I say Lennon *and* McCartney, because "A Day in the Life" is a genuine collaboration, which was rare by this point, if the two ever really worked together at all. Here, Martin grafts half a Lennon song onto half a McCartney song, then ties it all up and caps the album off with that big, impressive orchestral spiral and the slamming piano chord from hell that makes its point with all the subtlety of a nuclear detonation. The song is an effective evocation of an unexpected trip from the workaday to the cosmos, but holocaust ending or no, it's no "Tomorrow Never Knows," and it's not enough to make up for the rest of the album.

The Beatles have just given us thirty-nine minutes and fifty-two seconds of rather unremarkable, uninspired music with a central theme that's conservative, reactionary, and retrogressive. *To wit:* Embrace the past (it wasn't so bad) and celebrate the values of your parents and grandparents. Contrast this with some of the truly great albums of the same period, works that offer a glimpse of a brave new world, and which still sound fresh and inviting today: *The Psychedelic*

Sounds of the Thirteenth Floor Elevators, *The Velvet Underground and Nico*, *The Piper at the Gates of Dawn* by Pink Floyd, *Are You Experienced?* by Jimi Hendrix, *Pet Sounds* by the Beach Boys, *Fifth Dimension* by the Byrds, and *Forever Changes* by Love are all stronger, less contrived, more inventive, and more moving albums than *Sgt. Pepper's Lonely Hearts Club Band*. They all rock harder, too. And to say that they don't bring back the period the same way as the Beatles' alleged masterpiece is irrelevant.

You don't have to be a veteran who fought at Guernica to be affected by Picasso's painting. You don't need to know that the women in Shakespeare's plays were guys in drag in order to dig the beauty of his words. And being aware that Ricky and Lucy had marital problems in real life, or that Pee-Wee Herman whacked off at dirty movies, or that the gals on *Baywatch* are pneumatically inflated bottle blondes doesn't add to or detract from the joys of these TV farces. Great art stands on its own even if it's removed from the specific context of when and how it was made.

What's more, it matters not at all how many other artists are influenced by it when you're judging the thing itself. It's equally as valid to trace some of the worst, most indulgent music in rock history back to *Sgt. Pepper's Lonely Hearts Club Band*—it gave us the Electric Light Orchestra, fer chrissakes!—as it is to credit it with forever changing the way that rock albums were recorded. What matters in the here and now is what you hear when you press "play." When I listen to this album, I hear a mostly boring set of songs in love with the past and saying very little about the present or the future—music that is as much of an anachronism today as those marching band outfits were when the Beatles put them on back in 1967.

The good old days? Good riddance.

THE BEACH BOYS
Pet Sounds
Capitol, 1966
By Jeff Nordstedt

Though it pains me to engage in this sort of idol worship, what follows is a quick history of the Beach Boys and, more specifically, *Pet Sounds*. Be warned, the following statements do not necessarily reflect the attitude or opinions of the author. However, like Marley's death in *A Christmas Carol*, these are "facts" that must be understood if any of what I have to say is to make sense. I will keep it short and (relatively) painless.

Brian Wilson was *the* musical genius of his time. In the mid-'60s—a period that many people I've never met seem to agree was "the most creative in rock's history"—a war broke out between the ruling rock dinosaurs, the Beatles and the Beach Boys, though in truth, it wasn't really between the Beatles and the Beach Boys at all; certainly Mike Love had no real beef with Ringo Starr. This now-legendary "war" was between the two groups' auteurs, John Lennon and Paul McCartney versus Brian Wilson, with peripheral players such as Beatles producer George Martin and Wilson lyricist Tony Asher in the infantry. The real revolution in all of this came when the Beatles released a great album called *Rubber Soul*. The record company's marketing plan did not include releasing a single from this LP full of hits, and rock historians argue that this was the moment when the bar was raised for rock artists. No longer was their medium the 45 r.p.m. single; now it was the 33⅓ r.p.m. LP that separated the men from the boys.

Rubber Soul aroused the competitive spirit in Wilson. No longer could he be content with writing and recording singles such as "California Girls" or "Barbara Ann," perfect pop songs featuring the Beach Boys' "California Sound." *Rubber Soul* drove him to make an album that would be more personal and musically experimental than anything the world had heard before. The result was *Pet Sounds*: a thirteen-track album hailed by many as "a masterpiece" and "one of the most influential records in rock history."

Initially, the album was a commercial flop. It was too avant-garde to be accepted by the Beach Boys' fan base, who wanted their heroes to be the buttoned-down, clean-cut answer to the rowdiness of the British Invasion. Unfortunately for Wilson, their reputation as clean-cut, stand-up young fellows from California endured with hipper rock fans who were unwilling to give the group a fair chance with its first "high-art" offering. Sales of *Pet Sounds* paled in comparison to previous Beach Boys albums; Wilson had put his heart on a platter for public consumption, and it was basically rejected. He had already stopped touring with the group, and he deteriorated into mental illness after the album's release; he hasn't done anything since that approaches the artistic scope of *Pet Sounds* or his previous work's commercial success. Blah, blah, blah....

The funny thing about the "official history" of *Pet Sounds* is that it rarely discusses specific sounds or songs from the album. We are told of its impact, of its inventiveness, of its influence, but rarely do we hear about the actual music. In some ways, that is a disservice done by critics infatuated with the lore of the album. But it is also a convenient omission by those bent on creating legends where a more complicated piece of art rests. So let's get down to the heart of the matter: the songs.

THE SONGS

Wilson's ability to write hits is undeniable, even by me. On *Pet Sounds*, there are two "hits" that are really almost unassailable; I'm talking, of course, about "Wouldn't It Be Nice" and "God Only Knows."

"Wouldn't It Be Nice" starts the album with a walloping dose of the classic Beach Boys' "California Sound." Having had the misfortune of having been indoctrinated by a class on the history of rock 'n' roll in college, long before actually listening to the album, I was ready to be blown away. "Wouldn't It Be Nice" doesn't disappoint. The track clocks in at a cool two minutes and twenty seconds—perfect for radio consumption—and it features a driving beat that has always been central to good rock music, but it adds to the classic rock format with rich harmonies, a dense musical arrangement, and Brian Wilson's soaring voice, all signature Beach Boys sounds. The lyrics often contrast the bright, happy sounds of the track with a strange darkness; lines such as, "You know it seems the more we talk about it / It only makes it worse to live without it," are downright depressing. O.K., it's not really the "slit your wrists" sounds of Depeche Mode, but it isn't exactly the fun-in-the-sun image of the Beach Boys that I'd previously held. I got excited. Hey, maybe there's more depth to the Beach Boys than I knew! Maybe *Pet Sounds* really *is* all that it's cracked up to be!

The other stand-out track is "God Only Knows." It doesn't have the driving beat of "Wouldn't It Be Nice," but there are some sleigh bells that keep it progressing steadily. It is not lost on me that I'm on a slippery slope here: I mean, since when are sleigh bells an asset to a "great rock song," let alone one of the "greatest rock records ever?" But the beauty of the song's hook, the chorus, and the title line, "God only knows what I'd be without you," is so overwhelming that you can forget the sleigh bells and the strange Broadway breakdown at the bridge.

According to the highly reverent liner notes in the CD reissue, this was also the first time "God" was referenced in a pop song. Also, according to the liner notes, the recording session was preceded by a prayer session. O.K., so they weren't doing acid in India with Ravi Shankar, but this isn't God Rock like Stryper, either. I mean, the song doesn't seem to be about God: It feels dark and lonely, and it did require some courage on Wilson's part to put it out as a single after witnessing the hubbub that his rival, Lennon, caused when he compared himself to Jesus.

In truth, the fact that Wilson and Company put me in the very uncomfortable position of trying to defend the very un-rock 'n' roll prayer session that the liner notes are so proud of makes me realize that the album has already lost me. I am trying to make excuses for the record because I am supposed to like it. Or at least that's what *Rolling Stone* says.

The fact is, even the hits are disjointed, and the rest of the songs are downright insane. When you really listen to it, the emotional gap between the music—which is full of lush, über-happy instrumentation and soaring harmonies—and the lyrics—which are so depressing that they make Nick Drake sound like Captain Kangaroo—is bigger than Steven Tyler's *Rock In A Hard Place*-era drug habit. Case in point: On track two, "You Still Believe in Me," the last line of the song is simply, "I want to cry," a sad lyric paired with a beautiful melody. But the line is accompanied by the sounds of bicycle bells and clown horns. Then the song just ends. Are you kidding me? Every time I hear it, I lose my mind.

"Here Today" is another example. It sounds like the happiest of love songs: The opening lines paint a perfect portrait of beginning a new relationship. But by the pre-chorus, Wilson is telling us, "It makes you feel so bad / It makes your heart feel sad / It makes your days grow long." The second chorus segues into another musical theater-style bridge, which is followed by an uplifting and remarkable little bass solo. But then the song fades out with the lyrical warning, "Love is here today then it's gone tomorrow," just in case you were lulled into happiness by the bass solo.

The arrangement concocted for their cover of the old folk song, "Sloop John B.," is downright ecstatic, while the vocalist is singing of "the worst trip I've ever been on."

💀💀💀

THE LYRICS

For better or for worse, it is impossible to ignore the impact of the heart-broken lyrics that saturate *Pet Sounds*, but there are two major problems with the lyrics on the album. The first—that they seem wildly at odds with the over-the-top, happy musical arrangements—I have already touched on. I won't harp on it any more, other than to say that one half of this schizophrenic equation is wildly out of place.

The other lyrical problem is downright bizarre. Evidently, Wilson had a glut of overwhelming emotions that he wanted to express musically with the songs on *Pet Sounds*, but he struggled to find the words to represent the ideas. He sought the help of Asher to collaborate on the lyrics and give him the direction he desired. Now this is where the story gets weird. Asher's background was not as a poet or a songwriter; he was in advertising! And this wasn't an accident or a coincidence. Legend has it that Wilson's plan was to find an ad guy, because who knows more about making the public believe what you're saying more than someone in advertising? In a way, it's genius. But in another, very profound sense, it offends every notion of truth that I hold dear about rock 'n' roll. Knowing that the lyrics were cooked up advertising-style makes me feel like a sucker for having wondered, teary-eyed, "God only knows what I'd be without [her]."

What's more bizarre is that the "official history" of *Pet Sounds* celebrates this collaboration. If I were doing the spin on this album, I would make that a bigger secret than the CIA's involvement in the Kennedy assassination.

Think about what an artist like Moby has gone through. He was a former darling of critics, but then he sold every single song on his breakthrough album, *Play*, to a different commercial, and suddenly he is an enemy of the rock 'n' roll state. But at least he wrote his songs independently and then brought them to the advertising world. Wilson invited the advertising world into the creative process and is heralded by many of the same critics that shun someone like Moby. Am I missing something, or is this totally insane?

💀💀💀

THE SOUNDS

The only break from the lyrical insanity is found on the title track, "Pet Sounds." This is a two-minute, sixteen-second instrumental interlude which has me hard-pressed to identify any of the instruments being played. It also showcases the fact that Wilson is clearly trying too hard throughout the album. His absolute refusal to indulge in any of the standard rock devices muddies the album.

In order to achieve the desired sound—the one that was in Wilson's heart—on "You Still Believe In Me," he had to have a guy crawl into a piano and pluck the appropriate strings individually, while he sat at the keyboard and played the keys so the notes would ring out. These kinds of over-thought, over-produced sounds are all over the album. Later in the same track, there is the aforementioned jarring bicycle bell, followed by oddly spaced pauses and crescendos that keep listeners at arm's length from the guts of the song.

Engineers laud *Pet Sounds* as revolutionary from a recording standpoint. The ambitious layering of sounds on the album is something that no one had ever attempted previously, especially not on a pop album. That may make *Pet Sounds* one of the most important pieces of music engineering, but does excellence in recording equal excellence in rock? I don't think so; the over-wrought arrangements move the music too far from the visceral greatness of its rock roots. If Jerry Lee Lewis had had some guy inside the piano plucking every note he played, rock 'n' roll might have gone the way of the Hula-Hoop and died like every other fad.

Think about the impact this over-production had on rock albums to come. As the legend goes, *Pet Sounds* inspired *Sgt. Pepper's Lonely Hearts Club Band*. If you haven't already, be sure to read Jim DeRogatis's interpretation of that album before we line up to kiss Wilson's ass. Then think about all of the other over-produced albums that have marred the good name of rock 'n' roll since the Beach Boys unleashed this album: If you heard any music in the '80s, you know what I'm talking about. There are albums like *Born in the U.S.A.* (see Rob O'Connor's deconstruction of that one), which might have been classic Bruce had it not been for over-production. Then there's the real cheese that is all production and no substance at all: This is a problem that afflicts all styles of pop and rock music, from hair metal (Mutt Lange would probably be flipping burgers if not for Brian

Wilson) to the boy bands. A compelling argument can be made that it all started with *Pet Sounds*.

Then there's the disco problem. Another part of the *Pet Sounds* legend is that the recording process was partially responsible for the invention of synthesizers. Throughout the album, entirely new instrumental sounds were created by doubling and tripling notes with different instruments. If you are wondering how they got those crazy bass tones, they were achieved by doubling the bass with a tuba and sometimes tripling it with a French horn or timpani. This approach fueled the drive toward the synthesizer—a single electronic instrument which fuses the tones of multiple organic instruments to create an entirely new sound. Wilson maniacally synthesized sounds on *Pet Sounds* before such a device was available. Once the door was opened for synthesizers, disco danced right through it. I'm sure I don't have to detail what an evil development that was.

💀💀💀

THE REST

Now this may be nit-picky, but there is the problem with the cover, too. Lyrically, the album is the portrait of a tortured, lonely, heartbroken man. The only happy image of Brian Wilson comes not in the music, but in the bizarre smile on his face as he feeds a goat on the album cover. It kind of makes you wonder if he is barking up the wrong tree (no pun intended) with the women in his songs. Maybe if he'd given up on women and gone for animals (he clearly loves pets), he might have inspired the Beatles to make another album on par with *Rubber Soul*, instead of *Sgt. Pepper's*.

The biggest problem, though, is this: A great rock album should scare your parents. When rock 'n' roll first hit the scene, white suburban fathers honestly feared that this new music would cause their daughters to have sex with black men. The fear of rock's "jungle rhythms" was intense and exciting to the young people that loved it and the parents who loathed it. Thankfully, times changed, and today the parents' fears are about drug use and suicide and *Blackboard Jungle*-style deviancy. (Although if you consider hip-hop to be rock 'n' roll, it's still very much a race-inspired debate.) The problem with *Pet*

Sounds (to steal an analogy from another fellow contributor, Jim Testa) is that Brian Wilson is about as intimidating as an episode of *Seventh Heaven*, and the album hardly solicits a PMRC-style reaction from anyone. Revisiting "Wouldn't It Be Nice" for a moment, the heartache expressed in the song seems to stem from the fact that our hero is too young to be married and therefore can't have sex yet. I appreciate Wilson's depth, but this is clearly a man who needs to spend a few hours with David Lee Roth before he can make a *really* great rock album.

This is a problem that goes beyond the album's lack of controversy. It is about the fact that *Pet Sounds* is a completely cerebral work of art. It lacks the visceral charge that is found in great rock music. It is perfect as a document of Wilson's musical genius and madness. It may even be great art. But great rock 'n' roll it ain't.

THE BEACH BOYS
Smile
Unreleased, 1967
By Dawn Eden

I first heard what passes for the Beach Boys' *Smile*—better known as "the Beach Boys' legendary unreleased 1967 album, *Smile*"—not on one of the many bootlegs that have been making the rounds almost from the day the album was shelved, but on a friend's homemade cassette. Actually, I hear a lot of music on homemade cassettes and, now, on home-burned CDs. As a dedicated collector of '60s sounds, I can usually find some fellow loon who'll copy, say, a pricey Small Faces bootleg in exchange for a Shades Of Morley Brown 45 that I picked up for half a buck at some dusty hole-in-the-wall record shop. The strange thing about getting the *Smile* tape was that soon afterwards, all my other lunatic collector pals spontaneously felt it was their duty to turn me on to Brian Wilson's "lost masterwork." More *Smile* tapes came unsolicited from Wilson admirers across North America; it was as though someone had sent out a call.

Each taper selected his or her own favorite version of this album that never actually appeared—there is no official running order for *Smile*—and they all gave their compilation tapes some corny title. The most inspired, from a man in Missussauga, Ontario, who played Al Jardine in a popular Beach Boys clone band called Endless Summer, was *Life of Brian*. The worst was from a Florida gent who called it *Beautiful Music for a Beautiful Lady*. (Flattery got him nowhere.) The same friend who was first in line to tape *Smile* also taped Van Dyke

Parks's 1968 debut, *Song Cycle,* an album best known for inspiring what is either the best or worst advertisement ever placed by a major label, depending on your point of view. *Song Cycle* was praised by every rock magazine in existence at the time, but it only sold ten thousand copies, and the Warner Bros. ad attempted to explain "How We Lost $35,509.50 on 'The Album of the Year' (Dammit)." On first hearing these two mega-hyped but rather inaccessible albums, I decided that *Song Cycle* was the one I'd hate for life while *Smile* was the one I'd eventually learn to love. A decade later, I'm listening to a CD of *Song Cycle* as I write this and loving it. And all those *Smile* cassettes? They've found more appreciative owners.

Wilson and Parks began their ill-fated collaboration in late 1966. Wilson had already left the surf sound of the early Beach Boys behind on *Pet Sounds* and "Good Vibrations," the ambitious "pocket symphony" that followed. The new album was originally going to be called *Dumb Angel,* and Wilson optimistically described it as a "teenage symphony to God." But the recording sessions that ensued became notorious for their indulgence. Wilson was taking speed and smoking marijuana constantly, and he suffered bouts of depression and paranoia. He built the infamous sandbox in his living room, and he tried to destroy the tapes of a track called "Fire" because he was convinced that the song was starting conflagrations around Los Angeles. In May 1967, the Beach Boys' label, Capitol Records, announced that the album now called *Smile* had been abandoned, and the legend started building almost immediately.

It's been over a decade since Capitol released *Good Vibrations*, the box set that includes half an hour of *Smile* material, yet rumors still abound that the label will finally release an official version of the album. In January 2004, the British newspaper *The Guardian* reported that Wilson, at the behest of his wife, Melinda, sat down with Darian Sahanaja—the keyboardist of his backing band, the Wondermints—and at long last assembled a completed version of *Smile.* But whenever *Smile* fans get their hopes up, something happens. In this case, Brian's new mix was meant not for release, but as a template for his live performance of the album on a tour of the United Kingdom and Europe. Such a daunting undertaking would have been impossible in the '60s, but it can now be achieved via liberal use of samples and synthesizers.

Even as the tour plans were announced, all but Wilson's most rabid fans knew in their hearts that this would be more of a nostalgic experience than a revelatory one—at least from the standpoint of Wilson's vocals. During his successful *Pet Sounds* tours of the previous few years, where he and the Wondermints recreated that album in its entirety, it was obvious that his once-silky voice had turned to gravel. Once one of the greatest voices in pop music, he had become like Jayne Mansfield in *The Girl Can't Help It*, with the entire band existing to provide the framework for his one lonely note.

Meanwhile, the enduring popularity of Domenic Priore's 1988 fanzine-cum-book, *Look! Listen! Vibrate! Smile!*, plus a plethora of other *Smile*-inspired fanzines and online sites with titles such as "A Teenage Web Page to God," suggest that *Smile*'s myth looms larger than ever. But it's a myth that only true believers can buy into.

The very nature of *Smile*—the fact that it is and will forever remain unfinished—is irresistible to diehard Wilson fanatics. Through the numerous bootlegs and fan-generated reading material, they can listen to *Smile* tracks and make their own conclusions about how Wilson intended the album to sound. Never mind that the overall quality in terms of material, production, and performance doesn't hold an incense stick to the Beach Boys' best effort, *Pet Sounds*. Since *Smile* can never be properly finished—Wilson's muse and brain cells having been radically altered since 1967—fans can do with it what they can't do with any other Beach Boys album: Get into Brian Wilson's head.

Just how far fanatics will go is illustrated by *Look! Listen! Vibrate! Smile!* Put your finger down on any page and it'll land on a passage similar to this one: "There is some concern that the 'Child is Father to the Man' ending is not as Brian had intended. This estimation is wrong: The classic fade is from the original tape of Brian's solo version, and no splices were made." Any questions? Elsewhere in that same tome, in an essay called "The *Smile* Music (With Keen Perception and A Lot of Listening)," Priore spews the kind of ultra-opinionated bile that fits the dictionary definition of "Surf Nazi," threatening that, "The next person who goes around perpetuating the myth that *Smile* 'should be left in the can so that the legend remains' or that it's 'too far out, weird, and inaccessible' will dutifully receive ten Samoans pounding on their door, looking for the honky who stole their longboard."

Well, I guess Priore can send those Samoans over to my place, because I'd say "classic" albums don't come any less accessible than *Smile*. Granted, the two singles that emerged from the sessions, "Good Vibrations" and "Heroes and Villains" (which found a place on *Smiley Smile,* the altogether different 1967 album compiled after *Smile* was shelved) are gorgeous marriages of artistry and commercial accessibility. But Priore and other *Smile* fans will tell you that you haven't *really* heard those songs unless you've heard the unreleased versions, each with extra verses. That's like a Shakespeare scholar telling you that you haven't read one of the sonnets unless you've read the unreleased couplets. The whole point of a great pop single (and a great sonnet, for that matter) is to marvel at how much beauty its creator managed to cram into its restricted form. Add more verses, especially after the single's a hit, and it's interesting at best, and anticlimactic at worst. The *Good Vibrations* box set brings that point home with extended versions of "Good Vibrations" and "Heroes and Villains," previously available only on bootlegs.

The new and unimproved "Good Vibrations" does give some welcome insight into Wilson's inner workings, particularly his fascination with the modern composer Charles Ives. Unfortunately, the song's lyrics, which were never terribly profound to begin with, hardly benefit from additional lines such as, "It's weird how she comes in so strong." Likewise, the long-lost "cantina" section of "Heroes and Villains" is nice, but hardly the grand revelation whose impending release caused untold numbers of Wilson fans to lose sleep at night. In terms of a great historical discovery, the Dead Sea Scrolls it ain't.

Hell, I'm not even sure if it compares to the unearthing of the lost *Honeymooners* episodes.

When it comes down to it, the main benefit of hearing the unreleased *Smile* versions of "Good Vibrations" is the opportunity to hear the *bad* vibrations that were plaguing Wilson at the time. A *Smile* tape I have from someone who claims to have acquired it from "someone very close to the Wilson camp" has an unreleased version that's longer than the alternate one on the box set. The feeling changes completely when you hear the song without its trademark high-pitched theremin line but with the lower-pitched theremin plus lots of breaks on a fuzz bass so distorted that it sounds like a primitive Moog synthesizer. It goes from being a sunny ode to positive thinking, to a schizophrenic, even sinister, rendering of the inner and outer "vibrations" that Wilson both sought and feared.

A more convincing argument for the greatness of *Smile* is that Wilson, an untrained musician, arrived on his own at some remarkably complex and inventive musical ideas. The only problem here is that you could say the same of *Pet Sounds*, and *Pet Sounds* is a much better album. On *Pet Sounds*, Wilson was working with a fairly straightforward lyricist, Tony Asher, a former advertising copywriter, and in terms of melody, he kept to familiar pop song structures, with the occasional chord borrowed from classical music. *Smile*, like *Pet Sounds*, was based around "feels"—musical impressions that Wilson created at the piano. But where *Pet Sounds* had Asher's verse, chorus, B-section mentality to balance Wilson's more fanciful musical excesses, *Smile* had Parks, who encouraged the troubled, drug-addled composer to stretch further in the direction of his worst impulses.

Since Wilson has composed so many more classic tunes than Parks, it seems strange that Parks's own *Song Cycle* would be, on the whole, superior to *Smile*. The difference lies in the compositions and arrangements. While the lyrics Parks wrote for *Smile* were no worse than the ones for *Song Cycle*, he was essentially a creative manic, while Wilson was a depressive. No matter how blissed-out Parks was lyrically, his music was always precise, sometimes maddeningly so.

33

Carried along by razor-sharp melodies, his oblique poetry sounds almost meaningful. Conversely, sung over Wilson's dreamy textures, a Parks line such as, "Over and over the crow cries / Uncover the cornfield" sounds laughably pretentious. And, yes, I do realize this criticism puts me in the same camp as Mike Love.

It was the Beach Boys' lead vocalist who, upon returning from a tour and finding that Wilson had recorded most of *Smile* without the group, bristled at the thought of lines such as, "Columnated ruins domino" (from "Surf's Up") being released under the Beach Boys' moniker. "Don't fuck with the formula," Love allegedly warned Wilson. Not surprisingly, Wilson fans have demonized Love to the point where he's become a joke. Admittedly, it's hard to defend a guy who told *Goldmine* that he'd like to make a documentary about a Beach Boys tour from the point of view of their cheerleaders, or who called Brian "delusional" in the same interview while speaking of his own ability to levitate via transcendental meditation. Yet in the long run, Love may have the last laugh, as those who hear *Smile* in the sections that appear on the *Good Vibrations* box or on bootlegs long for the "formulaic" Wilson of *The Beach Boys Today* or the profound pop of *Pet Sounds*.

Pre-*Smile* tracks such as "She Knows Me Too Well," "In My Room," and "Surfer Girl" may lack the self-conscious depth of *Smile*, but their goose-bump-inducing effect hits harder and lasts longer. The truth is that by the time Wilson made *Smile*, drugs and mental problems had so drastically separated his emotions from his intellect that there was no way that his songs could capture the most intense and dramatic qualities of both. Listening to great songs such as the single versions of "Good Vibrations" and "Heroes and Villains" next to the *Smile* versions, or wading through stabbing-in-the-dark experiments such as "Do You Like Worms" and "Cabin Essence," the real tragedy of *Smile* becomes obvious. Parks was able to carry on and make a *Song Cycle*, while Wilson's creative wheels spun to a halt, and Brian never really got rolling again.

THE WHO
Tommy
MCA, 1969
By Steve Knopper

Captain Walker dies in the war. His wife gives birth to a son. Then she takes a lover. But it turns out Captain Walker didn't die. He comes back and murders Mrs. Walker's paramour. Their infant son Tommy watches the whole thing without reacting.

Discussion questions: Was Mrs. Walker cheating on Captain Walker, or was she free to court a new man because she thought her husband was dead? Why didn't they just send Tommy to his room?

Captain and Mrs. Walker browbeat Tommy into forgetting the whole ugly affair. Tommy goes deaf, dumb, and blind. While he's helpless, his cousin abuses him, his uncle fondles him, the Acid Queen gets him stoned, and he learns to play pinball really well.

Discussion questions: Is it really possible to yell at somebody so aggressively that you make him lose his senses? Why would you bring a deaf, dumb, and blind child into an arcade?

Tommy beats all the local lads at pinball with his spiritual concentration and crazy flipper fingers. Later, his parents smash a mirror and reawaken his senses. Tommy leads a mass of followers to spiritual enlightenment, but they rebel, and he goes deaf, dumb, and blind again.

Discussion questions…you know what? Forget it.

💀 💀 💀

The Who's former manager, Kit Lambert, once said that *Tommy*, the rock 'n' roll album attached to this story line, is "just like grand opera—it's incredibly difficult to follow the story." People seemed willing to

35

ignore this fact in the late '60s. The Beatles and the Beach Boys had stretched rock's artistic limits with *Sgt. Pepper's Lonely Hearts Club Band* and *Pet Sounds*, and rockers were starting to believe that they should be taken as seriously as classical composers. Shallow oxymorons such as "rock opera" seemed to have extreme cultural significance—it was rock *and* it was opera. If you insisted on being hung up with concepts like *plot* and *character*, maybe you just weren't cultured enough.

Rock 'n' roll began (more or less) as a two-minute Elvis Presley single about hillbilly love in Kentucky, but by the '60s, it was no longer allowed to tell a simple story and play on a jukebox. The Doors' Jim Morrison couldn't settle for bluesy rock songs full of good organ solos; he had to be the Lizard King. Bob Dylan opened the door for the Jefferson Airplane's *Surrealistic Pillow*, and rock had to *say* something. Otherwise, it was disposable junk culture, and the Baby Boomer free-love radical revolutionary youth culture simply couldn't have that. *Its* music had to endure as *high art*, whether or not it made sense.

Who guitarist, primary songwriter, and former art-school student Pete Townshend was vulnerable to the notion of pop music aspiring to classical music's cultural credibility. Until 1969, the Who was a blue-collar band of angry, destructive British teenagers with big noses, ugly hair, and mod clothes. To get attention, they hurled their guitars and drums on the floor, creating explosions and smoke and massive repair bills. Townshend wrote brilliant, raunchy pop songs about speed, masturbation, sexual frustration, and hoping he could die before he got old. But mega-fame on the level of the Rolling Stones was still outside the band's grasp as the decade ended. If the Who could only come up with a Big Statement. Townshend, by now an introspective follower of the Indian spiritual master, Meher Baba, was up for the challenge. And thus was born rock opera.

Despite its glaring conceptual weaknesses, tin-can production, and timeless inability to rock, *Tommy* was immediately accepted by the sort of mainstream critics that Townshend was hoping to impress. *The New Yorker*, in a 1969 "Talk of the Town" commentary, referred to Townshend as a "composer and librettist," but it noted that *Tommy*, "properly speaking, is not an opera but an oratorio." *Newsweek*'s Herbert Saal wrote: "From the rich Purcell-like overture—with [bassist John] Entwistle doubling expertly on the French horn—[the Who's] rock beat is as pliant as a trampoline and they somersault around at will, visiting the minuet, the waltz, and a march." Added Albert Goldman in *Life*, "Considered as music, *Tommy* is magnificent, the final crystallization of the hard-rock style in an art as dry, hard, lucid, as unashamedly conventional and finely impersonal as the music of the most severe classicist."

These reviews started the unending *Tommy* snow job. The album continues to hold a place in the minds of Baby Boomer fans and critics as a watershed document in the history of rock 'n' roll. "Not only a personal triumph for the Who," Paul Evans writes in *The Rolling Stone Album Guide*, "the record remains one of the rare fusions of classical music and rock that works." (His restraint in not using the words "librettist" and "Purcell-like" is admirable.) In fact, *Tommy* is a novelty, a classical-rock experiment as overwrought as the Electric Light Orchestra's version of "Roll Over Beethoven." It has its charms, but it's best if you accept it as camp and laugh at its indulgences. It's like the early episodes of *Star Trek*: Much of the show's appeal, then and now, is its dangling loose ends and corny contrivances—Captain Kirk's staccato speech patterns, and Lieutenant Uhuru's beehive hairdo. *Tommy*'s plot is as disjointed as the worst *Star Trek* episode, but, somehow, it was always perceived as deadly serious.

It has been said that if a writer could spend his career fine-tuning his worst novel, with people paying top dollar for each revision, he would revise the thing until he dropped dead. Townshend has said his life's curse was writing the line, "I hope I die before I get old" at age 20—it doesn't sound quite so charming once your hair falls out, your hearing begins to go, and punks start calling you an old fart. But *Tommy* is Townshend's real curse: He *still* isn't able to laugh at it, thirty-five years later. Even worse, he keeps tinkering with it, as if it's just a few tidied-up subplots away from being perfect.

When Townshend first pitched *Tommy* to the rest of the Who, his bandmates were skeptical. The group had always despised pretension. Singer Roger Daltrey, a former boxer, joined the band because he liked James Brown and wanted to pick up birds. Bassist Entwistle and drummer Keith Moon were clowns who loved to play pranks on people who took themselves too seriously. But while he wasn't a major fan of psychedelic drugs, Townshend *did* respond to the soul-searching of the late '60s. In Meher Baba, he found a spiritual center, a disciplined way of life that emphasized love and compassion. "It's something inside where all you want is for the things that seem so simple and fundamental to your life to mean something more than they appear to mean," he told writer Dave Marsh in the Who biography, *Before I Get Old*. Before Baba, Townshend went along with the Who's straightforward goal of rocking in brutal and funny fashion. After Baba, he wanted to become one with his fans in a real astral hootenanny. But his expanding vision made the album an unfocused mess.

The dominant songs are the bland New Age spirituals. The trippy "Amazing Journey" is full of proselytizing: Daltrey, trained as a straightforward R&B singer, sounds daft spitting out lines such as, "Love as one I am the light," "Loving life and becoming wise in simplicity," and especially, "Sparkle warm crystalline glances to show." (Go ahead: Close your eyes and try to envision a warm crystalline glance sparkling.) "Welcome," a song about a love-in where everybody is invited to Tommy's house for tea and companionship, is so silly that even Townshend has deleted it from subsequent versions of his opus. And of course the album closes with Daltrey's messianic mantra—"See me, feel me, touch me, heal me"—followed by the feel-good religious claptrap about getting excitement at your feet and seeing glory in your eyes.

Daltrey was the main dumping ground for Townshend's spiritual waste. By the late '60s, the singer was growing angry because Townshend was usurping his role as leader of the band and generally being recognized as the brilliant auteur. Then Townshend, in a genius stroke of office politics, gave Daltrey the lead role in his opera, stroking the singer's ego and giving him a vested stake in making this bloated epic work. Never exactly an Otis Redding, Daltrey had managed to stutter personably through "My Generation" and growl with adequate menace on "I Can't Explain" and "Substitute," but he tackled the *Tommy* tunes in a wavering whine. Repeating, "See me, feel me, touch me, heal me," his voice is unnaturally thin and incapable of complementing Townshend's Phil Spector aspirations.

Musically, *Tommy* uses three or four repetitive themes as a crutch. Whenever he's at a creative loss, Townshend inserts the frantic guitar strum that opens "Pinball Wizard," tells Daltrey to go into his "See me, feel me" bit, or rehashes the same five chords that fill up "Overture," "Underture," and "Sparks." "Tommy, Can You Hear Me?" devolves into a bouncy chant that repeats the name "Tommy" over and over until the band finally tires of it and fades out. And this comes *after* the Who has already run the chant into the ground during "Christmas."

Then there's the *filler*. "It's a Boy," "The Hawker," "There's a Doctor," "1921," and "Miracle Cure" are Townshend's flailing attempts to make the plot more cohesive. Instead, they make things even more complicated, and they're among the worst Who songs ever recorded. (A possible exception is "Now I'm a Farmer" from *Odds and Sods*, with the chorus, "And I'm diggin', diggin', diggin', diggin', diggin'.") How the Who progressed from "I'm a Boy," the wonderful 1966 single about psychological child abuse and forced cross-dressing, to *Tommy*'s "It's a Boy" is one of the great mysteries of the '60s. "It's a boy," a nurse sings to Mrs. Walker at the beginning of the opera. "It's a boy, Mrs. Walker, it's a boy." As if there was still some doubt, Townshend emphasizes the point with the chorus: "A son! A son! A son!"

These songs are intended to function onstage as narration explaining what has transpired, but on album, they just take up space.

Covering Sonny Boy Williamson's Chicago blues classic, "Eyesight to the Blind"—which Townshend renamed "The Hawker" and stuck in because of its references to being deaf, dumb, and blind—should have been a natural for a band that started out playing blues at smoky British nightclubs. But Daltrey sings it in a high-pitched but characterless voice, and Townshend's hooting backing vocals add only confusion. (Those vocals return with a horrible vengeance on "Christmas," when Townshend actually sings this chorus: "Hubba, hubba, hubba, hubba, hubba.") To say "The Hawker" robs Williamson's original of its grit is a serious understatement.

Much to the frustration of Daltrey, Moon, and Entwistle, *Tommy* took half a year to record, which was almost unprecedented for a rock album at the time. "I can't believe we spent six months doing it—that's studio time and that's talking about it, discussing it, arranging it, producing, and writing it," Moon said in Marsh's book. "Recording it and then saying we could do it better and recording it again. Six months, continuously, in the studio." But the album was scheduled to come out before a tour that had already been booked, and in the end, the band wound up rushing to finish it. Lambert was an "ideas man" who had very little technical studio skill. Entwistle's bass and Townshend's Spector-inspired string and piano arrangements sound as if they're being recorded simultaneously in different ZIP codes. (This was especially irritating for Entwistle, who was a big believer into post-recording overdubs, but here he didn't have the time to make crucial touch-ups.) The French horn is supposed to sound regal, but it comes across as scrawny. Recorded much too cleanly, Townshend's guitars have none of the wonderful punk-sludge effect of "My Generation." At least Moon's drumming sounds as messy as it's supposed to sound.

Whenever the songs get too repetitive, Moon invents new rhythms or tries as usual to play all of his drums and cymbals at once. His playing is the album's biggest reward for repeated listening, but there are also points where he seems to deliberately undermine the mood of the music. In "Overture," when a flock of pretty acoustic guitars swoops in, Moon sounds like a collapsing building. He's great, but he doesn't fit, and he often makes *Tommy* sound nervous and at odds with itself.

There *are* a few good songs here, but they account for only about twenty percent of the double album. "Pinball Wizard" is still all over classic-rock radio, in part because it uses Townshend's dramatic power chords at least as well as the early Who hits, "I Can't Explain" and "The Seeker." Divorced from the spiritual hoo-hah, the song's narrative about a deaf, dumb, and blind kid who crushes the local slackers at pinball works like a rock 'n' roll comic book, offering up a superhero to stand beside Chuck Berry's Johnny B. Goode or the Ramones' Sheena, the Punk Rocker. The Who's great strength was in writing straightforward rock anthems—rallying cries for disenfranchised youth that laid a foundation for the Sex Pistols and the Clash. "I'm Free" showcases Moon's explosive drumming and Daltrey's liberating screaming, and the album's convoluted story makes perfect sense in exactly one place, when Tommy's mother finally returns Tommy's senses with a dramatic crash in "Smash the Mirror."

The other standouts are Entwistle's demented songs, especially the sadistic "Cousin Kevin," during which Tommy's cousin lists all the clever forms of pain he plans to inflict on the child. (Pause for a fantasy: It's 1973 and a disgusted Entwistle drags Townshend into the bathroom to snuff a cigarette out on his arm, drag him around by the hair, and dunk his head under the scalding water from the bath.) Similarly, "Uncle Ernie" invents a derelict relative, a dirty old pedophile who offsets all of Townshend's holy pretensions with evil perversions, chanting "fiddle about" as he diddles with the helpless Tommy.

And about that Uncle Ernie: Until January 2003, I always interpreted "Fiddle About" as a *funny song,* envisioning a toothless, overcoat-wearing Moon clowning around in his most lovable role. But Townshend's arrest in England for allegedly accessing a pay-per-view child pornography Web site made me return to the lyrics with a more discerning eye. An excerpt: "I'm your wicked Uncle Ernie / I'm glad you won't see or hear me / As I fiddle about, fiddle about, fiddle about / Your mother left me here to mind you, now I'm doing what I want to / Fiddling about, fiddling about, fiddle about / Down with the bedclothes, up with your nightshirt / Fiddle about, fiddle about, fiddle about."

Now, I'm not the type to take rock lyrics too seriously, and I realize that, in the context of the convoluted *Tommy* story line, Uncle Ernie is an unsympathetic villain who violates the heroic narrator. But the song doesn't come across that way on the album or on live *Tommy* bootlegs from the '70s. (Check out the gleeful, Entwistle-sung version on *The Who: Live at the Isle of Wight Festival 1970,* which came out in 1996 with an excerpt of *Tommy* that stomps all over the original album.) Uncle Ernie is a cuddly cartoon character, and the Who often played him that way by letting the lovable Moon voice his parts on stage. Given Townshend's recent revelations—and it should be noted the British police eventually decided to drop their investigation—you have to wonder if Uncle Ernie was based on a real person in Townshend's life. (According to Who lore, Townshend conceived the character and gave the song to Entwistle, by then well-respected for his dark humor.) If that's the case, why didn't the Who render "Uncle Ernie" as a more frightening or angry song—one that frowned upon or raged against its evil subject? "Cousin Kevin," which is about physical and psychological, rather than sexual, child abuse, portrays its protagonist as a menacing criminal. When I first heard *Tommy* as a child, I remember laughing at Ernie while feeling a little scared and queasy about Kevin.

I was born the year that *Tommy* was released. My older brother, Mark, played it constantly, along with his other favorite progressive-rock LPs: *Tales of Topographic Oceans* by Yes, *Works* by Emerson, Lake and Palmer, and *Apostrophe* by Frank Zappa. His musical dogma, then and now, is that you have to know how to properly play your instrument in order to make great rock. (To his credit, he makes exceptions for the Ramones, the Velvet Underground, and occasional others.) For years, as I grew up with *Tommy* as aural wallpaper in our suburban Detroit home, I bought into that philosophy: Ringo Starr sucked! Neil Peart of Rush ruled! But when I got older and friends introduced me to the Replacements ("I hate music! It's got too many notes!"), the Ramones, and the Sex Pistols, I made a U-turn and stopped believing that you had to be schooled in classical music in order to be innovative in rock. Those lofty old albums he loved sound irritating and pompous today, divorced from their composers' then-widely documented ambitions. Yet I've maintained an obsession with the Who, and with *Tommy* in particular.

Like Townshend, I've gone through phases where I've longed to rewrite *Tommy* as a cohesive narrative, but I never quite got there because: 1) Somewhere during high school, you realize that sitting around rewriting old rock operas doesn't get you any dates; and 2) The central, maddening contradiction of *Tommy* is that it retains its musical power precisely *because the story makes no sense*. Townshend has, unfortunately, never come to this realization. The Who could have acknowledged this fatal glitch and moved on. Instead, Townshend kept fiddling about—with plot, presentation, characters, and the music itself—and he continues to this day. I wish he'd stop. Instead, every few years, he and the band offer variations. To wit:

• *Tommy as Performed by the London Symphony Orchestra and Chambre Choir with Guest Soloists* (**Ode, 1972**)

The Who's weak links were Daltrey's singing and Townshend's occasional indulgences. This 1972 triple album, with dreamy cover paintings of scenes from *Tommy*, cuts out Moon's drumming and Entwistle's bass playing and replaces Townshend's trademark power chords with violins. Who gets to stay? Daltrey, the star of the show. His voice sounds even weaker underneath the big orchestral arrangements, and guests Rod Stewart and Steve Winwood add nothing to the Who's originals. Folk singer Richie Havens, as he often does, turns "Eyesight to the Blind" into a children's sing-along.

• *Tommy*, **the movie** (**1975**)

In this laughable psychedelic trivia question of a movie, director Ken Russell asks aging actress Ann-Margaret to bite her lip and stare pensively into the camera as simulated Who music plays in the background. It's like a bad cartoon. The "Amazing Journey" scene is filled with Warholian statues and icons of Marilyn Monroe. Fighter planes morph into cemetery crosses, possibly making the point that war is bad. A confused Eric Clapton wears a flowing white robe and sings an unnatural version of "Eyesight to the Blind" as Russell's camera goes kaleidoscopic. Only the hungry Tina Turner manages an inspired performance as the Acid Queen, fondling young Tommy (played as always without charisma by nappy-headed Daltrey) and dosing him with hallucinogens. Then she puts on a giant silver Darth Vader helmet and things *really* get silly. The flick makes Ann-Margaret's last bad rock movie, *Viva Las Vegas* with Elvis Presley, seem like *The Deer Hunter.*

• The Who's 1989 tour

Out of ideas and frustrated with its lack of cash flow, the Who grudgingly agreed to one "last" lucrative spin through the stadium circuit. Guess what album they decided to revive? A far cry from the legendary fury of *Tommy* during shows in the late '60s, on this tour, Townshend was flanked by a platoon of session musicians, and he cowered in a quiet corner of the stage so he wouldn't aggravate his hearing problems. I kept envisioning Moon's ghost striding onstage to kick his boring mates in their rears and take the show to the next level. But these English gentlemen, like the Rolling Stones, were above that sort of primal rocking by this point.

• *Join Together* (MCA, 1990)

This terrible two-disc set is a collection of live recordings from the 1989 tour. The first disc contains *Tommy* in its entirety, minus a few of the filler songs. Imagine an old, boring Who with no Moon, no explosions, and no passion—and stupid me bought it anyway, even after the disappointment of the live show. It almost made me nostalgic for the London Symphony Orchestra.

• *The Who's Tommy*

The '90s dawned with Townshend searching desperately for his fading creative spark. He put out one bad album, *The Iron Man,* which proposed the sing-songy euphemism, "Live your future—be friendly!" ("No future?" Take that, Johnny Rotten!) His book, *Horse's Neck*, was famous only for its author's admission, "I know how it feels to be a woman because I *am* a woman." What to do? *Tommy* to the rescue, of course! This time, to great critical acclaim and lots of friendly publicity, Townshend stuck the old dog on Broadway. The plot still sucked, but producers added some more focused dialogue, fancy lights, loud sound effects, parachuting Army men, bucking broncos, and, of course, a stage full of giant pinball machines. The songs were spit-shined for the theater, and the plot was transformed into a feel-good fairy tale instead of an exercise in frustrating contradictions and troubling loose ends. It was a big hit, and it won five Tony Awards.

Moon's death should have broken up the band once and for all, but the Who continues. In recent years, the band has been more interested in revisiting its other rock operas than in returning to *Tommy*. In 1996, it returned to *Quadrophenia*, and in 2000, Townshend started talking about revisiting his long-aborted *Lifehouse* project, before Entwistle's death in late 2002 put things on hold for a while. But it's only a matter of time before the Who once again returns to the undead Tommy, his confused and confusing parents, and his lovable-molester uncle. There are still myriad approaches left untried, not to mention new and developing technologies: How about *Tommy: The Interactive CD-ROM*, or Tommy.com, where any schmo with a computer or a wireless device can plunge into the story and create his or her own plot twists? My suggestion: Tommy finally dies before he gets old.

THE MC5
Kick Out the Jams
Elektra, 1969
By Andy Wang

It's a manifesto that now reads like a parody, but you have to imagine that John Sinclair's mind was racing, his heart was throbbing, his dick was hard (assuming that his dick *could* get hard after all those drugs), and slobber was dripping from his mouth when he wrote it. The crazy motherfucker, leader of the White Panther Party (yes, you read that correctly; if you still need more convincing as to the silliness of this whole enterprise, read on), was declaring war on his world, on the government that oppressed him, on all the dumb fucks around him who were complicit in creating the bad place he wanted to crush from its very foundation. He wanted to change the nation, destroy the concepts of commerce and the military and the government. It was 1968, and civil unrest was brewing in Detroit. The mad hatters in power were evil, and somebody had to say something. That someone was Sinclair, and this is just a small part of what he declared in the White Panther statement released on November 1:

We are the mother country madmen in charge of our own lives, and we are taking this freedom to the people of America, in streets, in the ballrooms and teen clubs, in their front rooms watching TV, in their bedrooms reading underground newspapers, or masturbating, or smoking secret dope, in their schools where we come and talk to them or make our music, in their weird gymnasiums ... For the first time in America there is a generation of vision-

ary maniac white motherfucker country dope fiend rock 'n' roll freaks who are ready to get down and kick out the jams—ALL THE JAMS—break every-thing loose and free everybody from their very real and imaginary prisons—even the chumps and punks and honkies who are always fucking with us.... We are bad.

There's only two kinds of people on the planet: those who make up the problem and those who make up the solution. WE ARE THE SOLUTION.... Our program of rock 'n' roll, dope and fucking in the streets is a program of total freedom for everyone. We are totally committed to carrying out our pro-gram. We breathe revolution. We are LSD driven total maniacs of the uni-verse. We will do anything we can to drive people crazy out of their heads and into their bodies.

If this seems a little verbose and hard to follow, allow me to trans-late: "Since I was born they couldn't hold me down / Another misfit kid, another burned-out town / Never played by the rule, I never real-ly cared / My nasty reputation takes me everywhere / I look and see it's not only me / So many others have stood where I stand / We are the young so raise your hands / They call us problem child / We spend our lives on trial / We walk an endless mile / We are the youth gone wild."

There are few people who make Sebastian Bach seem like a lyri-cal genius, but John Sinclair's one of them. It's sad and somewhat appropriate to see this elderly man, who once called for the "free exchange of energy and materials—we demand the end of money," now charging five dollars for readings pimped by guys like John Strausbaugh, who wrote an entire fucking book about how rock shouldn't be for old guys, but that's another essay.

The thing is, thirty-five years ago, a bunch of smart people fell for Sinclair's bullshit. That's largely because there was this "incendiary" band at the center of his call for chaos. It was the MC5, a doped-up, long-haired, swaggering bunch of guilty white boys managed by Sinclair. On October 30–31, 1968, they recorded a live album, *Kick Out the Jams*, which is widely considered a masterpiece.

By "widely considered a masterpiece," I mean that a lot of rock critics, most notably Dave Marsh and Jaan Uhelzki, who were Detroit youngsters working at the venerated *Creem* magazine and talking about a revolution in 1968, loved the MC5. (The great Lester Bangs both admired them and saw through its hype.) The MC5, of course, is just a footnote in both pop-culture and political history, but to this day Marsh will insist that it transcended both its record sales and its actual social impact.

"It felt like a thousand-piece band," Marsh said during a panel about the MC5 at the South by Southwest Music and Media Conference in 1999. "It was as if a bomb had exploded and your pre-vious expectations of life had exploded around you."

Or maybe Marsh just needed better earplugs or more life experi-ence.

It's hard to find a lot of criticism about the MC5 online—it was-n't that big of a band—but the fervor of the writing that's out there is over the top. Veteran critic Barney Hoskyns's review on Amazon.com notes that, *"Kick Out the Jams* still sounds astonishingly powerful after almost thirty years...this relentless, aggressive set offers the frenzy of politicized garage punks blasting through giant stacks: a blitzkrieg of hard rock ignited from the dueling guitars of Wayne Kramer and Fred Sonic Smith and of the throttled vocals of Rob Tyner...the Five turned the Motor City into a Mecca of sonic excess and shattered the dazed dreams of hippie America. From the pounding of the title track to the eight-and-a half-minute weirdout of Sun Ra's 'Starship,' *Kick Out the Jams* will rip your head to shreds."

Get some better substances and some better music, man. Listening to it now, *Kick Out the Jams* has the effect of a monster-truck rally: It's rousing, no doubt, but it feels like a cartoon. It's fake bad-assness that has no goal except for pretending to be bad-ass, which is somewhat admirable, but not for very long.

I can see how Wayne Kramer and Fred "Sonic" Smith's guitar pyrotechnics could get kids off thirty-five years ago in the way that blowing up a pimp in Grand Theft Auto 3 gets kids off in 2003. But the nonstop bombast is like listening to Vinnie Vincent for half an hour. Yeah, dudes, it's impressive, but dial it the fuck down, please. As for singer Rob Tyner and his punk-rock-before-punk-rock braggadocio, it just pisses all over Sinclair's manifesto. It becomes clear quickly that all that talk about rock 'n' roll, dope and fucking in the streets is less about a revolution and more about justifying a Bohemian lifestyle and getting laid. It's *Maxim* masquerading as *The Atlantic Monthly*.

Consider these lyrics from the title track of *Kick Out the Jams*:

"Well, I feel pretty good / And I guess that I could get crazy now, baby / 'Cause we all got in tune / And when the dressing room got hazy now, baby / I know how you want it child / Hot, quick and tight / The girls can't stand it / When you're doin' it right."

The rest of the songs on this album are much the same. They mostly blend into one, and like, say, the Ramones and the White Stripes, there's little point in listening to the MC5 for more than nine minutes at a time. It's like Hamburger Helper (which I admit to enjoying from time to time): There are no layers of flavor here. It's blunt music full of energy but bereft of mystery.

The album opens with a bunch of clapping and a minute and a half of posturing (a "testimonial" by the White Panthers' "Spiritual Advisor") before "Brother" J.C. Crawford gets to the point: He asks the crowd if it's ready to testify, and then the guitars collide and the MC5 performs "Ramblin' Rose." It's messy garage rock, a decent effort about finding a wild woman, and it's over in about a minute. Then Tyner dives right into the forgettable title track, which sounds like glam-rock minus the fun. On "Come Together," he comes on like both a maniacal preacher and a lech, but there's no more meaning here than there is in an AC/DC song. Memorable lyrics: "Nipples stiffen / Nipples stiffen / Nipples stiffen, mama / Let me give tongue to it, yes."

The next song, "Rocket Reducer No. 62 (rama lama fa fa fa)," is the best five minutes on the record, a straight-ahead feel-good barroom anthem, but again, it's as if the band really does think that nights of crazy fucking and partying automatically equates with revolution. When Tyner sings, "I'm the man for you, baby," he sounds as if he wants nothing more than an orgy, which would be totally fine if he just stopped there, and there was no added pretense heaped upon it all by the band's mentor, Sinclair.

The next song, "Borderline," is just some boring chanting pretending to be a punk song, and before Tyner starts singing "Motor City is Burning" (a song that, unlike all of the preceding tracks, *is* overtly political), he rants against honkies, looks at the crowd, and declares that, *"This* is the high society." Then he sings about his city being torched, about evil cops and soldiers and fire bombs, but—get this—the song is so much sludgier than everything that came before that it seems as if it's in slow motion. Maybe the MC5 is trying to be purposefully deliberate, but the long bluesy guitar parts do nothing more than make you forget what the tune is supposed to be about. And the crowd sounds quieter, too. Maybe they were transfixed and reflecting and all that, but my bet is that they were getting bored.

The album concludes with some speedy filler in "I Want You Right Now," which is about exactly what you think it is. Then there's the cover of Sun Ra's "Starship," which isn't nearly as weird or as powerful as Tyner would have you believe. Part of the song even sounds like Def Leppard.

Do not misunderstand: I do not question the authenticity of the feelings of those who were at Russ Gibbs's Grande Ballroom when this record was made in 1968. And I have no doubt that when Marsh first heard the MC5, he wanted to save people and make out with half the world and tear stuff to pieces with his fingers. What I am saying is that the music leaves me wanting, and whatever message it was trying to convey was largely ignored for a very good reason: It made little sense. One of the weaknesses of Sinclair's manifesto was that he was totally sincere, which means his earnestness destroyed his basic logic. It's one thing to want to overthrow the president, and it's another to say that you want to end the ideas of money and soldiers and then charge people for shows where there are security guards. Even a thirteen-year-old working his way through his first dime bag can recognize this as hypocrisy, or at least something that wasn't thought out enough.

As for the tunes, Uhelszki herself has said that Iggy and the Stooges were greatly influenced by the MC5, which is to say that you can trace decades of bad, discordant punk to 1968. (Maybe we should thank Dave Marsh for the Hives.) And if you want to understand Iggy's legacy, just consider that when he played Jones Beach in 2003, some tickets were only five dollars and the crowd was full of middle-aged punks with pot bellies (read: *Blender* editors) pumping their fists and screaming along.

Listening to the obviously-influenced-by-Hendrix MC5, listening to Tyner telling his "brothers and sisters" that "honkies" are dickheads who are trying to keep him down, it's easy to wonder why these guys hate their own race so much. Consider that the first point of the White Panthers' Ten-Point Program was the "full endorsement and support of the Black Panther Party's Ten-Point Program." So let's be clear: Sinclair and the MC5 were not white supremacists in any way. They were also not original in any way. This in and of itself is not a bad thing—plenty of great art is derivative, appropriated, purloined—but the MC5 managed to be both unoriginal and uninteresting.

Maybe Sinclair and the band didn't even care about being original at all. Maybe they just wanted to be a collective, to find salvation by leading a group of like-minded cats. It seems that way, but the thing about collectives is that they sap away creative energy. They're often for people who have a piece missing, who want so badly to be part of something, because it is, admittedly, often hard to figure shit out on your own when you're young and full of hope and dope and juice and ideas and talent. There's a reason why geniuses like J.D. Salinger and Axl Rose and all those guys who wore masks in the World Wrestling Federation in the 1990s turned into recluses. It's not that they couldn't deal with the pressures of fame. It's that they were singularly extraordinary, and they quickly realized that the rest of the world is stupid. When critics write about people like Salinger or Rose, they often focus on how fucked-up these artists must be—how they're not quite whole—but I really believe that the opposite is true: These artists have given the world a singular accomplishment, and maybe they think that's enough, and they've earned the right to do whatever the fuck they want, even if that involves locking themselves in a cave or a wine cellar.

When you've actually changed the world, there's no need to remind anybody that you have. As for the MC5, its mindset is pretty much the antithesis of this. Shortly before he died in 1991, Tyner wrote liner notes for the re-release of *Kick Out the Jams*. His fervor for his music more than two decades after it was released was telling: He felt a need to make everyone understand the importance of his band and its live album.

"This music expresses the frustration and future shock of the soul of the '60s. This is a portrayal of the struggle to create a world that was destined never to be. An impossibly beautiful dream that was doomed by the nation's descent into the disco inferno of the seventies," Tyner writes (and it's lucky for him that he wasn't alive to see the Backstreet Boys or 'N Sync). "We were Punk, before Punk. We were New Wave, before New Wave. We were Metal, before Metal. We were even 'M.C.' before Hammer. Depending on your perspective, we were the electro-mechanical climax of the age, or some sort of a cruel counter-culture hoax. We were considered killer, righteous, high energy dudes who could pitch a whang dang doodle all night long."

This, depressingly, sounds a lot like Al Bundy talking about his high-school football days, like any number of fifty-year-olds in a bar discussing for the thousandth time that one time when they were twenty and they got in a fight in a brothel and smoked weed all night and stole the car and tipped the cow, and it was, glorious, man, glorious, and who's buying the next round?

At that South by Southwest panel about the MC5 in 1999, there were a handful of youngsters there, and many nodded their heads when Sinclair, this white-haired, hippie-looking dude, declared that everybody in the room would have been part of his White Panther party if they were in Detroit during the long hot summer of 1968. He spoke about his manifesto, reminding people of "rock 'n' roll, dope, and fucking in the streets," and the crowd of critics was enthralled. Marsh and Uhelszki, who were part of the discussion, took turns talking about how amazing this band was, how it had stirred them in ways they could barely express, and Kramer sat there, smiling like a proud papa who was finally being recognized for all his hard work.

What I felt, though, when I saw the accomplished Marsh and Uhelszki, as well as our own Jim DeRogatis, bobbing their heads in agreement, was confusion. Here were these successful writers, known for their (mostly) independent thoughts, acting as if they felt fortunate to be part of one of the most ineffectual cults in history.

Something else hit me a few years later. What media critic James Wolcott recently pointed about Robert Christgau and Greil Marcus also applies to Marsh and Uhelzski: Here are these literary and political geniuses who came of age during a turbulent time, who were going to become thought leaders and start revolutions, who had the power to write about changing the world and then actually do it. And now they're still writing about music, trying to attach importance to it that simply isn't there, and that simply never was there.

Maybe I'm just an asshole who wasn't there in 1968, or maybe, like Tyner says, it all just depends "on your perspective." To quote David Sedaris quoting his nutty brother, "That shit don't mean fuck to me." If it means something to you, I somewhat understand, but I've never heard *Kick Out the Jams* played on any radio station or any jukebox. I walk around New York City every day, and I've never seen any fucking in the streets. So where's the resonance, brothers and sisters?

Maybe people aren't fucking in the streets because they're worried about phony-ass authority control-addict creeps who want to put them down, or maybe they're worried about concrete burns or bacteria. Or maybe—and carefully consider this for a minute—the MC5 was just so goddamn serious and self-righteous that it obscured whatever it was trying to accomplish. Sometimes, being a little tongue-and-cheek and self-deprecating is necessary to set the world ablaze. Sometimes, it takes the realization that you shouldn't try to convince everyone to join you that makes you understand that you can convince many to join you. Getting others to accept and understand you does not and should not have to be the same thing as asking them to change their own lifestyle. You can't simply make people feel good by screaming, "Feel good!"

Being an effective leader often involves being subtle. Just consider the words of a poor Detroit kid fixated with black music who declared war on all around him largely by making jokes, often about himself. After he became one of the most important and successful artists in history, his career still largely seemed like a happy accident to him. On "White America," Eminem raps:

"I never would've dreamed in a million years I'd see / Soo many motherfuckin' people who feel like me / Who share the same views and the same exact beliefs / It's like a fuckin' army marchin' in back of me / So many lives I touch, so much anger aimed in no particular direction / Just sprays and sprays and straight through your radio waves it plays and plays / 'Til it stays stuck in your head for days and days."

Marshall Mathers is an egomaniac, but he's an egomaniac who understands that self-importance can only take you so far. There's a lesson there.

𝕴t was 1968, a time when America was as divided as it would be until the second Bush administration was ushered into the Oval Office thanks to what is politely referred to as a "contested" five-to-four Supreme Court decision. Foretelling the red/blue divide of the 2002 presidential election, on the right you had country music, exemplified by Buck Owens's Old Glory-striped guitar and George Jones's flattop haircut, while flying their freak flags on the left were the likes of Jimi Hendrix, who would soon refashion "The Star Spangled Banner" into a crash-and-burn anti-war anthem, and the Beatles, who, for Middle America, had ceased to be cuddly mop-top pop stars two years earlier when John Lennon made his "bigger than Jesus" remark.

Into the gulf that divided these two camps waded the remnants of America's first folk-rock group, though by then only two of the founding members of the quintet remained. Turning up in Nashville with a hipster producer in tow, they enlisted some of Music City's top session musicians to record what would come to be hailed as the "first country-rock record," a groundbreaking effort that, while generally ignored in its day, is now cited as one of the most influential recordings of the rock era. That band is the Beau Brummels, and the album is *Bradley's Barn*.

All of the above is true, except the last part: No one believes

Bradley's Barn built a bridge between the rock and country communities, thus changing the course of both genres. Nope, common wisdom holds that the *true* touchstone of country rock is *Sweetheart of the Rodeo* by the Byrds, which appeared a couple of months before the Beau Brummels' country-rock foray. That happens to be just about the same length of time with which the Brummels' 1965 folk-rock debut, *Introducing the Beau Brummels*, beat the Byrds' similarly Dylan-and-Beatles-inspired debut, *Mr. Tambourine Man*.

This begs the question: Is *Bradley's Barn* an unjustly ignored classic by pioneers who were overshadowed by the better-known Byrds? That really isn't the case. *Bradley's Barn* is a perfectly decent collection of songs, but hardly one that ranks with the elite albums in the rock canon—which is just one more thing it has in common with *Sweetheart of the Rodeo*.

Despite the fact that *Sweetheart* is championed as the album that ushered in the country-rock movement of the '70s and provided inspiration for the cow-punk and alt-country insurgencies of the '80s and '90s, a fresh listen reveals it to be something more prosaic—an O.K. collection of songs performed decently, if not commandingly. In that way, I suppose, it did play a vital role in shaping '70s country rock, a genre that produced one truly essential recording—the Flying Burrito Brothers' *The Gilded Palace of Sin*—and a whole lot of perfectly O.K. LPs that have been cluttering up the racks at used record stores since the Ford administration. When's the last time you found yourself wishing you had a Pure Prairie League or Poco album nearby? How many times have you wished the Eagles were still Linda Ronstadt's backup band?

Indeed, with the exception of the aforementioned debut from the Flying Burrito Brothers, even the best that country rock produced represented a watering down of the sounds the musicians were attempting to fuse. If this was the rock, where was the fire? And if it was country, where was the heart? Country rock seemed to exist to allow *Easy Rider*-era musicians to engage in some gentle mocking of straight country, while simultaneously paying guarded tribute to a few twangy artists who were acceptable in counterculture circles. When alt-country bands such as Uncle Tupelo and the Old 97's picked up the banner in the 1990s, the need for "rock" bands to justify an affection for country music had passed, and they were thankfully free of self-consciousness and preciousness.

Even the notion of country rock as defined by the Byrds and their brethren seems unnecessary. After all, rock 'n' roll was founded on elements of R & B and country. What were the likes of Elvis Presley, Jerry Lee Lewis, Chuck Berry, and Wanda Jackson if not country *and* rock performers? What did '60s country-influenced rockers bring to the show that was unique from the contributions of the Everly Brothers, Roy Orbison, and Charlie Rich? On the other side of the divide, Buck Owens went out on a limb in the spring of 1965 by taking out a full-page ad in a Nashville fan magazine in which he proclaimed, "I shall sing no song that is not a country song." He simultaneously released his version of black rocker Chuck Berry's "Memphis," later reasoning, "I see 'Memphis' as rockabilly. I didn't say I wasn't going to do rockabilly." Owens took it as self-evident that the lines dividing country and rock were blurry, if not nonexistent, from the time Presley cut Bill Monroe's "Blue Moon of Kentucky" for the B-side of his first single.

If a chasm began to develop with the popularity of the Beatles, the Fab Four were willing to bridge it, paying tribute to Owens with Ringo Starr's version of "Act Naturally." Around the same time, Bob Dylan cut his 1966 classic, *Blonde on Blonde*, with Nashville session cats who, in tandem with some of his New York recruits and members of the Band, created careening, caterwauling rock 'n' roll that sounded nothing like what was then coming out of Nashville. Dylan was back in 1968 to record another landmark album, the considerably more hushed *John Wesley Harding*, in the process opening up the floodgates for a slew of hipsters to lay down tracks in Tennessee. The Rolling Stones' smirking "Dear Doctor" signaled that they were at least clued in to country, if not quite ready to give it serious treatment.

Even within the Byrds' circle, *Sweetheart of the Rodeo* was hardly a daring leap into the precipice. Founding member Gene Clark left the group in 1966 and, one year later, put out the down-home-flavored *Gene Clark with the Gosdin Brothers*; Vern Gosdin, who'd worked with the Byrds' Chris Hillman earlier in his career, went on to score a series of honky-tonk hits in the '80s. And, of course, Gram Parsons, who became a Byrd a few months before *Sweetheart of the Rodeo* was released and was gone a few months after it appeared, was the force behind the International Submarine Band, which issued country-inflected singles as early as 1966, and put out a full post-breakup album, *Safe at Home*, in early '68.

Parsons, who was really more of a visionary than a virtuoso, was, strangely enough, hired to play jazz piano on what Roger McGuinn envisioned as the Byrds' most ambitious album to date—a two-record overview of 20th Century music. Despite his initial sideman status, Parsons quickly became a full-fledged Byrd and steered McGuinn, Hillman, and new drummer (and Hillman's cousin) Kevin Kelley in a more down-home direction.

The Florida-born, Georgia-reared Parsons was from a privileged background, and he hadn't always embraced country music; the Harvard dropout spent a stint as an awkward folkie before rediscovering his Dixie roots. Still, where the idiom was concerned, he displayed impeccable instincts. Drawn to hardcore country rather than its more tepid offshoots, but unafraid to toy with psychedelic and soul embellishments, he was just about ready to make his mark.

In March 1968, the reconfigured Byrds began recording in Nashville with help from steel guitarist Lloyd Green, banjo player John Hartford, pianist Earl Ball, and a handful of other ringers; they'd wrap up the record back home in Los Angeles. The eleven songs that made the final cut range from Dylan *Basement Tapes* covers, to Parsons originals, to songs culled from the catalogs of Roy Acuff, Woody Guthrie, the Louvin Brothers, and Merle Haggard. *Sweetheart of the Rodeo* is the only Byrds album without an original number from McGuinn. Initially, Parsons was at the mike for all but four songs, but contractual problems dating back to his days with the International

Submarine Band forced the Byrds to excise most of his vocals, most regrettably "The Christian Life."

The bonus disc on the 2003 Legacy Edition reissue of *Sweetheart of the Rodeo* features two takes of the track with Parsons handling vocals. He plays the Louvin Brothers' paean to Godly living straight, though his soon-to-be drug buddy, Keith Richards, was a hell raiser whose taste for excess led to his early demise. McGuinn, on the other hand, found lyrics such as, "My buddies shun me since I turned to Jesus / They say I'm missing a whole world of fun" to be "corny." In some ways, it's to his credit that his disrespect comes through clearly; at least he's honest. (Of course, Ira, the younger of the two Louvin Brothers, was an alcoholic, so one didn't really need to be particularly pure to sing the number with feeling.)

But the final version of "The Christian Life" is ultimately a telling misfire that points to the album's fundamental problem: McGuinn, a great folk-rock bandleader who'd guided the Byrds through a creative burst that produced five popular and innovative albums in three years, found his role as avatar of the band usurped by an ambitious, charming transient with his own very clear agenda. To add insult to injury, at a stage when McGuinn expected to be embarking on his most ambitious project yet, he found himself singing Parsons's vocal parts and trying to hold the increasingly flimsy lineup together. Sure, McGuinn's 20th Century overview as likely as not would have been a sprawling mess, but it was the '60s, and he had earned the right to take a shot at his *Tommy*.

For his part, Parsons couldn't have been pleased with the turn of events. *Sweetheart of the Rodeo* is viewed today as quite possibly *the* essential Byrds album, but the superior recordings that preceded it with the original five members rank with the best work of any American band. *Mr. Tambourine Man* and *Turn! Turn! Turn!*—both released in 1965—served as signposts for the folk-rock movement, and the title tracks were both hit singles. *Fifth Dimension* came out one year later and begat one of the most daring singles of the era, "Eight Miles High." *Younger Than Yesterday* set a standard for uniform excellence, and *The Notorious Byrd Brothers* was made when the lineup was in flux (by the time it appeared, only McGuinn and Hillman remained), but it holds up as progressive pop at its best.

Their commercial fortunes may have been falling a little with each release, but *Sweetheart of the Rodeo* considerably accelerated the Byrds' descent. Indeed, the squares at the Grand Ole Opry may have given the band the cold shoulder when it topped off its stay in Nashville with a two-song performance, but it wasn't much cooler then the reception their fans gave the country collection. *Sweetheart of the Rodeo* peaked at No. 77 on the *Billboard* albums chart, and it seemed destined to be lumped in with now-forgotten Byrds-in-descent albums such as *Dr. Byrds & Mr. Hyde* and *Byrdmaniax* in the telling of the band's story. When matched up against what came earlier, that was where it belonged. But history took a twist somewhere along the way.

Parsons left the Byrds in the fall of 1968 while they were on tour in London, proclaiming that he couldn't stomach performing before segregated crowds in apartheid South Africa, where the band was scheduled to tour. Noble sentiments, but Hillman, for one, thought Parsons's abrupt departure had a whole lot more to do with wanting to party with his new buddies, the Rolling Stones. Still, when Parsons finally got around to forming his dream band, rock's preeminent second banana was there at this side. Hillman and Parsons fleshed out the Flying Burrito Brothers' lineup with bassist Chris Ethridge and steel guitarist Sneaky Pete Kleinow. The quartet and some pickup drummers recorded and released *The Gilded Palace of Sin* in 1969; it did even worse commercially than *Sweetheart of the Rodeo*, peaking at No. 164, but it earned praise from a lot of prominent musicians who appreciated how Parsons and Hillman had deftly mixed and matched the pathos of country with the weirdness of psychedelia and the raw emotion of soul. It's an uncompromised *Sweetheart of the Rodeo,* and, for my money, the undisputed zenith of country rock.

An out-of-control Parsons was canned by Hillman after an unsatisfying sophomore album, *Burrito Deluxe,* which stiffed worse than the debut. Parsons's initial early '70s attempt at a solo LP was stillborn, and the inspired notion of recruiting Merle Haggard to produce a second attempt never came to fruition, but he eventually got around to recording a couple of fine solo albums before he died in 1973 of heart failure following a drug overdose. Two friends stole his corpse and burned it in the desert, which, apparently, was what Gram would have wanted.

McGuinn, the lone original Byrd following Hillman's departure, recruited the great guitarist Clarence White (who guests on *Sweetheart of the Rodeo*) and some less distinguished cohorts and managed to put out a handful of spotty albums before he gave up the Byrds name and went solo in 1971. There were reunions and partial reunions to come. In January 1991, the original quintet was inducted into the Rock and Roll Hall of Fame; four months later, Gene Clark died in Sherman Oaks, California. In 1993, Michael Clarke, who'd been scrapping with the other three surviving band members over the rights to the band's name, died in Florida.

The Beau Brummels broke up following *Bradley's Barn* and put out a comeback album in the mid-'70s that failed to cause much of a stir. They were a pretty good band, though.

CAPTAIN BEEFHEART
AND HIS MAGIC BAND
Trout Mask Replica
Straight, 1969
By Jason Gross

"**A**n assortment of observations took place."
A large part of the legend of painter, poet, singer, songwriter, and sculptor Don Van Vliet—a.k.a. Captain Beefheart—rests on his third album proper, *Trout Mask Replica*. After bouncing around on several different major labels in the mid- to late-'60s, Beefheart's reunion with his old chum, avant-rock misanthrope and producer Frank Zappa, seemed to signal the full flowering of the Captain's talents in many critics' minds. *Rolling Stone* put *Trout Mask Replica* on its 1987 list of the one hundred best rock albums, Greil Marcus called it "as unique and true a vision of America as rock and roll has produced," and *The Trouser Press Record Guide* hailed it as a "masterpiece." *Record Collector* called it "a major musical achievement," *The All-Music Guide* gave it five stars, and so on. But in addition to the fact that these accolades have never helped to spur sales, none of these publications ever really got around to saying why the damn thing is any good.

The problem with knocking an icon such as Captain Beefheart is that you run the risk of being seen as (the horror!) *uncool*. Merely name-checking *Trout Mask Replica* seems to grace any writer or musician with an aura of underground chic among the self-proclaimed cognoscenti. Sonic Youth, XTC, and the Buzzcocks covered his songs, PJ Harvey ("Rid of Me") and the Sex Pistols ("New York") quoted his lyrics, and former bandmates infiltrated the Pixies and the Red Hot

Chili Peppers. His fan club also includes the Talking Heads, Pere Ubu, the Residents, and Devo. Only an uptight, stuck-up, wimpy shithead couldn't appreciate *Trout Mask Replica,* their attitude says. Any album that pisses off and confuses so many people must be good, right? If it turns every cherished convention of pop music upside-down, it *has* to be a work of genius (even if the Shaggs did the same thing better—or worse, actually—the same year that Captain Beefheart's opus was released).

But no one ever stops to ask if the broken melodies and fractured rhythms which supposedly make the album so great might actually be its weakness. The music is more fun to talk about than to listen to—playing it end to end just gives you a throbbing headache.

When it came out in 1969, around the same time as another pretentious piece of art rock from the Who, *Trout Mask Replica* beguiled even the hippest minds simply because it was a sprawling double album. (Those were still a novelty at the time, and more *had* to be better, right?) After *Sgt. Pepper's Lonely Hearts Club Band, Tommy* took the lead in pushing rock into the realm of high art. Credit Beefheart with making a gesture that was on the surface less radical, but in essence, much more revolutionary than the Beatles or the Who ever dreamed.

While *Trout Mask Replica* had a very dry and unelaborate production, and it sported only guitars, drums, and two horns, it attempted to transform the idea of what rock could or should be. Lyrically, it cut through the flowery imagery spouted by progressive rock bands such as Procol Harum and King Crimson. While the hippies were demanding free love, Beefheart was agitating for freedom from every societal convention, including the confines of intelligible language (he resorted to field hollers—literal cries in the wilderness—and inventing his own slang instead). But like *Finnegans Wake* by James Joyce or the action paintings of Jackson Pollock, I'm convinced that it's ultimately something that's best admired from a distance, and that it's better in theory than in execution.

My skepticism hasn't stopped me from listening to *Trout Mask Replica* dozens of times over the years. When I was in high school, ten years after the album's release, it was a secret pleasure, a strange alternative to the Pink Floyd and Bruce Springsteen that my friends loved. I admired the whole contraption—still do (from a distance)—but I think I kept playing it because I was fascinated with the bizarre world that it conjured up, rather than the fact that I enjoyed the music. In time, I discovered and came to love the Captain's other albums, particularly *Strictly Personal* (1968), *Lick My Decals Off, Baby* (1970), and *Doc at the Radar Station* (1980). They seemed more self-assured but still infinitely crazed. Now, I wonder if people cite *Trout Mask Replica* whenever the subject of Beefheart comes up because that's the only album they can actually name. I still return to it occasionally, as a curiosity and something that I once respected for being so damn strange. But as any ex-flame can tell you, love and respect ain't the same thing—not by a long shot.

"I don't play lullabies."

To start with the best part, the lyrics on *Trout Mask Replica* play with broken, slurred, or invented words about the environment and the stupidity of mankind. This sounds like typical '60s bleeding-heart material, but Captain Beefheart was a cut above Jim Morrison, if not the Fugs. This was raw, down-home, bluesy Beat poetry. Many of the best blues lyrics (think of Willie Dixon's classics for the Chess label) dealt with romantic woes and alienation. While Beefheart didn't bother much with the former, he certainly knew a lot about the latter, and his brand of nostalgia for the country life wasn't exactly a Norman Rockwell painting or an Audubon landscape. We hear about moonlight, a riverboat, a smokestack, flowers, a barnyard, snow, worms, and a rabbit, but Beefheart mixes it together with wild imagery and unexpected poetic associations, creating a crazed prism. In his cranky tone, Beefheart sings about running away to the "Wild Life," not buying a "Veteran's Day Poppy," witnessing a disaster ("The Blimp") and the holocaust ("Dachau Blues"), escaping from "Frownland," and killing a "China Pig." He's down, but always looking for a way out of a world gone cuckoo, much like Samuel Beckett's most evocative characters.

Musically, the Captain pulls no punches. He created a cult-like atmosphere within his band, sequestering the musicians in a rural compound at Woodland Hills, California, subjecting them to endless mind games during the intense rehearsals, and keeping the musicians locked up together for finger-pointing sessions that wore away at all involved. He even rechristened them with alien names—Zoot Horn Rollo (guitarist Bill Harkleroad), Rockette Morton (bassist Mark Boston), Drumbo (drummer John French), Antennae Jimmy Semens (guitarist Jeff Cotton), and the Mascara Snake (clarinetist Victor Hayden)—to complete the transformation of his brave new world. In the process of this brainwashing, he managed to free them from most of the conventions of popular music.

A left-channel guitar plays something close to rhythm, while a right-channel guitar does wailing slides. Both deliver distinct leads, occasionally soloing in sync, but usually going off on their own with no relation to the drums or vocals. This was the exact opposite of the minimalist approach of the early Velvet Underground: Groups of different rhythms jump up and disappear in each song. The "beat" can get pretty sludgy at times, even when the band raves up, especially compared to the relative tightness of Beefheart's later albums. Meanwhile, the Captain screams, howls, bellows with the abandon of a wounded child, and plays flurries of cascading notes on his saxophone.

But as the legend holds (and the musicians confirm), what sounds like a bunch of sloppy dip shits is actually a well-tuned machine. The Captain meticulously wrote out many of the instrumental parts, and dictated carefully mapped boundaries for other sections that were improvised. Each band member repeats a riff a few times, and then does another unrelated one, usually without repeating himself during the song. Sometimes, they sound as if they're playing different songs at the same time. "Learning the material for *Trout Mask Replica* had been everything—a sometimes fun but often excruciating experience," Harkleroad writes in *Lunar Notes: Zoot Horn Rollo's Captain Beefheart Experience.* "Even so, after all that rehearsing, there were only two recording sessions for the whole album."

Trout Mask Replica is full of moments of audio vérité, as if to underscore this fact and point out that this is a recording and not some trip where the listener can lose him- or herself. The tapes capture spoken intros and outros, flubbed and unfinished takes, and conversations with engineers and passersby. But there's never anything as great as Sonny Boy Williamson calling label boss Leonard Chess a "motherfucker" and a "son of a bitch" on "Little Village," and this approach remains unique to *Trout Mask Replica* in Beefheart's work. (Maybe it was Zappa's doing? In any case, the two boyhood friends had a famous falling out shortly after the album's release on Zappa's own label.)

The whole problem with experiments is that sometimes they don't work, and here, Beefheart's batting average isn't always major-league material. "Well" is a great solo reading thanks to Beefheart's majestic chanting. "Orange Claw Hammer" is another good field holler driven by his rising and falling voice. "When Big Joan Sets Up" sports a fine wailing sax solo; "Sugar 'N Spikes" finds the guitars dueling throughout; "Pachuco Cadaver" is a wild stomp, and "Moonlight on Vermont" features a cool buzzing guitar sound. But "The Dust Blows Forward 'N the Dust Blows Back" is an uninspired reading; "Dachau Blues" and "Old Fart At Play" mix the guitars down to no great effect; "Ant Man Bee" and "China Pig" are stumbling blues; "Pena" finds Semens cackling like an old lady; "Dali's Car" is just synchronized guitar scales; "The Blimp" is a cute novelty, and "Veteran's Day Poppy" starts as a blues stomp then swings then falls into a long, plodding riff.

Elsewhere, the coy dialogue and missed takes detract even more from the proceedings. None of the four sides are consistent enough to embrace without qualification, unless you agree with James Joyce that mistakes are really the portholes of discovery. I think mistakes are mostly just fuck-ups.

💀 💀 💀

"We're the only people doing anything significant in modern music."

Maybe if someone was raised on a steady diet of *Trout Mask Replica* in a lab experiment without ever hearing nursery rhymes or the radio, this music wouldn't seem so mysterious or strange. I blame the radio, which fooled me in the '70s into believing that *Born to Run* and *The Dark Side of the Moon* were the end-all and be-all of modern music. The problem with realizing that such fare is just mainstream crap is that you can rebel in the opposite extreme and begin to think that any noisy, discombobulated, screaming horror show is *good*. Extremism in the defense of anti-commercialism is the opposite side of the same self-defeating coin.

Like the Grateful Dead or Beck, Captain Beefheart absorbed many musical styles and tried to transform them into something new. Howlin' Wolf reading the poetry of Ishmael Reed with backing by Ornette Coleman's band might be a decent start at attempting to conjure up his work, but who ever said that all of these diverse elements belonged in the same realm at once? It's a damn shame that many of the Captain's fans aren't equally enamored of Coleman, who started about a decade before Beefheart and is still active today. (The Captain retired from music in the early '80s, disgusted after twenty years in the biz.)

Beefheart took Coleman's ideas of rearranging melody and rhythm and brought them into rock, but Coleman explored these notions more thoroughly, more thoughtfully, and more consistently. In the process, he spurred violent reactions from the musical establishment of the mid- to late-'50s. Charles Mingus disdained his so-called "free jazz" and was never shy about excoriating it. At one infamous show, Mingus presented a "free" group performing behind a screen. After a time, he removed the barrier to expose a group of children trying to play their instruments for the first time. His point was that these kids weren't any better than the "avant-garde" musicians that some people in the jazz world were taking so seriously.

Of course, there's a flip side to this argument—an obsession with "musicianship" can stifle the creativity and drain the life out of music. The reason that a lot of early rock 'n' roll sounds so alive is that guitarists, singers, horn players, and drummers had a lot of "unprofessional" fury, momentum, and sweat that was driving their music past its origins in country and R&B. As the Mekons pointed out, rock is one of the few places where expertise and experience work against you. But what the hell are you trying to prove when you carefully pick a group of virtuoso musicians, painstakingly proscribe purposely atonal or primitive parts for them to play, rehearse this music with an obsessive and joyless attention to detail, then record it all sloppily and haphazardly in an attempt to simulate the passion that you've long since drained out of it?

💀💀💀

"God, please fuck my mind for good."

It's no different with other examples of intentionally "difficult" art. If you're used to watching movies like *Die Hard* or *Terminator* and then run across *Dog Star Man* (with the film out of focus and painted on) or *Un Chien Andalou* (with its disconnected, nightmarish images and infamous scene of a knife slicing through an eyeball) or *Empire* (twenty-four hours of a single shot of the Empire State Building), you'll no doubt think, "What the fuck?!" and spit out your greasy popcorn. Stan Brakhage, Luis Buñuel, and Andy Warhol took the basics of film (story, characters, action) and turned them inside-out to make an abstraction, much as Beefheart does with blues rock. These experiences can screw with your expectations of what you think *ought* to be happening, and they can open up the old gray matter so you see things in a different way. But that doesn't mean you'll necessarily enjoy them.

While the ideas behind them can be fascinating to read about, sitting through the films mentioned above is as difficult, annoying, and wearing as listening to *Trout Mask Replica*. So what's the real worth of this music? Are theoretical ideas something to champion when the sounds that result from their execution make you want to run screaming from the room whenever the album is played? If you want to argue that *Trout Mask Replica* "works on its own terms," you can say that about anything—go listen to some composer's limited-edition release of a field recording of the train screaming by or a jackhammer pummeling the earth at a construction site (these do exist, folks). In the end, you might find those just as pleasurable, if not more educational.

DEREK AND THE DOMINOS
Layla and Other Assorted Love Songs
RSO, 1970
By Marc Weingarten

When I was fourteen, in 1978, my sister and I made a pact: For Christmas we would exchange albums as gifts. She chose an Elton John record—*Capt. Fantastic and the Brown Dirt Cowboy*, I think it was–and I picked Derek and the Dominos' *Layla and Other Assorted Love Songs*, which had always been just beyond the reach of my weekly allowance, due to the fact that it was a double album, and I was too profligate to save up for it. This was a yearly ritual for us; even though we knew what we'd be receiving, we went through the gift-wrap rigmarole to maintain some holiday decorum for our parents' benefit. But that year, I couldn't wait. One night, I snuck into her bedroom and spirited *Layla* away, carefully pried the paper open, and laid the needle on "Bell Bottom Blues," the second-most popular track on the record.

It was one of the most bitter disappointments of my young life. Here was a cherished song from a record that I had internalized from repeated glue-sniffing sessions in friends' bedrooms, and suddenly it sounded…quaint. Not quaint like my mom's Herb Alpert records; more like the sound of middle-aged men trying hard to be intense. Had the punks rendered Clapton obsolete? Not in my world. We all lived in Manhattan, but C.B.G.B. might as well have been in Pacoima. Still, it was in the air, some of the more palatable stuff like Elvis Costello was being played on WNEW-FM, which was a kind of proto-classic rock station ten years before the fact, and the worm had definitely turned. I knew, right there in the dark, that I had no use in my life for Eric Clapton any more. On December 27th, I exchanged the record for *Armed Forces* and *Talking Heads '77*.

This was a heretical move on my part, like a Jew who one day decides to proselytize for the Jehovah's Witnesses. I hung out with whack jobs who got loaded in Central Park blasting Boston's first album, guys who thought Boz Scaggs was a great soul singer. At first, I had to keep my Clapton aversion a secret, because I didn't know how to broach it. Music was so crucial to us that it cancelled everything else out; our shared passion for certain artists formed the parameters of our stony clique. To just barge into school one day and declare that Clapton was irrelevant would bring a fallout that I was afraid to face.

Clapton was God. Sure, I bought into it for a while. There had been an early compilation that we all owned, because it had the solos that we expertly picked out on our wooden Jack Kramer tennis rackets: That explosive starburst break on the Yardbirds' "I Ain't Got You," the elegant bob-and-weave of "Hideaway," which he recorded as a member of John Mayall's Bluesbreakers, and the mother of them all, his amped-up shrapnel attack on Robert Johnson's "Crossroads."

Those three touchstones were enough to place Clapton in the pantheon, but he was also cool by association, because he had played on "While My Guitar Gently Weeps" by the Beatles, and provided that weird "Are You Hung Up?" spoken intro to *We're Only In It for the Money* by Frank Zappa and the Mothers of Invention. That, and he looked great—a central casting rock star with his fabulous blazers and scraggly beard. Plus, he did a lot of drugs, and that was always cool.

Clapton was strictly heavy rotation, and *Layla and Other Assorted Love Songs* was the acknowledged artistic triumph, his only five-star album in *The Rolling Stone Record Guide* (and that meant something to us in those days). He has never, before or since, written anything nearly as great as the title song, but it wasn't his alone. Drummer Jim Gordon is responsible for writing that lovely piano coda that closes it out. (In the '80s, Gordon was diagnosed as a paranoid schizophrenic and institutionalized for hammering his mother to death. Try squaring that madness with the languid beauty of "Layla.")

Clapton is shown up a lot on *Layla and Other Assorted Love Songs*; he's not even the best guitarist on it. Duane Allman was introduced to Clapton by the album's producer, Tom Dowd, who had also produced the Allman Brothers' first two albums. Allman was asked to sit in on the *Layla* sessions as a de facto Domino, which in retrospect has served only to enhance his rep at the expense of Clapton's. Allman's strident but lyrical leads are foregrounded in Dowd's muddy mix for good reason: He smokes Clapton all over the place. Listening to the album now, I can hear Allman as an intuitive artist furiously trying to keep pace with his own ideas, and Clapton as a conscientious blues student, eagerly transcribing from his internal fake book. Even to my weed-befogged teenage ears that Christmas Eve in 1978, Clapton's playing sounded embalmed and entombed, an archival excavation of traditional Chicago blues guitar.

That was Clapton's gig all along—to introduce the blues to benighted white kids who thought Chess was a boring game, kids like me that really couldn't distinguish authentic artistry from canny simulacra. It was a clever bunco game, and for a while there he had all of us hooked. It just took a little research to figure out that the slick, high-on-the-fretboard riffage was yellowed and shopworn, stolen from his venerated Three Kings (Albert, Freddie, and B.B.) and processed into "Are you ready to rock?" pabulum.

It was kind of thrilling at first, because he was smart enough to do it and popularize it before his peers caught on. Cream at its best was a shock to the system, particularly when Clapton took a trowel to stuff like "Crossroads." That solo on *Wheels of Fire* is probably the best sustained work of his career, one long, flowing burst of inspiration. There was dark energy and mystery there; for four minutes and eighteen seconds, you could actually convince yourself that, yes, here was Hendrix's closest rival. Not "God," necessarily, but at least a dutiful apostle.

But Clapton was too ambitious, too much the showman, to sub-
sume himself in a band concept, to look sullen near the Marshall
stack while Jack Bruce took his turn at the mic. By 1970, he was a
giant star, but he wanted to pull back, to woodshed and learn how to
become a singer-songwriter and soak up lessons from white R&B kids
Delaney and Bonnie, who welcomed Clapton on the road with them
to boost their buzz. Clapton, to his credit, was leaning towards the
quiet, unassuming songcraft of the Band and J.J. Cale, but that was a
bad fit for him, like adding fabric softener to steel wool. Songwriting
was never his strong suit; he could write simple sentiments and keep
it light, but without the nuance and narrative verve of, say, the Band's
Robbie Robertson. His self-titled debut was pretty modest, considering the momentousness of the occasion, a handful of so-so country-
and R&B-tinged rock songs. Instead of reaching for some connection
with his times or his audience, he just underachieved, slouching
towards Muscle Shoals to be reborn.

It's been ever thus for Clapton, who is one of the few '60s icons
that doesn't possess a large self-written oeuvre, a body of work that
will outlive him. That's why *Layla and Other Assorted Love Songs* is such
an important album for him and his fans: They can always point to it
and say, "looka-here now! Real classic rock-like songs, a few of them
immortals, no doubt!" It remains his best album, but that's only a testament to how weakly he has negotiated his subsequent career. No
music icon has recorded more stinkers than ol' Slowhand.

Like *Eric Clapton*, *Layla and Other Assorted Love Songs* is a minor-
key album, with a few exceptions. The first thing you hear is
Clapton's delicate finger-picking over Gordon's elemental beat. It's
the opening figure of "I Looked Away," a gentle breeze that you
might have expected to find on a Poco record. The song's "She done
me wrong" lyrics establishes the album's theme, whose well-known
subtext was Clapton's unrequited love for his friend George
Harrison's wife, Patti Boyd. (The album's emotional resonance cur-
dled when Clapton subsequently married, then divorced, Boyd.) The
second track, "Bell Bottom Blues," carries the theme further ("I don't

wanna fade away"). It's the other undeniable song on the album, because Allman's guitar actually sounds like it's crying. Despite Dowd's bona fides as an engineer of genius, the album has always sounded awfully muddled to me (the "remastered from the original master tapes" CD that I bought to reacquaint myself with it for this essay sounds just as rotten, like there's a garden snake hissing next to Clapton's amp), but it works to the song's advantage in this case. There's something about all that desperate clamor, the two guitars fighting for space over Gordon's inverted "on the one" pattern, that gets me in the throat. (It might be a good time to mention the other members of Derek and the Dominos: bassist Carl Radle and key-boardist Bobby Whitlock, both fine, seasoned sidemen, although Whitlock's strained blooze voice is a liability.)

The album climaxes early. From "Bell Bottom Blues" on, it meanders and sags and only occasionally uplifts, and then never enough to justify its length. This is the record that gave double albums a bad name, Exhibit A for the "too thin for two albums" argument that has rarely been refuted. There are roughly two musical statements to be found here: "We're in the studio crashed out on dope and Red Stripe and we want to lay back nice and easy," and "We're here to play some real blooze for y'all!" The four traditional blues songs—Jimmie Cox's "Nobody Knows You When You're Down and Out," Big Bill Broonzy's "Key to The Highway," Freddie King's "Have You Ever Loved A Woman," and Chuck Willis's R&B shuffle, "It's Too Late"— are properly mournful but prim as an altar boy on Sunday morning. You get the feeling that Clapton has something in reserve that he's holding back, some part of himself that he won't reveal. That reticence has bugged me since 1978, and it only became more acute as the years and the albums slogged on.

There's one flat-out guitar tour de force on the album, and it's Allman's moment completely. For an artist that set down a good number of astonishing performances in a truncated career, "Why Does Love Got to Be So Sad?" might be the high watermark. Amid the frenetic rush and drive of the rhythm section, Allman just lets it rip in one big gulp, and he never comes up for air. Clapton creeps in near the end, but it's like a paperboy trying to catch up with Lance Armstrong: "Eat my dust, Slowhand!" Clapton's cover of Hendrix's "Little Wing" was a gauntlet thrown down—an homage, sure, but also a chance for Clapton to measure up. His interpretation is a dumbing-down of one of Hendrix's most delicate and moving compositions. Clapton just papers over Hendrix's filigreed melody with big, dumb power chords, kind of like the way bedroom amateurs approach Jimi—just play the chord progression.

Imagine my disappointment upon hearing the album in *toto* on that most hallowed night, coming through my Sennheiser headphones like electric sludge, the songs offering the tonal and dramatic range of white semi-gloss. I lost my faith in Clapton then and there as an artist that could change me, rock me, make me pick up a tennis racket. But it wasn't easy; an infidel doesn't just stop paying his tithes to the church. I had some explaining to do.

Layla was among a handful of albums (you can guess the others) that got heavy rotation on the Panasonic boombox that my friends and I used to lug to Central Park during recess and after school, smoking Camel Lights and fumbling awkwardly with girls. It soundtracked our leisure time so ubiquitously that there was really no need to ever comment on the music. It just existed, like the trees and the big fountain where the pot dealers hung out. But now I didn't want to listen to it anymore—it just annoyed the hell out of me. The final break came during one overcast Friday, and it went something like this:

"Hey, Mike, what's the deal with Clapton anyway? This shit is so played-out, man."

"What the fuck are you talking about? Clapton rules."

"I don't know, man. It kinda sounds like Jimmy Buffett to me. I think he spends too much time in Miami."

"But he's like the greatest guitarist in the history of rock!"

"No, he's not. Come on, Neil Young plays better than that warmed-over blues shit."

"That's fucked up, Marc!"

Mike, Billy, and Toby were all really pissed off at me for a week or so; I mean, glowering looks and everything. They got over it, of course, because by 1979, Clapton, along with all the rest of the '60s holdovers (except Young, who was still making relevant music), had been rendered obsolete by progressive rock, at least in our world. Now, we parsed *The Lamb Lies Down on Broadway* to figure out what the hell it all meant and marveled at Rick Wakeman's tower of keyboards when Yes played in the round at Madison Square Garden. That's the way it went with music—you lived for it for a brief time, and then you had to move on. Hey, it wasn't easy for Martin Luther, either, but some things are worth fighting for.

LED ZEPPELIN
Untitled ("IV")
Atlantic, 1971
By Adrian Brijbassi

For seven minutes and fifty-five seconds, I held Michelle Kellerman. I grew intimate with her hair, an astonishing swath of DNA the color and texture of a Twinkie; her smell, a fragrance not unlike strawberry yogurt once it's been stirred rapidly and the fruit coerces to the top; the small of her back, which pressed into the palm of my hand as the spine of a paperback novel would; her toes. I stepped on her toes, which were inside her little black shoes. Then I stepped back and uttered the most sincere and pleading apology I had ever uttered, and was willing to drop to my knees and clutch my hands together, begging to continue in her arms.

Michelle Kellerman never complained. In fact, when I stepped on her toes, she did the most generous and wish-fulfilling thing Michelle Kellerman could do: She said it was O.K.—and she reaffirmed her grip around my scrawny neck and pulled me closer.

Michelle Kellerman wanted me! And boy did I come forth.

My palm reached around and applied itself more firmly on her waist, and at a position slightly lower, my fingers eager to reach the good parts of this book. We were so close, her gold earring shaped like a clover nudged my nose, and her neck—my God, her neck was right there like vanilla ice cream waiting to be lapped up. When she breathed, her breasts rose and fell against my chest in an undulating motion that was exquisite in the rapture and the pain it caused.

Led Zeppelin – Untitled ("IV")

The song, meanwhile, settled over us like a blanket. It lilted and lolled and like any sappy song was full of "s" sounds: "whisper," "stores," "a songbird who sings." Sort of like "Careless Whisper" by Wham!

Keep playing, keep playing. Don't stop, I thought. If I had any telepathic powers laying dormant in me, I urged them to come alive and reach out to the singer. *Buddy, whatever you're screeching about, just keep going. Make sure it's a long climb up for that lady.* The longer the tune, the longer I got to graze against Michelle Kellerman's amusement park of a body. And Michelle Kellerman, God love her, was grazing back.

We stepped in circles in the dark gym, grazing together like we were scratching one another's itch. The tip of my nose nuzzled her precious hair and sometimes dipped down to her earlobe and her clover-shaped jewelry, her cheek pressed against my shoulder, and the inside of her left thigh rubbed against the outside of my right leg. Did it feel good? Oh, did it ever. It felt real good…it felt…it felt…ooh… aah…uh…. It felt *too* good.

Whatever hormones in my body urged me to cross the room, to reach out my hand and clumsily ask her to dance, were now making me flex a part of my body in a way it only did in the cloistered sanctuary of my bedroom—and sometimes the shower. But being where I was—within Michelle Kellerman's sacred arms—I couldn't step back. No way. That might seem like I was pushing Michelle Kellerman away, and after months of machinations toward this moment, it would be a cruel irony for me to be the one to pull back.

Michelle Kellerman was a year older, and I was an advanced student taking a couple of courses ahead of my grade. We shared chemistry class, which was a good class to share. Instead of being stuck in our seats for an hour listening to some teacher prattle on about a topic like the history of aeronautics, telling us in arcane terms why the Hindenburg was built and how it exploded, we actually got to move about, put on lab coats and goggles, flick water on each other when no one was looking, and create sparks of our own.

One day before Eastwood Collegiate's annual Christmas dance,

Michelle Kellerman had asked to use my Bunsen burner. Her Bunsen burner had run out of gas, the poor thing. Having spent the first three months of the semester ogling her and scheming for a way to off her lab partner, I was overjoyed to help. I carried my Bunsen burner to her station and wiggled its plug into her outlet and gently turned it on so the gas could rise through the shaft and Michelle Kellerman could ignite it with her match.

She thanked me and said I was fantastic. I grinned and bumped into a stool behind me as I stepped back like an obedient hunchback. *Yes, my lady, anything else? Anything at all, I would be happy....*

Of all the people in the class, Michelle Kellerman had asked me for help. Yes, it was convenient; I was sitting right behind her and her lab partner, plus my lab partner was sick that day, so the experiment took half the time for me, and that's why my Bunsen burner was available. But isn't that how destiny works? Through simple coincidences that appear innocuous at the time?

Convinced that fate was with me and I was just its conduit, I prepared for the dance by repeating the inspirational mantra Nike had drummed into my head: *Just Do It.*

Still, for a good part of the dance, I simply stared at Michelle Kellerman as I did in class. As the night progressed, though, and the moment of opportunity diminished, desperation kicked in like an instinct. *Next slow song,* I said, and sidled up to her, anticipating the moment. When I heard the soft guitar strum of a vaguely familiar tune, I made my move, and she said yes, and we danced, sending my body into its overexcited state.

After all of what I had gone through to get into that position, I had no choice, hard-on or not. I stayed close, my pinky finger invading the back pocket of her Jordache jeans, and our torsos pressing together to form a prophylactic wall of denim. Our stilted steps shuffled on the gymnasium floor as we turned in place. Each movement caused her body to rise and fall against me, which, in turn, increased the blood flow to the growing extremity in my pants. I closed my eyes and cursed fate. Even now, I can hardly believe it. Being close to

Led Zeppelin – Untitled ("IV")

Michelle Kellerman was both excruciating and ecstatic. The relentless friction caused by our close dancing made me wish for a numbing agent—and for the bloody song to stop already. *Forget what I said earlier, boys. Time to cut the number and dig into some meatier material.*

But the song, I was afraid, had just begun. As ludicrous as it seemed, this was the truth. The very same song that I began dancing to when I was sweating and limp was still building, not winding down as it should have been. The singer—who I swore sounded like he had his pants on tighter than the Hulk—continued to caterwaul, the guitar player plucked away, and the drummer began to hammer on his snare.

I rolled back my eyes and told myself to *hold it, hold it*, even as Michelle Kellerman picked up her pace. *Oh, God, don't go faster.* But she did. Why would she do this? Why would she speed up? The answer, of course, was because the song had. The band kicked into a rocking stretch, a lengthy one, when the guitars strummed like a Metallica tune and the singer shrieked like the dude from AC/DC. Michelle Kellerman kept up with them without letting go of me, grazing and grazing and grazing.

I couldn't take it. My body needed relief. I grazed back, faster and faster, pushing against Michelle Kellerman like a frisky dog against a leg. Around and around we went, wearing out our little spot on the floor as the spiteful band jammed on.

Why would they do this to me? Anyone who records a slow song must know that there's a good chance of it being played at a dance, and that some kid who'd been sucking up the courage then letting it out then sucking it up again might finally—upon hearing the sentimental notes of a ballad—stride over to the girl of his obsession and give it his best shot. To then pull a one-eighty and go full bore into a mayhem of metal is more twisted than Dee Snider. *How do you lead a girl to that?*

I didn't know. I just held Michelle Kellerman and prayed for the song to stop or someone to change it. But the song… it remained the same. The sadistic bastards. They were going to play until I seeded the entire gym like a coked-up bee. Did they not understand the physiology of an adolescent male?

Seeing that the band wouldn't relent, I longed for any intervention. For the tape to snag, or the speakers to conk out, or the fire alarm to be pulled, or the principal to walk in and get a whiff of the pot being smoked in the corner. Anything. Any distraction that would stop the dance and get me away from Michelle Kellerman and the agonizing way she kept rubbing against me like she was in on it.

Eventually, the song slowed down again and so did we, but by then I had felt a spasm and bit my lip and inhaled deeply, and wished my dearest wish that Michelle Kellerman didn't know what had just happened. She wouldn't, I was convinced, if I could just get away right then, before a stain had time to form and seep through to stick on her denim as well. The song, though, wouldn't allow it.

The singer dragged out the final verses. By this time, the man had become particularly aggravating. He sounded like a starved cat. Instead of going on about the stairway, couldn't he just do Bryan Adams's "Heaven," a sweet-enough song that's a merciful four minutes?

As I was busy cursing him, my partner raised back her head and let out a howl that terrified me. I cringed and waited for the slap to my face or whatever punishment a woman metes out when she discovers she's been soiled. That didn't happen, though. She simply stopped dancing and released me. Her arms removed themselves from around my neck with the slow elegance with which they had arrived.

The song had ended—it really had—and Michelle Kellerman was giddy. Apparently, she enjoyed it. She clapped her hands in front of my ashen face, grinned, and yelped, "I love that song." In her joy and with her somewhat lopsided smile, all fascination I had with her ended.

She turned her back and returned to her friends, obviously unaware of what I had done. I thanked her and fast-walked to the nearest boys' room, grateful that the paper-towel dispenser wasn't in need of a refill.

Up until that moment, I'd thought I wanted to be with Michelle

Kellerman for eternity. But I realized it was really only for about four minutes and thirty seconds, roughly half the length of the so-called greatest song in the history of rock 'n' roll. From then on, I despised Led Zeppelin, smug English pricks who wished they were Rush or the Who.

Like anyone who grew up with a radio, I'd heard "Stairway to Heaven" before that night, which was a cold one in 1987. But I contend no man has really experienced that song until he's had to endure it in a close, public embrace with a sexual woman and contain himself for the full, torturous seven minutes and fifty-five God-awful seconds.

"Stairway" closing the high school dance is a gesture that's been romanticized and heralded. That notion, though, has always been foreign to me. By the time I was sixteen and growing up in southern Ontario, it was just another example of a grievous genre—the power ballad, which Zeppelin spawned with its opus—and the members of the band, for a few reasons, were more weird than cool.

Led Zeppelin is an enigma, and its enigmaticness is best exemplified by its fourth album. For one thing, no one knows what to call it. Prior to its release on November 8, 1971, Jimmy Page contended that the music would speak for itself, and he fought with executives at Atlantic Records to release the album without a title, the name of the band, or any other labels. Some referred to it as "Untitled," while an Atlantic representative, believing Page's tactic would devastate sales, called it "The Suicide Album." The cover features a tattered wall and a picture hanging on it of an old man bent over with a bushel of straw tied to his back; on the inside sleeve are symbols that resemble medieval lettering intended to represent each member of Zeppelin. For this reason, it's been called "Four Symbols" or the "Rune" album. One of these symbols, the one that marks Page, appears to spell "ZoSo," and some have dubbed the album with that name (although "So-So" may be more appropriate). Page, whose interest in the occult is well documented, created the symbol, and it features astrological forms with meaning only to him. In Chris Welch's book, *Led Zeppelin: Dazed and Confused*, Page said the symbol doesn't spell ZoSo or anything else, and he called the confusion "a pity." So the album is now most commonly referred to as "Zeppelin IV," or, more importantly to pop culturists and fringe fans, the one that contains "Stairway."

Sure, there are seven other songs on the album, but come on, no discussion of the band—let alone this recording—can be had without *that* song dominating the conversation. Indeed, "Zeppelin IV" lives and has some stature because of one seven-minute-fifty-five-second moment in time that seems destined to never go away.

The rest of the album contains hints of genius, particularly on "The Battle of Evermore," and triumphant displays of talent, especially on the album's best track, "When the Levee Breaks." But ultimately, it's uneven, disjointed, and falls short of its ambition and potential. "Stairway to Heaven" rescues it from forgettability. The song has been so celebrated that there are only two positions on it: It is either the greatest rock song ever written, recorded, and played, or it isn't.

The best argument that it's not is based on the old, thorny matter of authorship that has plagued Led Zeppelin from the beginning, when critics labeled it a too-loud blues rip-off. Zeppelin, as the years have further revealed, is not so original, and its penchant for plagiarism is the primary reason why it's expelled from the top of any credible list that ranks importance to modern music. The band incorporated songs created by others, didn't credit the original writers, and became rich for it. The defense that it was following a tradition of bluesmen by "borrowing" riffs and lyrics is ludicrous. The "tradition" existed because there was no alternative, not until companies owned by white men went around delivering cheap, lump-sum payments to blues musicians in return for the rights to their songs. Even then, many musicians received no royalties and in some cases were denied songwriting recognition. It's an injustice that persists.

Page and Robert Plant seemed to think of this practice as something musicians did as long as they could get away with it. Blues great Willie Dixon sued Zeppelin in 1985 for plagiarizing the lyrics to his song "You Need Love" on "Whole Lotta Love," a tune from *Led Zeppelin II* that gives songwriting credit to Page, Plant, John Bonham, and John Paul Jones. The suit was settled out of court, and later Plant said, "Well, you only get caught when you're successful. That's the game." Not an endearing attitude, nor an apologetic sentiment.

What really hurts Zeppelin, though, is that blues musicians aren't the only ones whose songs it misappropriated. The greatest heist in rock history, in fact, may very well be the opening chords of "Stairway to Heaven." The notes apparently were taken from the instrumental "Taurus" by Spirit, a band Zeppelin toured with prior to recording "IV." Never mind that Page and Plant have praised Spirit, and that one member of Spirit has said Page asked for permission to use the riff. The truth is the most played song in radio is credited to Page and Plant, neither of whom, it seems, composed the finest and most important bars within it.

Critic Will Shade has dogged Zeppelin for its unscrupulousness, and in a recent article for the e-zine *Furious*, he writes, "There is no doubt that Page appropriated the opening guitar lines note for note on 'Stairway to Heaven.' Further, the chord progression in 'Stairway to Heaven' is incredibly similar to a song by the Chocolate Watch Band, 'And She's Lonely.'" The Chocolate Watch Band, Shade points out, had toured with Page's old band, the Yardbirds.

That's what it comes down to with Zeppelin: Every note of every tune scrutinized, reasons to speculate sought out. Finger-pointing and askance looks, they're what greet the infamous.

So well-known are Zeppelin's hijinks that several Web sites catalogue the band's alleged and proven infractions. Also, an album called *Led Astray* features the original songs (with proper songwriting credits) that "inspired" and "influenced" the band. In addition to "Stairway," there are three other songs on "Zeppelin IV" with questionable authorship: "Black Dog," the opening track, features a vocal arrangement reminiscent of Fleetwood Mac's "Oh Well," though it's credited to Page, Plant, Bonham, and Jones; "Rock and Roll," also credited to the four members of Zeppelin, is suspiciously close in its chord progression and drum line to Little Richard's "Good Golly, Miss Molly / Keep A Knockin'," and "When the Levee Breaks," the album's last song, is an interpretation of an old blues number by Memphis Minnie and Kansas Joe McCoy. (In this instance, Memphis Minnie is given credit—along with the members of Zeppelin. About the band's input on this collaboration, Shade writes, "What they contributed to the song is once again debatable.")

With so much of the work already done for them, you would think Led Zeppelin—with the talent it had—would have turned out disc after disc of remarkable music, but none of the nine studio albums it produced are close to flawless. "Zeppelin IV" is its supposed peak, the album it made after it had enough money and record-company backing to take the time to perfect its sound, and before the hedonistic lifestyle its members were notorious for did them in with the death of Bonham in 1980. As a whole, the record is a mishmash of styles and musical stabs that no listener could believe was heavy metal. There are folk songs, straightforward rock 'n' roll numbers, an experimental tune ("Four Sticks") that's more percussive bombast than substance. Worse yet, over them all is the wailing, grating screech that passes as Plant's voice, an instrument with all the subtlety of the Jaws of Life operating at full force.

Despite its shortcomings, "Zeppelin IV" has sold twenty-two million copies—the most of any rock album other than the Eagles' *Greatest Hits*, Michael Jackson's *Thriller*, and Pink Floyd's *The Dark Side of the Moon*. If Zeppelin has proved anything, it's that criticism isn't going to slow album sales or fan obsession. The reason the band retains its appeal is simple: Its music speaks to the main contingent of rock fans, teenage boys and young men lacking in self-esteem and desperate to be tough and cool. The music can be dark and brooding, with elements of fantasy, and Page, more than Plant, has a persona of power that resonates with men.

Rock 'n' roll is changing, though. It's no longer just the rebellious expression of youth. For many of us in our twenties and thirties, we listen to and admire music from our parents' generation, and will do the same to certain selections from our children's. Rock, once wholly controversial, is now ubiquitous, and it has risen to become a true art form. Musicians who practice perfecting their art are reaping more of the acclaim of critics and aficionados who compile such things as lists of greatest albums, songs, and bands. That's a good thing. A professional group such as Rush continues to rise in prominence, and Led Zeppelin, which was never as serious about the music part of rock 'n' roll as it should have been, slides. Even prior to Bonham's death, Zeppelin was a band burned out on excess.

With that and all other things said, what can't ever be overlooked when discussing Led Zeppelin is that before its decline, Page, Plant, Bonham, and Jones did manage to touch people. That's not a statement meant to balance the argument. It's an undeniable, unavoidable fact, and there's more value in that accomplishment than in any criticism or analysis of their music. Their fans are loyal, and that loyalty, more than "Stairway to Heaven," is Led Zeppelin's legacy. People feel compelled to share the band's music at the significant moments of their lives—weddings, funerals, graduations and, yes, at the close of the high school dance. To have your creation so adored that people weave it into the fabric of their existence is the goal of anyone who picks up a pen, paintbrush, or guitar. Once gained, no critic can take such intimate meaning away, nor should any try.

NEIL YOUNG
Harvest
Reprise, 1972
By Fred Mills

*L*et's start with a selected time line:

- **10 Bazillion B.C.—1969:** God creates the cosmos; Jesus dies for mankind's sins; McDonald's serves its first cheeseburger; Charles Manson kills off the hippie dream, and Neil Young is inducted into the superstar club by Crosby, Stills & Nash.

- **1970:** The perennially-waffling Young can't decide which he prefers, being a hippie poet laureate or serving as the "Y" at the ass-end of "CSN&Y." He does decide that L.A. sucks, however, and he moves up north to a ranch.

- **1971:** Thanks to a nasty back injury, Young spends much of the year in bed, popping pain pills, but he still manages to assemble his fourth solo album.

- **February, 1972:** *Harvest* is issued by Reprise Records. Both the album and the single, "Heart of Gold," shoot to the top of the charts.

- **1973—2003:** The music world is overrun by simpering singer-songwriters obsessed with the D chord and first-person pronouns.

- **2004:** Charles Manson is denied parole once again.

Calling *Harvest* a lesser Neil Young effort isn't that much of a stretch. Hell, a preliminary warning to that effect appeared shortly after the album's release, when critic John Mendelssohn, in the March 30, 1972, issue of *Rolling Stone*, submitted a dryly hilarious but pointed assessment of its dubious charms. Among his chief complaints was that nearly every song bears a "discomfortingly unmistakable resemblance" to earlier Young compositions, that the stiff musical performances are "restrained for restraint's sake, and ultimately monotonous," and that the lyrics are oftentimes "flatulent and portentous nonsense" routinely plagued by "rhyme-scheme forced silliness" and offering "few rewards to the ponderer."

Mendelssohn concluded that Young's superstar status ensured that his audience "will eagerly gobble up whatever half-assed baloney he pleases to record." I'm here to tell you that his prediction came true, and that—*Oh, the shame!*—back in the day, I, too, gobbled up my share of Youngian half-assedness.

My seventeenth birthday occurred right after *Harvest* appeared in stores. Do the math and you'll quickly realize that, as a Baby Boomer, I was primo demographic material for an album such as *Harvest*. Along with my Boomer peers, I kept it in the Top 40 for twenty-five weeks and made it the best-selling album of 1972. Blame me for its ensuing cultural ubiquity, if you wish, but understand that in 1972, for a liberal-minded teenager with inclinations toward hirsute grooming, sucking down doobs, and pursuing those elusive young fillies in their peasant dresses, denim jackets, and cowgirl (in the sand) boots, falling under the spell of a cultural totem like *Harvest* was a forgone conclusion.

As Johnny Rogan, in his 2000 critical bio, *Neil Young: Zero To Sixty*, put it, "Young's name was synonymous with the sound of the moment and he was increasingly perceived by the record-buying public as the hippie troubadour, blessed with a songbook of catchy, carefully crafted compositions and pleasing bittersweet melodies."

My initial encounter with *Harvest* actually left me a tad underwhelmed; in retrospect, I should have listened with my head and not my headphones. "Heart of Gold" sounded *O.K.,* but it didn't "rock," and even the "righteous jam" of "Alabama" paled in comparison to the similarly-themed and -arranged "Southern Man" from an earlier

Young album. I also recall being sorta creeped out by the textured, chalky, grainy feel of the sleeve: Give me the *faux*-leatherette album cover of *Déjà Vu* any day. Still, it was Neil, and like most everyone who bought *Harvest*, I accepted it as my duty to embrace the album and proselytize in the name of you-know-who.

Blind faith, of course, always extracts a price.

Thirty-odd years of hindsight and a couple of hundred Neil Young bootlegs later, I view *Harvest* as an unexpected but not altogether unexplainable artistic low sandwiched in between a pair of notable, three-album highs.

The first of these—which I'll call the Laurel-Topanga Canyons Trilogy (1969's *Neil Young* and *Everyone Knows This is Nowhere* plus 1970's *After the Gold Rush*)—has long been acknowledged as one of rock's most impressive early-career sunbursts. The second (assuming we omit the 1972 film soundtrack, *Journey Through the Past*), is an equally brilliant but different kind of supernova, a booze- and chemical-fueled one, comprising 1973's rolling drunk revue live album, *Time Fades Away*, 1974's moody but epochal *On the Beach*, and the black hole of nihilism that is *Tonight's the Night*, recorded in '73 but held back for two years. You get rock, you get revolution, you get sex, you get drugs—sometimes all at once—on a six-album roller-coaster ride across the counterculture that still conjures the mood of the era while sounding fresh and provocative. Somebody should do a box set.

Leave *Harvest* out of it, however. In his 2002 biography, *Shakey*, Jimmy McDonough pointed out how much of the album now sounds "heavy as in *turgid*," and that's as good a description as any. What should have been an engaging, back-to-the-roots project turned out instead to be a meandering, unfocused affair characterized by plodding-to-the-point-of-anesthetized rhythms, slight (if, on the surface, pleasant) melodies, and a lyrical outlook that could charitably be described as relentlessly narcissistic.

Speaking to writer Cameron Crowe for a 1979 *Rolling Stone* profile, Young himself candidly admitted how "being laid up in bed [following his back injury] … I became really reclusive. There was a long time when I felt connected with the outer world 'cause I was still looking. Then you get everything the way you want it. You stop looking out so much and start looking in. And that's why in my head I felt something change.… I was lying on my back a long time. It affected my music. My whole spirit was prone."

The Cliffs Notes version of the making of *Harvest* goes roughly like this: In the fall of 1970, following a massively successful CSN&Y tour and a breakup with his first wife, Young bought a ranch so that he could get back to the country and "get his head together." A subsequent back injury incurred while working on the farm, coupled with an aggravated spinal disc problem, forced him to spend a fair amount of time in bed and on heavy pain medication. Wearing an uncomfortable back brace, he went out on a solo tour in late '70 and early '71, during which time he premiered a number of new tunes, several of them hinting at his blossoming romance with actress Carrie Snodgress.

Shortly after the tour, Young went to Nashville to appear on the "Johnny Cash on Campus" TV show. While he was there, he hooked up with local producer and studio operator Elliot Mazer, who rounded up drummer Kenny Buttrey, bassist Tim Drummond, and pedal steel player Ben Keith—Young dubbed 'em the Stray Gators—and commenced recording *Harvest*. He returned to Nashville later in the year to cut some more material, holding additional sessions back at his ranch when his ongoing back ailments precluded travel. Also in the Gators: Young's old friend and producer, Jack Nitzsche, on piano and slide guitar, who'd previously overseen a February recording session in London featuring Young on piano, backed by the London Symphony Orchestra.

Reprise initially wanted to release *Harvest* in time for Christmas. Those plans were scotched while Young dithered over matters involving the track listing (at the last minute, he decided to include an acoustic song, "The Needle and the Damage Done," recorded during

89

the earlier solo tour) and sleeve design (a gatefold affair, it featured a fragile and strangely-textured oatmeal paper for both the sleeve and the lyric insert). The album was finally issued the following February.

Harvest, then, represents a mishmash of material culled from multiple recording sources: There are four songs from the Nashville sessions, three cut at Young's ranch, recorded in London with the orchestra, and the live solo number. Therein lies one of the album's chief flaws: its maddening lack of consistency.

Now, it should go without saying that Neil Young is among a select few artists—Bob Dylan, in particular—who is revered for his very inconsistency. Fans have come to accept, for example, that the cost of getting a *Freedom* or a *Ragged Glory* is having to first sit through a *Landing on Water* or a *Life.* For their part, critics cite Young's damn-the-marketplace approach to record-making as evidence of a fearless, uncompromising muse constantly shifting gears in a quest for new artistic strategies.

I'm not so sure any of that applies to *Harvest.* Bloody single-mindedness is one thing, but Percodan-fueled indecision is another matter entirely. Above and beyond some of the problems ticked off above— plodding tempos, overly reigned-in performances, etc.—*Harvest's* internal inconsistency makes for a bumpy and at times downright jarring ride. One minute, we're in mellow-yellow la-la-land ("Heart of Gold"), then the next we're tossing back shots and getting rowdy with the crew out in Neil's barn ("Are You Ready for the Country?"). Or the reflective mood of "Old Man" is abruptly shattered by the orchestral bombast of "There's a World."

The actual sound quality of *Harvest* is equally schizophrenic. One challenge for Young, Mazer, and Nitzsche was to make the Nashville, London, and ranch material all synch up sonically, but if that crossed their minds at all, they were still too lazy to put much effort into doing it. A striking example of this is when the audience claps at the conclusion of "The Needle and the Damage Done"; instead of fading out or cutting the applause entirely, a sudden edit boots the listener headfirst into the opening chords of "Words." While I have no doubt the effect was intentional, it just comes across as sloppy.

What really bugs me about the album is what it *could* have been. "Country-rock Neil," maybe, comprising an entire set of the Nashville material—and there are a number of viable contenders in circulation as bootlegged outtakes, notably the woozy "Bad Fog of Loneliness" and the sweet "Dance Dance Dance." Perhaps by keeping the overall vibe consistent with what Young presumably intended as a laid-back, autumnal theme, some of the performance flaws wouldn't have been as glaring. In effect, Young attempted to right his own wrong some twenty years later by reconvening the Stray Gators and creating *Harvest Moon*, a vastly superior and more aesthetically pleasing effort than its namesake.

Personally, I would have preferred "Jamming-in-the-barn-Neil": Take the slide-guitar rocker, "Are You Ready for the Country?", the gospel-blooze "Alabama," and the complete sixteen-minute version of "Words" (which would later surface on *Journey Through the Past*), then throw in a couple more tight-but-loose honky-tonkers, and you'd have—um, well, you'd probably have a studio variation on *Time Fades Away*, recorded on tour with the Stray Gators in early '73. But you get the point.

💀 💀 💀

In one sense, lyric analysis is a sucker's game. One can take words and lines out of context to back up or illustrate practically any claim, pro or con. But some of the sitting ducks that Young floats on the *Harvest* pond are too irresistible not to take a pull or two at 'em.

As right-on as the sentiments expressed in "Alabama" are (yes, slavery and racism *are* bad!), the metaphor, "Your Cadillac has got a wheel in the ditch / And a wheel on the track" seems slightly askew; shouldn't that second wheel be on the road, since ditches, not tracks, are usually found beside roadways? Of course, "road" doesn't rhyme with "back" in the couplet that precedes it. The famous titular metaphor in "Heart of Gold" fares somewhat better: It's kinda romantic-sounding, and it's also gussied up all nice and purty with burnished acoustic guitar chords, sweetly humming pedal steel, and a subtly yearning bass line. But try popping this line on a gal at a bar sometime: "Looking at you makes me realize I've been a miner for a heart of gold." Don't forget to duck—she's either gonna take a swing at you, or beer will squirt from her nose because of the laughter.

And what about that nifty little simile bobbing in the middle of "Old Man"—"Love lost, such a cost / Give me things that don't get lost / Like a coin that won't get tossed / Rolling home to you." I think I catch Neil's drift: He's talking about needing stability in life and love, right? But the whole coin thing eludes me. Does he mean the untossed coin is desirable, because it's safe in your pocket and won't get lost, or is he saying an untossed coin is cool because the coin (representing Neil, who presumably doesn't like making his decisions based on a coin toss) is free to roll on home? Oy; my head hurts. Maybe he should have used "stone" in place of "coin"—then he could rhyme it with "home." But I digress.

I must admit that I'm attached to the simile in "The Needle and the Damage Done," the tagline, "Every junkie's like a setting sun." Far from being a lazy rhyme ("sun" with "done") or an uneven poetic image (one critic huffed that setting suns are beautiful, whereas junkies most assuredly are not), it seems dead-on, as anyone who has ever observed a junkie nodding out (or, in the large sense, watched his spirit slowly close down) can attest.

While I'm giving Young some due, let me also say that my favorite song on the album also seems to have the strongest or least flawed lyrics. For *Harvest* to be considered such a classic singer-song-writer album, it's remarkably devoid of epiphanies or universal truths. I defy anyone to make sense of "Words between the lines of age" from "Words"; Nitzsche famously pilloried that song's lyrics as "dumb." But Young partly redeems himself in "Are You Ready for the Country?" It's worth pointing out that to this day, the song is routinely misconstrued as him announcing his "new" country-rock direction. Blame lazy reviewers who just look at the song title, or country king Waylon Jennings, who covered the song, or Young himself, who frequently whips it out at the annual Farm Aid concert. In fact, it's so clearly a song about the war that was still raging in Vietnam—with direct references to the Left, the Right, the domino theory of Southeast Asia, dying for God and country, etc.—that it's hard to fathom how anyone could get it wrong. While not as potent as "Ohio," it's still a compact, uncluttered anti-war number, a tale about a kid about to ship out who talks first to a preacher (who lets him know that God will be on his side), then to the hangman (who tells him unequivocally, "It's time to die").

Some have cited "A Man Needs a Maid" as an example of Young being on top of his game. Admittedly, it does carry a certain emotional heft, particularly at the end, when he sings in a tiny, plaintive voice, "When will I see you again?" It's a wonderful, nakedly vulnerable moment. But the whole housekeeper image, even as a metaphor for Young's insecurity and neediness, strikes me as slightly banal. I'm no poet, but maybe he could have considered some other lyrical options: "Hmm, let's see... 'A ma-a-an needs a mechanic,' and, uh ... 'Someone to keep my gears turning and my motor running.' Naw, naw. How's about ... 'A beekeeper, someone to keep my hive warm, bring me sweet nectar, and buzz around all day...'? Yeah, that works." Hey, it could have happened.

Earlier, I called *Harvest* "relentlessly narcissistic." Writing from one's own point of view certainly isn't a crime; part of any good songwriter's appeal is how he translates his interior life to the lyric sheet. That said, methinks the man's ego doth runneth over here. I ran the lyrics though my trusty old Schlock-O-Meter and arrived at some telling stats: "I" and "my" are the first words of three songs; "I," "my," and "I'm" appear in the first line of three other songs; and in three others more, "I" is prominently positioned as a line's first word. That's nine out of ten songs. After giving passes to "Alabama" and "Are You Ready for the Country" for being political, not personal, we're still left with a whopping seventy percent of *Harvest* being an exercise in solipsism, not storytelling.

The last thing I want to touch on might best be addressed in a court of law, but here goes anyway: Can Young be sued for what he spawned with *Harvest*? The album gave every half-assed folkie on the scene license to whine. Thirty-two years later, we're still knee-deep in legions of groveling, me-fixated singer-songwriters whose sole stock in trade basically boils down to this: "I got up today / I fixed a cup of coffee / Looked around / And saw you were gone / My heart was heavy / So I wrote this song about you / It kinda made me feel better." Your honor, we're willing to stipulate lifetime probation for Mr. Young, but absolutely no charity concerts in lieu of his community service.

☠ ☠ ☠

It's interesting to note that *Harvest* was recently the sole focus of an entire book, published in 2003 as part of Continuum's "33 ⅓" series, in which albums are dissected but generally praised as classics. Sam Inglis claims to love the album, although one wonders how loyal to *Harvest* he truly is, given that he voices many reservations similar to those expressed above. (A probing of *Tonight's the Night* would have made for far better reading.) If the best defense one can mount of an album comes across that conflicted, why bother in the first place?

If *Harvest*'s faults are so glaring, if critics routinely savage the album, or, in the case of Inglis, if they damn it with faint praise, and if its creator even tries to atone for his lapse by redoing it years later, what accounts for the fact that it continues to sell by the truckload? (Fun Fact #1: *Harvest* was the first album in Young's back catalog to be reissued on CD, while last year, it became the first Young title to be sonically overhauled for the DVD-A format.) As recently as last year, Aimee Mann, a gifted songwriter who's hardly your garden-variety, mainstream, Best Buy-shopping schmuck, was talking to *Entertainment Weekly* about essential albums, and she gushed, "My babysitter brought [*Harvest*] over one night when I was a kid and I was fascinated. It had such a haunting and mournful quality."

I'm tempted to take the easy way out to explain all of this by playing the Baby-Boomer nostalgia card: You just hadda be there. (Fun Fact #2: In August, 2003, a second-stringer named Josh Rouse issued an album of half-baked lite-rock entitled *1972*.) But maybe the nobler approach is to simply call *Harvest*'s enduring appeal a mystery, throw

Harvest

up my arms, and say, "It beats the hell out of me." Besides, I have a story to finish.

Back in the summer of '72, I'd become deeply smitten by a hippie chick whom I privately referred to as "my Cinnamon Girl." After finally screwing up the courage to ask her if she wanted to go out some night and smoke some dope, I rushed out and bought a second copy of *Harvest*, this one on eight-track tape (for the car, natch). I mean, how could these sensitive, tuneful songs about maids and men, about weekends and words—about *hearts of gold!* —fail to get me to first... second... maybe even third base?

Somewhere in between "Harvest" and the theoretically surefire "Heart of Gold," however, my Cinnamon Girl turned into the Cynical Girl. I sensed that I was losing ground when she mocked my air-piano-playing during "A Man Needs a Maid." Thirty seconds into "Heart of Gold," she complained, "Gawd, he is *soo* whiny-sounding; you don't have *Deep Purple In Rock,* do ya?" Then she summarily eject- ed the eight-track, and I deduced that tonight was *not* gonna be the night. With no Deep Purple on hand, I shoved in *Wheels of Fire* and lit up another joint. I think we both passed out during the drum solo in "Toad."

For a long time afterwards, I held a grudge against Young for delaying the loss of my virginity by at least six months. (That's an eternity in teenage time.) I eventually got over it, though, and Neil is still my favorite all-time artist. Picks to click: *Everybody Knows This is Nowhere, Sleeps with Angels,* and bootlegs of the 1991 tour with Sonic Youth as the opening act. To this day, however, I can't pick up a copy of *Harvest* and touch that textured sleeve without cringing.

THE ROLLING STONES
Exile on Main St.
Rolling Stones, 1972
By Keith Moerer

$\mathfrak{Y}$ou've heard it, read it, maybe even said it yourself: *Exile on Main St.* is one of the ten best rock albums of all time. It may be the best double album ever. I mean, c'mon, it's the Rolling Stones at their peak, their unqualified masterpiece. There's only one problem with these pronouncements: They're dead wrong.

To cut through the myth, let's start with an acid splash of reality. By the middle of 1971, the Stones had survived but were still haunted by the death of Brian Jones and the apocalyptic nightmare that was Altamont. To rid themselves of their longtime manager, Allen Klein, they were embroiled in a lawsuit that would force them to cede control of their catalog through 1969. Adding to their troubles, they were heavily in debt and faced enormous tax liabilities in England. On the advice of their financial advisor, Prince Rupert Lowenstein, they hustled off to the French Riviera, where they hoped to escape their crushing tax bills and record the follow-up to *Sticky Fingers* at Nellcôte, a sprawling villa rented by Keith Richards and Anita Pallenberg.

So far so good. From *London Calling* to *In Utero*, many great albums are made in the face of enormous strain. The storyline is universally appealing: Band members who have their backs to the wall join together and make a defiant statement, proving both their substance and their mettle.

But the "band" that recorded *Exile on Main St.* can scarcely be

96

called that in any real, meaningful sense. Keith was already deeply addicted to heroin, and his erratic work habits dictated the recording schedule—if that word can even be used to describe the scene as set by Stones biographer Stephen Davis in *Old Gods Almost Dead*. Charlie Watts and Bill Wyman would show up in the basement studio at the appointed time of 8 PM and wait around for hours for Keith to arrive, as though—shades of *Spinal Tap*—he somehow got lost making his way down the stairs. Once Richards made it to the studio, there was no guarantee that he wouldn't pop back out to, um, help Anita deal with their fussy baby, Marlon, and promptly vanish again for hours.

Pissed off by Keith's unreliability, Mick Jagger would often bolt for Paris, disappearing for days at a time to be with his pregnant wife, Bianca, then living in an exile of her own choosing at L'Hôtel. According to Davis, Richards despised Bianca, seeing her as Mick's pretty, vapid trophy wife, but it's hard to argue with her reluctance to be sucked into the rock 'n' roll suicide that was Nellcôte at the time. Like Richards, Pallenberg was doing a lot of heroin, even though she was pregnant with her second child. Not that anyone else staying at Nellcôte—a cast of about thirty—intervened too strenuously. With few exceptions, they were drinking and drugging heavily, too, helping themselves to the half kilos of heroin that were delivered to the villa as casually as Friday-night pizza.

With Mick largely absent, Keith at first welcomed the chance to hang with Gram Parsons, a musical ally and drug buddy since the summer of 1968. But Parsons consumed so many drugs so quickly that Richards told him to leave. Wyman, in particular, grew so unnerved by Nellcôte's heavy-duty drug haze that he retreated to his own villa, whiling his time away in a comparatively benign cloud of pot smoke.

During four-and-a-half months of recording at Nellcôte, most of the basic tracks were laid down by everyone's all-time favorite Stones lineup: Richards on guitar, producer Jimmy Miller on drums, Mick Taylor on bass, and Bobby Keys on saxophone. With a drug bust imminent—Pallenberg had injected her chef's daughter with heroin,

97

and the police were circling after the band refused to pay off her father—the band members scattered in late November of '71, fleeing the country before the *gendarmes* came calling with handcuffs.

By January, the Stones had regrouped in Los Angeles for final mixing, and this is where some of the album's undeniable magic emerges through the murk. Keyboardist Billy Preston invited Jagger to the church of Reverand James Cleveland, which probably inspired the strong gospel flavor that suffuses "Shine a Light." And Richards invited Dr. John and a few of his backup singers to sprinkle a little gris-gris on the proceedings.

During this phase, Jagger regained control of the band, largely out of necessity. By March, Richards and Pallenberg had jetted off to Switzerland to detox prior to the birth of their second child. Richards returned to finish recording, but was unable to function, so pedal steel guitarist Al Perkins was brought in to complete one of *Exile on Main St.*'s final songs, "Torn and Frayed." (The song is about a guitarist and his ragged coat, a little worse for the wear, but still rough and ready. Talk about denial.) When the album was released in May 1972, it featured all five members of the band—Jagger, Richards, Wyman, Watts, and Mick Taylor—on only two tracks, "Rocks Off" and "Ventilator Blues."

But wait, you say. Never mind the studio bollocks. What about the final, unsurpassed results? It's true, of course, that *Exile on Main St.* features a handful of Stones classics—"Rocks Off," "Happy," and "Tumblin' Dice"—and lots of great *sounds*. It's also true there's an awful lot of genre filler (and worse) for any album claiming to be the best of all time.

The blues tracks weigh down the album the most. In 1962, there was something charming about English teenagers trying to imitate American bluesmen two or three times their age. A decade later, it's creepy to hear a rock star spend tens of thousands of dollars trying to slur his words in a way that came considerably cheaper to Slim Harpo, as Jagger does on "Hip Shake." Heard today, the Stones' version of Robert Johnson's "Stop Breaking Down" sounds more like a pretty good Chicago bar band than the mid-period masters the Stones had supposedly become. And both "Ventilator Blues" and "Casino Boogie" wallow too much in their druggy, drag-ass grooves to be truly remarkable. Save yourself the trouble and track down some old Howlin' Wolf or Elmore James instead.

I'll admit that "Sweet Virginia" is one of the Stones' better attempts at country—infinitely preferable to the parody of, say, "Faraway Eyes"—but Jagger's voice is still too mannered as he scrapes the shit off cowboy boots he's probably never worn. ("Wild Horses" may be the only time Jagger's been able to hide or fully forget his embarrassment while singing cracker soul.) As for the loose-limbed swing of "Rip This Joint," it's a fine vintage rock 'n' roll rave-up, but not nearly distinctive enough to mark it as an indelible Stones gem.

However, I'll take any of the songs above over *Exile on Main St.*'s lowest moment, "Sweet Black Angel," a deeply offensive "tribute" to black radical Angela Davis that combines lovely acoustic guitar, light, lilting marimbas, and a jaw-dropping set of blackface lyrics: "Ten little niggers / Sitting on de wall / Her brothers been a fallin' / Fallin' one by one / For a judge they murdered / And a judge they stole / Now de judge he gonna judge her / For all dat he's worth / Well de gal in danger / De gal in chains / But she keep on pushin' / Would you do the same?" In the rousing climax to this timeless political protest, still heard occasionally behind closed doors at U.C. Santa Cruz, Jagger pleads to "Free de sweet black slave." It's enough to drive any tenured African Studies professor to justifiable homicide.

About a third of *Exile on Main St.*'s songs had been lying around in some form or another since 1969 or '70, among them "Loving Cup," "All Down the Line," "Sweet Virginia," "Shine a Light," and "Stop Breaking Down." Most of the other tracks emerged from endless jams at Nellcôte, and a lot of them retain their loose, unfinished feel on the final album. "Soul Survivor" isn't much more than a couple of cool guitar riffs and some furious syncopated piano from Nicky Hopkins. "Turd on the Run" is "Rip This Joint" fed through a country-punk grinder. And "Let it Loose" meanders over five minutes, with lovely vocals, but no particular place to go or any rush to get there.

But then *Exile on Main St.* is probably best heard as a glorious smear of sound rather than as a tightly focused collection of cohesive songs. For example, "Just Wanna See His Face" is a remarkable, spooky blueprint for a great gospel song, heard here through the leaky walls of some imaginary church, but it wasn't finished until twenty-nine years later, when the Blind Boys of Alabama turned it into a full-throated jubilee shout on *Spirit of the Century*.

I won't resort to the cliché that *Exile on Main St.* is a good double album that would've made a great single disc, 'cause it's not true. It's a great six-song EP, with a bonus disc of excellent demos begging to be fleshed out and mixed better. And yet, in the thirty-plus years since its release, the album has gathered so much critical momentum that it is routinely touted as the band's best, with little effort expended to explain why, other than, well, it rocks hard, baby.

A large part of this adulation has to do with the Cult of Keith. *Exile on Main St.* is unquestionably Keith's album, more than any other Stones effort. This fits nicely into the tidy worldview that Richards is the embodiment of rock 'n' roll purity, while Jagger is simply the careerist singer who benefits most when hanging on to one of Keef's gypsy scarves. Although glibly reductive, there's probably always been some truth to this formulation, and it's particularly easy to believe after watching the Stones' career trajectory over the past twenty years—ever more bloodless albums, followed by ever more meticulously planned and financially rewarding tours. But can anyone really think that Keith's jagged riffs alone are responsible for the Stones' finest moments? Or even, for that matter, that it's Keith alone who carries Mick over the top on *Exile on Main St.*?

Listening to the album near the end of 2003, what's remarkable is how much of the heavy load is carried by honorary band members and studio guests. Try to imagine "Rocks Off" or "Tumblin' Dice" without the horns of Bobby Keys and Jim Price. Listen to "Let it Loose" or "Tumblin' Dice" after you've mentally stripped out the sexy backing vocals of Vanetta Field and and Clydie King. Take away Billy Preston's organ and piano on "Shine a Light" and attempt to conjure up what's left. Pianist Nicky Hopkins deserves praise for his playing throughout, but he earns a particular shout-out for the intro that opens and propels "Loving Cup."

As for the band's contributions, this is clearly a Keith and Mick (Taylor) album. Jagger sounds great and fully engaged on some tracks, mumbly and perfunctory on others. As for one of the greatest rhythm sections in rock, you rarely hear Wyman and Watts together. In fact, you hear almost as much of session bassist Bill Plummer and producer-percussionist Miller as you do of the rhythmic duo that anchored the Stones—even when Keith was in rehab or Mick was busy preening for the paparazzi—through most of the band's first thirty years.

To believe that *Exile on Main St.* is the Stones' best album, you have to accept that the band was at its best when playing together the least and relying more heavily than ever on session players. You also have to acknowledge that it's an album whose songs—excepting "Rocks Off," "Happy," "All Down the Line," and "Tumblin' Dice"—are largely frozen on disc in their specific time, since the Stones rarely trot out most of these tunes in concert. Of course, there are great songs that don't get played live, but usually they're complicated studio concoctions impossible to recreate faithfully on stage, not three-quarters finished grooves that can't be played in stadiums.

Boosters routinely cite *Exile on Main St.* as the final great work of the Stones' four-album middle period, the glorious capper to a string that began with *Beggars Banquet, Let it Bleed,* and *Sticky Fingers.* I hear it as the first (if undeniably best) album in a songwriting and musical decline that deepened quickly with *Goat's Head Soup, It's Only Rock 'n' Roll,* and *Black and Blue.*

But even I have to admit that this sort of revisionism may be off the mark. Unlike the Beatles, the Clash, Bob Dylan, and Nirvana, the Stones have always been a great singles band rather than full-length album virtuosos. So what? Forced to choose, what true music lover

wouldn't take one great single off a later, weaker Stones album—
"Start Me Up," "Fool to Cry," "Waiting on a Friend"—over two of the
jams off *Exile on Main Street*—say, "Casino Boogie" or "Hip Shake"?
Only a rock critic, that's who.

The Stones' STP Tour, which immediately followed *Exile*'s release,
found the band playing ragged and out of tune most nights, with the
increasingly celebrity-riddled crowds loving it just the same. As Davis
recounts in *Old Gods Almost Dead*, tour keyboardist Nicky Hopkins was
disgusted by how poorly the band performed, but even more revolted
by the backstage sycophants who told the Stones otherwise.

If Jagger agreed with Hopkins, or even noticed, he didn't seem to
mind—there was always another post-show party to attend. After one
of the band's tour-closing shows in New York, Atlantic Records chair-
man Ahmet Ertegun threw a twenty-ninth birthday bash for Jagger.
Sure, Muddy Waters and Bob Dylan showed up, but so did Andy
Warhol, Woody Allen, Truman Capote, and Zsa Zsa Gabor. The
Stones' first full-scale U.S. trek since Altamont, the STP Tour was also
the beginning of the band's lengthy run as a slightly off Broadway
spectacle.

Shortly after its release, Lester Bangs ripped *Exile on Main St.* as a
"mass of admittedly scalding gruel" before recanting a few months
later: "Hard to hear at first, the precision and the fury behind the
murk ensure you'll come back, hearing more with each playing. *Exile*
is about casualties, and partying in the face of them. The party is obvious. So are the casualties."

Judging from the body count, *Exile on Main St.* was one hell of a
party. Richards nodded off for most of the '70s, too smacked out to
do much more than croak "Happy" once a night and inspire ghoul-
pool bets on when he'd join Brian Jones in Rock 'n' Roll Hell. But at
least he's survived, and quite handsomely, as the Stones' 2002–2003
tour proved, with nearly three-hundred million dollars in grosses.

Not everyone involved with the Stones at this time was so fortunate. Gram Parsons would end up dead and scattered to the desert
wind a year after *Exile on Main St.*'s release. A month after this, Bobby

Keys collapsed on stage, unable to continue touring because of his own smack habit. Deeply addicted himself, Miller would be brought back to produce the Stones' next album, but he was dumped before *Goat's Head Soup* was completed. He'd drift for most of the next two decades before dying of liver failure in 1994, still in his early fifties. Bangs himself would die in 1982, unable to resist the sort of *Exile*-style party that he first said "no" to.

Sorry, but *Exile on Main St.* doesn't come close to being the Stones' grandest achievement. In fact, its debauchery all but guaranteed that they would eventually flame out for good, or be forced to reinvent themselves as a sleek corporate machine to survive. Don't blame Mick Jagger for turning the Stones into a bloodless rock 'n' roll circus; fault Keith Richards's absurdly outsized appetites for preventing any other option from being possible.

But the true legacy of *Exile on Main St.* is far more sinister than this. Besides the toll it took on so many directly involved with it, the album endures today as bullshit inspiration to countless musicians who romanticize excess, glorify self-destruction, and lie to themselves that their latest murky-sounding, half-finished work is the best thing they've ever done. Unless you're a sheltered multimillionaire like Richards, that kind of lie usually leads to the nut house or death. How cool is that?

THE EAGLES
Desperado
Asylum, 1973
By Bobby Reed

he first song on *Desperado* opens with the strumming of an acoustic guitar and a cinematic, campfire harmonica riff. On "Doolin-Dalton," the Eagles' Don Henley and Glenn Frey share the lead vocals, singing, "Go down Bill Dalton, it must be God's will / Two brothers lyin' dead in Coffeyville / Two voices call to you from where they stood / Lay down your law books now, they're no damn good."

The Eagles were tapping into the history and mythology of the Old West. The deceased brothers mentioned in the lyrics are presumably Bill Dalton's siblings, Bob and Grat, who died in a gunfight following an attempt to simultaneously rob two banks in Coffeyville, Kansas, in 1892. Born in 1858, Bill Doolin left his native Arkansas and worked as a cowhand in Oklahoma in the 1880s. There he met some folks in a more lucrative business, so he joined these desperadoes and started robbing trains. Western lore is peppered with the exploits of the infamous Doolin-Dalton Gang.

By dressing as outlaws for the photos adorning the cover and back jacket of *Desperado,* the Eagles encouraged fans to make connections between a gang of nineteenth-century, gun-toting bandits and a quartet of twentieth-century, Los Angeles-based rock musicians. Their eponymous 1972 debut had yielded three flaccid hit singles: "Take It Easy," "Witchy Woman," and "Peaceful Easy Feeling." *Desperado* was the follow-up, and the lineup at the time was Henley, Frey, Randy Meisner, and Bernie Leadon. The producer for both albums was Glyn Johns, who....

Hold on, wait a second. I'm getting ahead of myself. Maybe I ought to start by explaining why the hell I'm doing this—not only deconstructing *Desperado*, but writing about popular music in the first place.

I was a smart kid. I paid attention. I did my homework. I obeyed my mother. I could've been somebody. Instead, I wound up writing about country and rock music. What happened?

When I was thirteen or fourteen, during a periodic visit to the local mall, I spent five bucks on *Rock Critics' Choice: The Top 200 Albums,* compiled by Paul Gambaccini with Susan Ready and published by Quick Fox in 1978. The cover featured a color photo of a Wurlitzer jukebox, superimposed with text that proclaimed, "THE ALL-TIME GREATEST ROCK ALBUMS CHOSEN BY THE WORLDS [*sic*] TOP DJs AND CRITICS." Gambaccini had gathered a top-ten list from forty-eight contributors, then used a points system to rank the albums.

I devoured the book, reading it over and over. I learned the names of acts I'd never heard of: the Stooges, Robert Johnson, the MC5, the Wailers, David Ackles, King Crimson, John Stewart, Love, Can, Traffic, the Sir Douglas Quintet, Gram Parsons, and the New York Dolls. Gambaccini's introductory essay instigated my downfall, pushing me onto a circuitous career path by claiming that rock critics serve an important function: "Without them we are at the mercy of record company advertising, the squeals of the loudest fans, and that inaccurate barometer of quality, reputation. Without rock critics, there would be anarchy in the browser bins."

Before I bought this book, I hadn't thought of the Eagles as belonging to the elite in rock history, but lo and behold, *Their Greatest Hits (1971–1975)* was ranked at No. 141. This placed it ahead of Pink Floyd's *Wish You Were Here* (No. 146), the *Woodstock* soundtrack (No. 150), and Patti Smith's *Horses* (No. 182). Coming in at No. 190 was another Eagles album, *One of These Nights.* Two titles in *Top 200* indicated that the Eagles were responsible for exactly one percent of the best rock music of all time.

The book concluded with a section that revealed the top-ten list for each contributor. The Eagles fared well here. Rosalie Trombley put *Their Greatest Hits (1971–1975)* at No. 5; Joel Whitburn put *One of These Nights* at No. 7; Chuck Blore put *Hotel California* at No. 8; and Cameron Crowe put *Desperado* at No. 9 (tied with Little Feat's *Dixie Chicken*). During my late teens, it didn't occur to me to view rock critics as frustrated musicians, pompous assholes, self-absorbed nitwits, or socially inept misfits. They were my teachers and mentors—or at least people with cool jobs. So I went to college to become a rock critic. Didn't work out like I planned. I started out in journalism, then switched my major to English, wrote some music criticism for the school newspaper, graduated, then went straight to grad school to study American Literature, got an M.A., and wound up working full-time in a record store.

In the noble profession of retail clerk, I helped people discover new music. Plus, I could (legitimately) take home part of my meager paycheck in the form of vinyl. By then, I no longer referred to Gambaccini's book—I had developed my own aesthetic. I knew what constituted great rock 'n' roll, and I didn't need some dumb-ass music critic to explain it to me.

I became reacquainted with my mentors, however, when I read Greil Marcus's 1979 collection, *Stranded: Rock and Roll for a Desert Island.* Finding this book was like running into a group of old friends at a party. Six important contributors to *Top 200*—Marcus, Robert Christgau, Ellen Willis, Simon Frith, Dave Marsh, and Ed Ward—wrote pieces for this collection, which was based on the premise of Marcus asking rock writers to pen an essay on the one album they would take to a desert island.

One of the *Stranded* contributors, Grace Lichtenstein, devoted an essay to *Desperado.* Her writing was so persuasive that it made me reexamine my stance on the Eagles, whom I'd dismissed (despite the advice of the Gambaccini book) as boring millionaires. Lichtenstein made a passionate and articulate case for *Desperado,* not as the finest album ever recorded, but as a work of art that was deeply important to her. She described it as "deliciously melodic throughout." She even bought the "concept" aspect of the album: "The themes are all of a piece, more like a musical comedy/drama than a rock performance. Only the Who's *Tommy* seems to have been conceived with such close lyric connections and a coherent story line."

Coherent story line? I've listened to *Desperado* plenty of times, and I've studied the lyrics, but it has never struck me as a cohesive tale with a compelling plot. I do like Lichtenstein's comparison to a musical comedy/drama, because elements of *Desperado* are so meticulously calculated that they're reminiscent of Broadway schlock. Lichtenstein argues that the album can be interpreted as the saga of Bill Doolin, as well as the story of the Eagles and "every young hotshot rock-and-roller with a quick draw on his guitar."

In 1973, listeners may have found grandeur in *Desperado,* but thirty years on, it comes across as dated, pretentious, and dull. If, when I die, it turns out that I am an unforgiven sinner in the hands of an angry God, I will be banished to a desert island where the only sound will be that of *Desperado* playing in its entirety, repeatedly, for eternity.

The thirty-six-minute song cycle begins with the aforementioned "Doolin-Dalton." That's followed by "Twenty-One," a faux-country ditty anchored by Leadon's banjo work. Sample simplistic lyric: "I'm young and fast as I can be / I know what freedom means to me." The next number starts with Frey screaming, which is definitely a bad sign. "Out of Control" is a carefully constructed studio attempt at rocking out, an ode to being reckless, getting drunk, and bedding a slutty barmaid. This song is as "out of control" as a kitten full of milk. In the context of a relatively mellow album, this track's fast tempo and wailing electric geetar parts sound incongruous.

"Tequila Sunrise" is the most effective cut, a gently swaying, countryish tune that exudes regret. The band tries to ruin it with some putrid "ooh-ooh" backing vocals—and someone should have stomped on Frey's foot to prevent him from humming "Mmmmm" at the very end—but if you're looking for a pretty tune to stimulate the growth of your houseplants, this will do the trick.

Side one of the old vinyl LP closes with the famous title track. There's no palpable emotional investment in Henley's vocal delivery, which is so measured that he might as well be singing about a new brand of margarine instead of telling a desperado to stop ridin' fences and doing those pleasin' things that could hurt him somehow. Jim Ed Norman was responsible for the lush, syrupy string arrangements, which add a sticky gauze to the proceedings. (Norman, who was Henley's former bandmate in the group Shiloh, would later become president of the Warner Bros./Reprise label in Nashville.) Henley and Frey cowrote "Desperado," and they'll be cashing checks for a long time thanks to subsequent covers by acts as diverse as Lynn Anderson, the Carpenters, Judy Collins, Randy Crawford, Chris LeDoux, Johnny Rodriguez, Kenny Rogers, and that brutal rawk 'n' roll keyboard pounder, John Tesh.

Side two begins with Meisner singing "Certain Kind of Fool," which concerns a feller who wants to git himself a gun. Once he scores, he develops a fondness for stroking the barrel: "He kinda liked the feeling, so shiny and smooth in his hand / He took it to the country, and practiced for days without rest." The poor boy becomes a criminal, as many chronic masturbators do.

Next up is a completely unnecessary forty-eight-second instrumental version of "Doolin-Dalton," followed by the David Blue composition, "Outlaw Man," which was probably included because it fit the thematic underpinnings. The narrator tells his woman that she better not love him—he's gotta hit the road because, you know, that's the life of an outlaw man. Like the title cut, this tune invites the listener to see the common ground between a ne'er-do-well gunslinger and a coked-up musician trying to hump a teenage groupie. The problem is that Frey sings as though we're supposed to take this shit seriously. When Jon Bon Jovi screeches, "I'm a cowboy, on a steel horse I ride / I'm wanted dead or alive," it's okay to sing along because you know that Jon knows that you know it's all just show-biz non-sense.

Then there's a cloying waltz that never fails to nauseate me. "Saturday Night" is a lament about lost love that was written by all four band members, who should have pawned it off on Seals & Crofts.

Critiquing *Desperado* in the April 26, 1973, issue of *Rolling Stone*, my ol' pal Gambaccini gave the album a favorable review, but he singled out "Bitter Creek" with this comment: "It wasn't until halfway through recording the album that the Eagles and Glyn Johns realized they could string in order as an entity what they were putting down, and as a result only one of the songs, the 'Bitter Creek' written after that realization, seems strained."

The Eagles wanted to cast themselves as outlaws; now that the band has become synonymous with outrageous ticket prices, the role finally fits. When they reunited for a tour in 1994 after initially splitting up in 1981, they were widely criticized for setting their ticket prices in the triple-digit range. Nine years later, the lineup of Henley, Frey, Timothy B. Schmit, and Joe Walsh played Chicago as part of "The Farewell I Tour," and the best seats were one hundred eighty-eight dollars and sixty cents apiece, including Ticketmaster service charges. A couplet from "Bitter Creek" now seems prophetic: "We're gonna hit the road for one last time / We can walk right in and steal 'em blind." Amen, brothers.

The album ends with a pretentious slab of dross called "Doolin-Dalton / Desperado (Reprise)." It's ostensibly designed to give the listener a sense of closure, but it just seems like filler. The album ends with eighty seconds of the Eagles solemnly harmonizing, singing the word "desperado" ten times in a row.

When *Desperado* was released, it did not generate a hit, but the title track, which was never released as a single, eventually became wildly popular at FM rock stations and junior proms all across the nation. Clint Black recorded it for *Common Thread: The Songs of the Eagles,* a country disc that miraculously manages to make nearly all the material even more bland than the originals; if you want to hear where the Eagles' influence is most manifest today, just turn on your local mainstream country radio station.

There are a few covers of "Desperado" worth recommending, however. Johnny Cash gave it a potent, austere reading on *American IV: The Man Comes Around*. Linda Ronstadt nailed it on her 1973 album, *Don't Cry Now*. My favorite version is on a 2001 album by the Langley Schools Music Project titled *Innocence & Despair*.

In 1976-'77, a Canadian music teacher named Hans Fenger tried to inspire his students in the grammar schools of Langley, British Columbia, by having them sing tunes by the Beach Boys, David Bowie, and other pop acts of the day. He recorded this sixty-voice choir in a school gymnasium, and the students paid the cost for pressing up a few hundred LPs. A quarter-century later, music archivist Irwin Chusid heard the recordings and produced them for commercial release

Unlike most of the tracks on *Innocence & Despair*, the version of "Desperado" is a solo vocal performance with piano accompaniment by Fenger. In the liner notes, he writes, "Sheila Behman, who sang it, was only nine, and her delivery evoked such innocence and despair. She sang it without a trace of sentimentality, a literal reading. She had no idea about the romantic cowboy stuff; she just heard it as sad, the way a child does—the way Mahler, another genius with innocence and despair, might have."

Behman is wholeheartedly convincing in a way that Henley is not because she *feels* the lyrics.

In the original, the narrator wags a finger at the desperado, chastising him: "Now it seems to me some fine things / Have been laid upon your table / But you only want the ones that you can't get." This message is consistent with a line that appears twice in the song: "Desperado, why don't you come to your senses?"

Being a kiddie genius, Behman alters the lyrics: "Now it seems to me some bad things / Have been laid upon your table / And you only want things you can't get." Behman's version is more conversational, and changing the word "fine" to "bad" is a vast improvement—a crucial edit that conveys the narrator's empathy for the desperado.

You should really hear Sheila Behman sing "Desperado." But, hey, don't take my word for it. I'm just a dumb-ass music critic.

LYNYRD SKYNYRD
Pronounced Leh-nerd Skin-nerd
MCA, 1973
By Leanne Potts

Most encyclopedias of rock will tell you as gospel that Lynyrd Skynyrd was the Quintessential Southern Rock Band, the triple guitar-wielding ambassadors of bubba. The entry will go something like this: "Chroniclers of the workingman's dreams and frustrations, these kick-ass musicians combined swamp blues, country, and rock into joyous songs about a magical, pastoral place where skies are blue and necks are red. Their career was cut short in a made-for-*Behind the Music* plane crash that killed nearly half the band. Fly on, free bird!"

Well, I was born and raised in Alabama, y'all, and not once did I ever cut the rug at a colorfully named juke joint, tote my pistols in my pocket (when it comes to firearms, we Southerners favor deer rifles), hear any female referred to as a "little queenie," or go down to the swamp and watch my hound dog catch a coon. I wouldn't dare go into a Southern wetland, because most are so poisoned with industrial pollutants, you might get cancer just wading in, much less eating some poor critter that had the misfortune to live there before you shot it.

Don't tell that to Lynyrd Skynyrd. In Skynyrd's South, folks have escaped the dehumanizing forces of modernity and are still as one with the land. They fetch—yes, fetch—their dinner with a cane pole or a rifle; drink whiskey on Saturday night, and are simple kind of men the rest of the week. They're authentic sorts who play blues harmonica on the porch while mama shells peas and daddy picks a banjo in between sips of sweet tea.

Sounds like a right peaceful way to live, Ellie Mae, but I'm here to tell you that the definitive Southern rock band is handing you an F-350 truckload of bombastic, sentimental bullshit. Its vision of the South as a land of rebels resisting all things modern, intellectual, and Northern is as outdated as hoop skirts, and was even when the band made its debut in 1973.

Lynyrd Skynyrd introduced its Southern-fried hokum to the record-buying masses with *Pronounced Leh-nerd Skin-nerd*, eight songs of pastoral fantasy fueled by a three-guitar attack of country blues and rock. Initially, the album was an underground phenomenon, selling only about a hundred thousand copies and getting good but not great reviews. "'Free Bird' offers a tour of blues guitar expertise," Jim Miller wrote in *Rolling Stone*, adding that Skynyrd had "modest proportions but considerable promise." At this point, it was regarded as a rock band from the South, not a Southern rock band. But as the years passed, critics and fans decided that Skynyrd was the voice of Dixie—a bunch of long-haired nature boys who celebrated the South's quaint separatism from the rest of the country and, most important to etching a myth into the rock canon, behaved like a bunch of bikers during Hell Week. Robert Christgau called them "the most joyously unreconstructed of all Southern bands."

Your exposure to the South would have to be limited to *The Dukes of Hazzard* to believe that *Pronounced Leh-nerd Skin-nerd* was an accurate reflection of the region. By 1970, when Ronnie Van Zant was writing songs about trains and rough country bars and old black men who played dobros 'cross their knees, Lynyrd Skynyrd's hometown of Jacksonville, Florida, was home to more than six hundred thousand people, most of whom lived in tract houses and worked in reeking paper mills and widget-making factories. The city sprawled over seven hundred fifty square miles because it had essentially annexed the entire surrounding county to make it easier for the bulldozers to knock down the piney woods and build strip malls. And Duval

County, Florida, wasn't alone in its march to progress. The entire South had been reborn as "the Sunbelt," thanks to the invention of a little thing called air conditioning in the 1950s. Dixie was becoming urbanized faster than you could say, "Knock down that farm so we can build a superhighway."

Lynyrd Skynyrd's South certainly doesn't exist now. Jacksonville is home to more than a million people and more than seventy potential Superfund sites. (Ol' Ronnie wouldn't want to eat those bass he caught on his fishing pole these days.) The city has twice as many people per square mile as New York City. Atlanta has out-gridlocked Los Angeles, Wal-Marts line the Southern countryside from Little Rock to Charlotte, suburbs have replaced hunting grounds, and you're more likely to get a drink at a TGI Friday's® with a girl named Amber than at a honky-tonk with a girl named Linda Lu.

Despite this—or maybe because of it—I own every Ronnie Van Zant-era Lynyrd Skynyrd album, and I stayed up until the wee hours to watch *Free Bird: The Movie* on cable TV. Why? Because I write about rock music for a living, and I have to listen to all of it, good and bad. I've endured entire Backstreet Boys albums in the name of being informed. But my interest in Skynyrd goes beyond the merely professional. Because I am a vacant-souled child of the mall culture, I need to believe that the place I come from is as exotic as Skynyrd makes it sound. Fantasizing that I hail from people brassy enough to say, "Oak tree, you're in my way" helps me get through another day in a cubicle.

Even though I'm about to launch into an anti-Skynyrd rant, I have to say that I like the band. The original band—not the gang of historical re-enactors impersonating Lynyrd Skynyrd these days, with only Gary Rossington and Billy Powell remaining from the glory days. I still appreciate the roaring guitar assaults of Rossington, Allen Collins, and Steve Gaines, Powell's rolling boogie-woogie piano, the unbridled (if maudlin) passion of the epic "Free Bird," and Ronnie's growling vocals and earnest lyrics. I love that Ronnie performed barefoot. But because I still needed a babysitter when Skynyrd was in its prime, I hear the songs in a different context than those Jacksonville roughnecks intended.

"Gimme Back My Bullets" is macho and anachronistic to the point of silliness, but I delight in hearing a fellow product of the working-class South tell all those pencil pushers they better get outta his way, even if I have become one of the sedentary nebbishes that Van Zant despised. It's such a simplistic rebellion against the Man that it glows. But like walking around in a Dale Earnhardt T-shirt, buying into Skynyrd's Southern mythology marks you as sentimental, low-brow—a sucker even. The band ladles up enough moonlight-and-magnolias pap to rot your teeth, but for me, it's a ragged but cherished souvenir from a Southern childhood in the '70s.

I was seven years old when *Pronounced Leh-nerd Skin-nerd* was released in the fall of 1973. I didn't buy the album, but I heard it anyway, blasting continually out of car windows, the teen next door's bedroom, and the radio. Lynyrd Skynyrd hovered in the humid air of my hometown of Mobile, Alabama, for most of the decade, particularly after the band released the single, "Sweet Home Alabama."

Even then I was aware that the rest of the country viewed Southerners as quaint ruffians who talked funny but produced cool music. Southerners in the '70s were what the Irish became in the '90s: Agrarian exotics who were romanticized and patronized by a mainstream America who believed we hailed from a simpler, more colorful, and therefore lower culture.

I didn't really listen to the album intently until I was 15 and had a boyfriend who was a Lynyrd Skynyrd fanatic. His name was Steve Normand, and he wore his dark hair Skynyrd-long in the early '80s when everybody else was sporting short, spiky, MTV-inspired 'dos. He even dressed entirely in black every October 20th, the day the plane went down, to show his grief for his heroes' loss. He was uncool to the point of being cool, really cute, and fervent in his devotion to Allen and Ronnie, so I listened to Skynyrd with him.

I didn't like *Pronounced Leh-nerd Skin-nerd*, because by that time it was ludicrous to play the tiresome "Free Bird" of your own volition. The eleven-minute anthem had already been turned into a cliché by FM radio, and when you're a teenager, eleven minutes feels like sixty unless you're stoned. But mostly I didn't like the whole American-by-birth, Southern-by-grace of God ethos that had come to be associated with Southern rock bands like Skynyrd. By the early '80s, only .38 Special, the Charlie Daniels Band, and Molly Hatchett remained of the Southern rock movement. The Southern renaissance that had propelled Jimmy Carter into the White House had hardened into the conservatism of the Reagan era, and I wanted none of Skynyrd's talk of down-home values. It sounded like Moral Majority code speak, and this teenaged member of Greenpeace and fan of musical minimalists such as the Ramones and Devo was having none of this Confederate flag waving, axe-wielding mob of rednecks in bell-bottoms.

Ronnie Van Zant wrote the lyrics for all of the songs on the band's debut. They're tersely worded vignettes about life in a rural South straight out of that PBS blues documentary, a place where men flee the scene of failed romance on trains (trains! in 1973!), but not before sitting by their mama's side to listen to her warnings about being too ambitious. From start to finish, *Pronounced Leh-nerd Skinnerd* was pure good ol' boy hokum, and the public and the critics lapped it up.

Broad tales of love gone wrong, wanderlust, and partying that would make Keith Richards worry about his health, Van Zant's lyrics lack the sort of telling details that make a good song great. Fans and critics saw this vagueness as Zen-like simplicity. Christgau compared the lyrics to "the spare vocabulary of the best Southern folk rock." I'd say they're more skeletal than spare. Let's look past the inevitable guitars and listen to the words on this album.

In "Things Goin' On," a message song about society's problems, Ronnie sings, "Have you ever been in the ghetto? / Have you ever felt the cold wind blow? / If you don't know what I mean / Won't you just stand up and scream?" Well, Ronnie, we don't know what you mean, and we'd like a more articulate explanation before we start shouting. What specific aspects of ghetto life are you citing as problematic? (I doubt that Ronnie really wanted us to scream, but it rhymed with "mean," so into the song it went.) The fuzzy social analysis continues in the next verse: "Too much money being spent on the moon." What does NASA have to do with these unnamed problems in the ghetto?

This is the same guy who expected the masses to grasp that the impossible-to-understand chorus, "Boo, boo, boo," negated the praise for George Wallace supporters in "Sweet Home Alabama." Until I was in college, I thought he was singing, "Ooh, ooh, ooh." I'm not alone: I did an informal poll of some of my thirty-something Southern-born friends, and not one knew the chorus was, "Boo, boo, boo." Most people, if they're honest, will admit they have no idea what Van Zant meant when he sang, "In Birmingham they love the governor / Boo, boo, boo / Well we all did what we could do / Well Watergate does not bother me / Does your conscience bother you?"

Compare "Things Goin' On" to, say, "Pineola" by fellow Southerner Lucinda Williams. Lu gives razor-sharp details about a friend who blows his brains out and then suffers the final indignation of his mother giving him a Pentecostal funeral. "Pineola" is poetry; "Things Goin' On" is Cliffs Notes.

Ronnie tells us to listen to our parents, or at least to mom, in "Simple Man." How uncool is that? Everybody under thirty thinks their parents are morons; those of us over thirty are certain of it. We've spent thousands of dollars on psychotherapy and self-help books trying to forget the baloney our parents told us. Not Van Zant. His mom was an oracle. "Forget your lust for rich man's gold, all that you need is your soul," he quotes her as telling him, which makes me think Mama Van Zant missed her calling as a writer for Hallmark cards. The painfully earnest Cameron Crowe liked this song so much he included it on the soundtrack for *Almost Famous*, his icky-sweet film about the rock business in the '70s, which was based on that most annoying of Boomer tenets, "Things were so wonderful and pure back then, but you don't understand because you weren't there."

Then there's "Mississippi Kid," a genuine imitation blues song. "I've got my pistols in my pockets, boys / I'm Alabama bound," goes the opening line. Its theme sounds an awful lot like a 1961 John D.

117

Loudermilk song called "Big Daddy," which goes like this: "Who's on the loose but can't be found? / Big Daddy's Alabama bound." It also sounds like a zillion blues songs written in the 1930s and '40s. There's the requisite blues double entendre involving food: "'Cause she was raised up on that cornbread and I know she's gonna give me some." Jellyroll, with three syllables, didn't fit the meter, so Ronnie gives us another carbohydrate metaphor. The song is anachronistic to the point of being meaningless—a mere novelty.

We get an update on the traditional Appalachian murder ballad with "I Ain't the One." In Skynyrd's version, the guy claims he's being railroaded and hightails it out of town instead of killing the pregnant woman who is about to haul his freebootin' butt to the altar. "Your daddy's rich, mama, and you're overdue / But I ain't the one, baby, been messing with you," Van Zant growls. It's one of the few times Skynyrd skips the Southern gothic melodrama and gives us a peek at what life was really like in the South circa 1973: mundane and unheroic.

There is more of Van Zant's lame narrative detail in "Gimme Three Steps," in which he tells us that the man who pulled a .44 on him at the Jug was "lean, mean, big, and bad." Is the sort of man who totes a handgun into a bar and threatens to kill a fellow patron ever small and nice? And when Van Zant sings that the "water fell on the floor," does he mean the protagonist was sweating profusely, or was he peeing in his pants?

A Mellotron swirls mawkishly in the background of "Tuesday's Gone," on which the production screams, "Easy listening!" You can imagine producer Al Kooper thinking, "I need to squeeze a song outta these bruisers that might work as a single." And Christ on a crutch, the banality of the lyrics! The chorus doesn't refer to the existential passing of time or to the inability to relive the past, as you might think based on a less-than-close listening. Tuesday is not the day of the week, but the name of a woman who has gone with the wind. "Tuesday, you see, she had to be free," Ronnie sings in the last verse, one of those "Gotcha!" hooks that schmaltzy country songwriters manufacture by the truckload. How hokey is that? Tuesday sounds like the sort of hippie-chick name that Stevie Nicks would bestow on Rhiannon's sister.

We all know that too much whiskey will curdle your liver, but too many songs about whiskey will wreck your brain. "Poison Whiskey" offers yet another tale of the evils of liquor, filled with the usual unheeded warnings to quit the stuff and the requisite reference to Satan's role in the matter. I'd like to hear a song about a self-destructive Southerner who just can't lay off the Little Debbies; given that the South routinely leads the nation in obesity rates, food seems to be as much of a health problem as liquor. But oatmeal creme pies just don't have the same cache as Johnny Walker Red. Mercifully, at three minutes and eleven seconds, "Poison Whiskey" is the shortest cut on the album.

"Free Bird"—where to begin? A bombastic and maudlin display of guitar excess that has become an aural punch line for a Jeff Foxworthy joke. "A perfect example of technopastoral counterculture transcendence," blathered Christgau, whatever the hell that means. I say the song is just too long for the 21st Century, the age of the short attention span and fragmented consciousness. Maybe it's time to pare "Free Bird" down to a more tolerable and modern three minutes. Perhaps there could be a "Free Bird" remix, deconstructing the song into its essentials: Guy scared of commitment goes away; guitar solo.

Pronounced Leh-nerd Skin-nerd is an album of backwards-looking music that was more reactionary than innovative. On it, Skynyrd pretends that the '70s—or, for that matter, the '60s—never happened. The battle for civil rights, the women's movement, and the sexual revolution never took place. The world was still a paradise for manly white men with manly ways. The band didn't yet have the female backup singers who would join later on, so there's enough testosterone to fuel a college football team. Throw in all that Confederate flag waving and the fact that it opened its concerts with "Dixie," and you have a band that is retro to the point of retrograde. Rock 'n' roll is supposed to fight the powers that be, not reinforce them. Yet here's Skynyrd telling you to listen to your mother and stay away from liquor, and doing it in musical forms that were half a century old. It was trying to redraw the boundaries that the '60s stretched or erased, and it was claiming its Southern identity as the reason for this desire to go backwards.

Compare *Pronounced Leh-nerd Skin-nerd* to the work of other Southern-born musicians who are willing to live in their times. R.E.M., Steve Earle, the B-52's, and Lucinda Williams have all made albums that are less contrived and far more reflective of their native region. Yes, the B-52's: They represent an entire demographic of arty Southerners who put a contemporary spin on the region's tradition of eccentricity. As for Williams, I'm only praising her pre-"Car Wheels on a Gravel Road" work. Since she won a Grammy, her music has become increasingly mannered and self-consciously Suh-thun, as if she has to prove to herself and the world that she is still an agrarian exotic and not a pop star. (Don't be surprised to find her singing in an Uncle Remus dialect on an upcoming release.) If you want to hear the voice of the South circa 2004, listen to the Drive-By Truckers: "Throw another log on the fire, boys / George Wallace is coming to stay / When he met Saint Peter at the pearly gates / I'd like to think a black man stood in the way."

Pronounced Leh-nerd Skin-nerd is an irrelevant album glorifying a past that wasn't as idyllic as Ronnie and the boys would have you believe. It's an album that sold a myth of white Southerners as noble rustics to a nation weary of the '60s and ready for the false comfort of a bucolic fairytale. It's an image we reconstructed children of the South wear like an albatross, or a wife-beater with a Skynyrd logo on it. Boo, boo, boo, indeed.

GRAM PARSONS
GP / Grievous Angel
Warner Bros., 1990;
original releases 1973, 1974
By Chrissie Dickinson

hen alt-country holy man Gram Parsons died in 1973 at the age of twenty-six, his corpse was set afire in the Mojave Desert.

Too bad nobody saw fit to light a fire under Saint Gram's ass when he was still alive. Dead before he could burn off the baby fat or excise his encroaching debauched bloat, he died young, but he didn't die pretty. Or good. Nevertheless, this trust-fund hippie has inspired a cult-like critical devotion in the decades since Phil "the Road Mangler" Kaufman absconded with Gram's casket at the airport and hauled it back to Joshua Tree, where it met with a partial immolation nearly as sloppy as Parsons's itself. Parsons has been hailed as the great "inventor" of country-rock, an artist ahead of his time, the hipster genius who single-handedly bridged the gap between rock and country music. To this I say: Have any of these critics ever actually listened to the fucker's horrible solo records?

Parsons's bewildering status as an icon defies some pretty painful evidence, unless of course you consider mastering the flat note an achievement worthy of canonization. It would be charitable to call him a half-assed talent in his (thankfully) limited recording time on this earth. As for the deification he's achieved in relation to his supposedly groundbreaking "country-rock" fusion, the sad fact is that this privileged dilettante was too removed from the true shit-kicker

121

life to create even passable country. On the other side of that hybrid musical equation, he couldn't rock his way out of a wet paper sack. To borrow from Comedy Central, the dude wallowed in lameness.

During his life, Parsons never had a hit, a plus for any critically-correct cult god. Obscurity and a drug-overdose death—ah, the romance!—only enhanced his iconic status. Like fellow obscure heroes Nick Drake and Tim Buckley, his name served for many years as a trump card to toss out in those tedious games of one-upmanship beloved by record geeks and gassy critics looking to out-wank one another's references to Tim Hardin. None of which can hide this primary, salient fact: THE GUY COULD NOT SING.

Sure, neither could (or can) Bob Dylan. But Dylan can't sing in that can't-sing-singer kind of way that works. Parsons just flat out could not put a song across. And it is painful to hear him try.

I first heard *GP* as a thirteen-year-old in 1973, when I came across it while pilfering through my elder sister's hippie-chick LP collection. A music-nut since the age of six and the youngest of eight siblings, I devoured anything and everything that came my way, from Phil Ochs's *All the News That's Fit to Sing* to the Band's *The Band* to 45s of "The Lonely Bull" by Herb Alpert & the Tijuana Brass and "The West Point Dress Parade" by Jaye P. Morgan (later of "The Gong Show" fame). I listened to it all, thanks to the various record collections of my older brothers and sisters: Dylan, the Beatles, and the Stones existed next to Frank Sinatra, Petula Clark, and Jim Nabors.

When I first heard Parsons, I knew nothing about him, only that I thought he sucked. Three decades on, I still cannot detect a discernible pulse in this supposed watershed recording.

Born in 1960, I technically fall into the tail end of the Baby Boom generation, but as a seven year old in 1967, I was hardly diving headlong into the Summer of Love. There's that saying about the 1960s: If you can remember them, you weren't really there. Well, I was there, but I was just a kid. All the arguments about Parsons's great achievement in turning idiot hippies on to country music are lost on me. I was a kid and I dug what I dug musically, regardless of context, whether it was Merle Haggard or Buffy Saint-Marie or the Womenfolk. Gram Parsons was one of the few artists I heard back then that I immediately loathed, and time has not changed my assessment.

That said, I'm sure anyone who lived through the redneck diner scene in *Easy Rider* recalls all too well and bitterly the political chasm between country and rock in the late '60s and early '70s. I've heard repeatedly from elder Baby Boomers how the right-wing conservative politics so associated with country music back in the day kept that genre anathema to many hippies. That is, until shag-haired Parsons came along in his rhinestone marijuana Nudie suits and hepped his fellow bong-suckers to the coolness of Hank Williams.

All of this just makes many hippies look like exactly what they were: a big herd of cows, immersed in group-think, too afraid to listen to country music unless it was wrapped up in Gram's dope-smoke aesthetics or safely spoon-fed to them from the reverent stages of the Newport Folk Festival. Parsons was a debauched Southern boy, but a politically correct debauched Southern boy.

Parsons's defenders speak vociferously about how important a figure he was at the time. So he made the water safe for hippies to get past their preconceived notions about country and actually listen to the Louvin Brothers? So fucking what? If you needed a numb-nut longhair like Gram Parsons to take your hand and open your ears to the joys of Charlie and Ira, how pathetic and lemming-like were you? Any real music fan will see past the image of a genre and let the music speak for itself, whether it's punk or rap or bluegrass. So fucking what if Parsons stitched pot plants on his Nudie suit? So, like, that made it safe for hippies to finally dig bona fide country greats and validate the likes of Hank Snow, the Buckaroos, or Webb Pierce?

Yes, Parsons was certainly an undeniable presence in the emergent West Coast country-rock scene. Besides his unlistenable solo output near the end of his life, there was his work with the International Submarine Band, the Byrds, and the Flying Burrito Brothers. But his vocals moved at the speed of Thorazine, making him a wimp of the first order. At his top-dollar best, he sounds like a bush-league folk-singer clearing out the coffeehouse circa 1972. And he ate the wrong drugs to play good country rock (oh, I'm sorry, "Cosmic American Music," to use his own pretentious term). His droopy-lidded heroin aesthetic was directly at odds with the substances of choice of most of country's genuine greats. The whiskey-and-amphetamine drive of Johnny Cash, the new white-lightning diet favored by George Jones—these are the true hillbilly cocktails.

Parsons's L.A. turnaround sure wasn't the twenty-four-hour stay-awake pill; it was the Buddhahead snooze alarm. There's no doubt that he did it all when it came to illegal substances, but if he ingested any uppers, you can't hear it in the downer that is his solo oeuvre. That would be his two solo albums, the combo platter of 1973's *GP* followed by *Grievous Angel* in 1974. What a paltry sum it is, considering the legend that it spawned. And what is most enraging about both these albums is that Parsons had the wherewithal to assemble an extraordinary bunch of musicians for the recording sessions, but he had no earthly idea how to marshal, direct, and exploit their world-class talent. (Parsons reportedly approached Merle Haggard to produce *GP*, but the Hag passed.) He is joined by stellar sidemen including Glen D. Hardin and James Burton, who were both backing Elvis at the time. But even these primo players can't prop his lame ass up.

This is a talented studio band without an anchor, devoid of a central vision, bereft of a leader. On *GP*, the song "Still Feeling Blue," an original Parsons composition, is too busy musically. There's plenty of decent pedal steel and fiddle and banjo going on; trouble is, it's all going on at the same time, with no guiding force. That guiding force should've been Parsons, but he was apparently too blotto to guide his own butt, let alone lead a real band. Though the musicians sound willing, this song lacks the tightly wound coil that Haggard coaxed from his Strangers or the symbiotic cohesion between Buck Owens and his guitarist, Don Rich, which guided the Buckaroos.

And, of course, there are those much-venerated "harmony duets" between Parsons and the young Emmylou Harris, which in reality amount to little more than sour caterwauling between a guy who can't sing and a woman who's still learning how. If you're still learning how to sing, how can you harmonize with someone who can't? This didn't stop these two. Harris's high, quavering voice is often reduced to a shrill wail when paired against Parsons' flat, draggy singing. "We'll Sweep Out the Ashes in the Morning" is almost listenable when Harris solos in mid-song, but then there's Gram coming back in to muck it all up. It's cringe-inducing.

To cut Harris a lot of slack here, how could one possibly stay harmonically on point with the likes of Parsons? Harris went on to make some fine albums and put together a stellar band of her own. She's also remained Gram's earthly messenger and the primary keeper of his flame, keeping a big hand in maintaining his mythology. In her folkie maxi-dresses and long hair split down the middle, she was every hippie's wet dream. Her undeniable allure made it easier for longhairs to embrace the country part of Parsons's equation, as opposed to the perceived bad acid trip of Appalachian drag queendom that was vintage Dolly Parton.

Despite Harris's input, *GP* is the mother lode of unlistenable Parsons moments. "A Song For You" reminds me of something you'd hear on those horrid, herbal-tea-swillin' female folk albums you'd find in hipper record stores in the 1970s, the "sensitive," overly earnest LPs always filed under the embarrassing rubric, "Women's Music." Likewise, "She" (cowritten by Parsons and Chris Ethridge) is a creepy, easy-listening excursion, a debacle of meandering melody and twee lyricism. It makes one long for the beefy Mel Street—a big, soulful, country galoot who could sing—to barge through the door and stomp on Gram's brainpan. The irony of "She" is this recurring line: "Oh, but she sure could sing / Oh, she sure could sing." This, sung by a man who can't sing. Painful.

But wait, there's more. Parsons also butchers some otherwise great songs. Tompall Glaser and Harlan Howard's "Streets of Baltimore" becomes a numbing exercise as he wobbles around the lyrics like a retarded cat. What's most confounding about this recording is that it's been held up by some critics as some sort of seminal event in country.

GP was followed a year later by *Grievous Angel*, an album that is almost but not quite as bad. "Pick it for me, James," Parsons feebly instructs James Burton on "Return of the Grievous Angel." The normally inventive guitarist responds to the tepid command with a pro forma "doo-doo-doo-dink-dinkity-dink" lick that is as memorable as the length of time it took him to noodle out this perfunctory "lead."

What's called for here is a taste test. Compare Parsons's pathetic "call and response" moment on "Return of the Grievous Angel" to a similar moment on Merle Haggard's monumental recording of "Workin' Man Blues." Listen to the radical difference between the guitar work by Burton, who performed on both cuts. Recorded in Hollywood in 1969 and produced by Ken Nelson, Hag's self-penned blue-collar epic snarls with hard-country intensity, and yet it cooks along on a tense rock muscle. Hmm … isn't that what "country-rock" is supposed to do? "Here comes that workin' man," the Hag calls to Burton, and the guitar lead snaps and hammers down with authority.

The point here is that Haggard is great, and Parsons just sucked. Haggard knew the proper use of talented sidemen, having been one himself. He is the master of the form, assured in phrasing and intent. As a singer, songwriter, musician, and bandleader, he remains the most complete artist country music has ever produced. "Workin' Man Blues" is a bona fide masterwork, and it grease-spots Parsons's work so wildly on every count that it feels almost blasphemous to mention the two men in the same sentence.

But there are several reasons to compare and contrast "Workin' Man Blues" and "Return of the Grievous Angel." Where Haggard creates an environment for Burton to do some of his greatest guitar work, Burton with Parsons can only manage a generic lead at best. Then there's the difference between the singers' recitations: Hag sounds like what he is, a world-class artist at the top of his game. And Parsons sounds like what he is—a green kid playing at being a hillbilly artiste. Thirdly and most importantly, "Workin' Man Blues" still kicks ass three decades on, as fresh and teeth-baring as the day it was recorded. Then as now, "Return of the Grievous Angel" sounds draggy, dusty, and amateurish.

There are several musical exceptions on *Grievous Angel* where the band cuts loose and even the noxious Parsons can't choke them down. "Ooh Las Vegas" (a Parsons/Rik Grech number) actually does what it's supposed to do, i.e. "rock," and if Haggard was on the mic, this would actually be worth a listen. But Merle isn't on the album—Parsons is—and Gram is a dabbler merely trying to sound worldly and tough.

Gram in fact sounds like a child—an idiot child mumbling into a Mr. Microphone. One glance at the reviews of the day reveals critics either artfully dancing around this glaring fact or appearing to have gone outright fucking insane. Here are two "critical" observations of *GP*, pulled from Ben Fong-Torres' Parsons biography, *Hickory Wind*. Robert Hilburn at the *Los Angeles Times* hailed Gram's vocals as coming "straight from the sentimental, George Jones heart of country music." Bud Scoppa at *Rolling Stone* fulminated that, "That amazing voice, with its warring qualities of sweetness and dissipation, makes for a stunning emotional experience."

Huh? What? Was Hilburn actually, with a straight face, comparing Parsons's work to that of the Possum, perhaps the greatest pure singer of country music? As for Scoppa's assessment, all I can say is the only thing "stunning" about Gram was his ability to inspire the unwarranted critical tongue bath.

There's no denying that Parsons knew his country history. From all accounts, he had a deep knowledge of everyone from Jimmie Rodgers, to the Louvin Brothers, to George Jones, to Merle Haggard. But so what? He can't lick the boots of any of those artists.

So who actually "invented" country rock? Well, that is a tedious hair-splitting argument, one that could easily rise to the level of the great Reese's Peanut Butter Cup debate. ("Hey, you put your peanut butter in my chocolate!" "No, you put your chocolate in my peanut butter!") There were many who rocked up their country, just as there were many who countrified their rock. Country had already been rocking its ass off for decades by the time Parsons came along. Give a listen to the crazed cackles and goosed-up rhythms of the Maddox

Brothers & Rose's classic hillbilly boogie recordings in the 1940s and you'll hear the most colorful hillbilly band in America cranking out country that was suffused with emergent rock 'n' roll. To borrow from the late Lee Atwater, it strips the bark off that little man.

Of course, Gram Parsons was doing something different: He was fusing country not with rock 'n' roll, but with "rock," as in rock music post-Dylan. Or, to put a finer point on it, he was fusing country with a rock mentality, i.e., a definite '60s countercultural vibe. Or to put a finer point on it still, a longhair hippie spin.

There is never just any one figure at the center of any "movement." Like the invasion of Normandy, a lot of guys hit the beach that day. Some didn't make it out of the water. Some got mowed down on the shore. And some passed through the fire to the other side. It's the same with bands and musicians. Whether it's hair-metal bands or country rockers, any "scene" teems with people trying to do something similar or sharing a set of interests. A few get the glory and the cred. Most of them don't. But that doesn't mean they all weren't important in creating the scene in the first place.

Parsons was certainly a central figure in the West Coast country-rock scene, but he gets way more credit for "inventing" country rock than is historically accurate. There were lots of guys doing the same mix in the same place at the same time: Roger McGuinn, Chris Hillman, Vern and Rex Gosdin, the Dillards, Mike Nesmith, et al. Parsons collaborated with some of them and knew many of them. Rick Nelson (who had been tapping into the vast talents of James Burton since his terrific rockabilly sides in the late '50s and early '60s) was an important figure in the scene, but when was the last time you heard somebody giving him props? Never mind that the teenage star of "The Adventures of Ozzie and Harriet" went on to outshine Parsons in terms of his ability to play country rock. Nelson's 1972 hit, "Garden Party," tops anything Gram could even conceive. But his earlier teeny-bopper image was apparently too uncool for a bunch of spliff-sucking hippies.

What gets remembered is oh-so-hip Gram. Oh yeah, and the ultimate imprimatur of cool, Gram's friendship with his party-pal and the coolest Stone, Keith Richards.

Much has been made of the fact that Parsons's greatest achievement was that he influenced hordes of musicians who took up his grail and ran with it. I DON'T CARE. The guy is unlistenable to this day. His great legacy to today's alt-country music is this: You don't have to be able to sing to sing country! And this is something to wet your critical pants over?

THE DOORS
The Best of the Doors
Elektra, 1985
By Lorraine Ali
(with Jim DeRogatis)

DeRo: So, Lorraine, we decided to do something different with this essay: You and I are just gonna have a chat about why *The Best of the Doors* sucks. Here you are, a dyed-in-the-wool punk-rock chick born and bred in Los Angeles; it seems as if you should love the Doors. What's your problem with them?

Ali: I have to say that, yes, I'm an L.A. woman, and I hate the Doors. First off, Jim Morrison wasn't a good poet. He wasn't smart—in fact, he was really stupid, *and* he couldn't sing. It's amazing that he's become this mystical icon of rock, when he was really your run-of-the-mill, faux-poet trying to pick up on girls at a party with oh-so-spooky, enigmatic lines like, "I am the lizard king / I can do anything."

DeRo: He's got a line of mystical crap.

Ali: Exactly. The fact that people fall for the whole "dark poet of his generation, voice of the '60s" thing is just another one of those shockingly clueless phenoms—like voting for Bush—that makes you feel ashamed of humanity.

DeRo: I listen to Morrison and I hear Robert Bly. I hate the Doors, too—mainly for musical reasons, but also because of the lyrical pretensions. I'm curious to hear what you think as a woman, because it's this chest-thumping, testosterone-laden, ultra-heavy guy bullshit. Bly started a whole cult of stupid middle-aged guys with beer bellies and bald heads going into the woods to beat on drums and read poetry like Morrison's.

130

Ali: First, I'd like to applaud you for hating the Doors; a man like you is hard to find. Now, as a woman, his faux man-of-many-thoughtful-words pose is not so much offensive as it is annoyingly condescending. Didn't he think we'd see through this? Am I supposed to be dazzled that, A.) He's such a free-thinking intellectual, yet B.) He's still so in touch with his primal man? Really, if he had to work so hard to show me these things, clearly he wasn't in touch with either of them.

DeRo: He was over-compensating.

Ali: True; it's the total small-dick syndrome. The guy drives a big truck, therefore we can only assume …

DeRo: I've always thought that the only people who think Morrison is a real poet are people who've never read real poetry.

Ali: But even when I was thirteen and thought poetry was only for wussbags who carried flute cases through the school quad—O.K., so I was mean and ignorant—I still thought his lyrics were incredibly shallow, just awful stuff.

DeRo: Lester Bangs is quoted entirely too many times in this book, but he had a brilliant line about Morrison. Bangs liked him, but as a bubblegum joke; he called Morrison "Bozo Dionysus."

Ali: That is fine. To me, if he was taken for what he was—which was basically a pop sensation—I wouldn't have such a problem with the Doors. But it's this legacy of greatness that kills me. He was a cute guy who scored on the pop charts. O.K., so he wasn't singing "Feelin' Groovy"; it was a *little* scarier than your typical AM radio fare at the time, but he was no brooding lyrical genius. He's the cute guy at the party who also wants the ladies to know there's actually danger—*ohhhh!*—under that pretty exterior.

DeRo: He was a cute guy at the *L.A. party.* Isn't there something innately California about this line of mystical mumbo-jumbo?

Ali: There are enough things you have to battle when you come from L.A.—"Ah, land of the beautiful people!"—without having the fucking Doors making it even harder. Black Flag was from L.A.; how come it didn't go down in rock history as the band with "the L.A. sound?" Maybe if you were growing up somewhere in the Midwest, and you heard Morrison's mystical, I-feel-your-vibe bullshit, you'd be like, "Ooh, California dreamin'!"

DeRo: The Doors do seem to have a largely male following—aside from people like Patti Smith, and Melanie Haupt does a good job in this book of nailing Smith's own poetic pretensions.

Ali: I also have a problem with Patti Smith. Again, if you have to stand up in your leather pants and scream, "I'm a poet!" then, clearly, you're not. I can't stand that whole thing of, "I'm having a nervous breakdown in front of your eyes; I'm the screaming insane woman." I know that it's a stereotype that Smith was sort of railing against, but she was also fulfilling it, and that really bothers me. She was trying to exploit this side of womanhood that men are terrified of, but I think there's too much drama. It rings insincere to me. She's certainly not as ham-fisted as Jim Morrison, though, whose stage theatrics were just embarrassing. They were clumsy attempts to break social mores, piss off parents, stick it to the man, etc. All that stuff is fine, if it doesn't go down in history as some act of rebellion with deep, intense meaning. I remember this TV special, something like *A Look Back at the Doors*, and they were interviewing "rock experts" about the band. Someone—a male critic, of course—was speaking about Morrison, the Artiste: "It was in 1970 that Jim Morrison really began to expand his boundaries." Sure, because he was fat, bloated, and ready to die—he was expanding *physically*! I mean, come on!

DeRo: The other thing that's always gotten me is that the music is so lame: You have this bad, faux-flamenco guitarist, a jazzy, cocktail-lounge drummer, and a cheesy, ivory-tinkling keyboardist, and the music just doesn't rock.

Ali: "Light My Fire" is the ultimate lounge tune! *"Dee-dee-dee, do-do, dee-dee-dee."* I can just see my parents clinking their martini glasses, my dad with his paisley cravat and sideburns trimmed just-so, my mom with the little bouffant and the lovely cocktail dress. They were so embarrassingly un-hip! The Doors should have been their music, but, alas, they preferred the Tijuana Brass, which I'll pick over Morrison and Company any day. "Light My Fire" is the ultimate lounge song, and the lyrics are perfect to hum when you're scamming the room for chicks: "Girl, we couldn't get much higher / Come on, baby, light my fire." And what about "People Are Strange"? Can I just say: I hate it! "People are strange / When you're a stranger." It's like, "Aaagghh!" It's something you would see scrawled on your desk in high school!

DeRo: It's literally sophomore poetry.

Ali: It's so bad, it should only be seen on a Pee-Chee folder!

DeRo: I love the way that every classic-rock radio station in America plays "Riders on the Storm" whenever it's about to rain.

Ali: And you could say, "Well, that wasn't their intention." But really, was it not?

DeRo: Of course it was! You have the thunder-and-lightning sound effects, the tinkling of the keyboard evoking the raindrops . . .

Ali: "Like a dog without a bone"?

DeRo: "An actor out alone."

Ali: God, an actor! It's so faux-L.A., and it's so bad! All those people who contend, "You really hadda be there"—well, would I have "gotten it" if I *was* there in the '60s? Would I have liked it because I would have gotten higher?

DeRo: Then they would have lit your fire.

Ali: "Riders on the Storm" would have seemed more profound because I was stoned and devoid of all taste.

DeRo: I reviewed Oliver Stone's Morrison hagiography, *The Doors*, when the film was released, and I couldn't help thinking that a great movie could have been made about the Doors' contemporaries, the Velvet Underground—here was music that was genuinely dark and scary—but instead, we got this one. For all of Lou Reed's professorial pretensions these days, standing on stage reading his lyrics from a music stand, some of the Velvets' songs legitimately hold up as poetry, whereas Morrison's don't. The Doors are a B-movie version of the Velvets at best.

Ali: Oliver Stone is a victim of all of this; he's the guy who falls for it. He's your archetypal Baby Boomer, and he's not a particularly

smart one: He buys into all of the "cutting-edge" pop-culture phenoms of the moment. Remember *Natural Born Killers*? He fell for that
shtick that Viacom must have paid millions to promote: "MTV is rev-
olutionizing the way we see and hear things!" Sure, it changed some
things, but "revolutionized"? Ollie tried to make the film a fresh visual experience, but he wound up looking like an idiot who was two
years behind MTV. Or his thing with the Kennedy conspiracy . . .

DeRo: So why do you think that Boomers buy this line of bullshit? Is it just that romantic, phony nonsense about the "nobility" of
self-destruction? Kurt Cobain be damned—it's *not* better to burn out
than to fade away! It's better to grow old and continue to be creative,
even if you start to suck.

Ali: Unless you're Rod Stewart, and then you *should* kill yourself.
I have to disagree, though—the Neil Youngs and the Bob Dylans are
few and far between. I think if Jim Morrison was alive today, he'd be
doing infomercials, selling inspirational tapes. Or maybe he'd be out-
selling John Tesh on the New Age charts. He'd be a New Age guru
who peddles his poetry on QVC: "Ladies, you should call in now,
because copies are limited!" He'd be the Thomas Kinkade of poetry.

DeRo: So why do people still praise the Doors?

Ali: They're a safe choice for being dangerous. You don't really
have to stretch your musical tastes to like them, because they're playing pop, and you don't have to really bend your mind to get the lyrics.
"Come on, come on, come on, now / Touch me, babe"—you don't
have to think too hard to get that.

DeRo: The Troggs wrote that song and it was a hundred times
better.

Ali: Then there's the naughty-boy theatrics: "Ooh, he pulled
down his pants onstage." And the whole Oedipal drama in "The
End"—that's what all these fans who talk about "the danger of Jim
Morrison" hang their hats on, and it's just so silly. It reminds me of a
college production of *Equus*. Like, "Ooh, they're naked, they're dis-
turbed...."

DeRo: Do you think that it's the death trip that gives Morrison the added credence? Clearly, even if Jimi Hendrix had lived and gone off into horrible jazz fusion, what he created on those first three albums would have stood up as brilliant because of the mix of psychedelia, rock, funk, soul, jazz, and blues. We don't revere Hendrix just because he's dead, whereas Morrison ... remember the famous *Rolling Stone* cover: "He's Hot, He's Sexy, He's Dead"?

Ali: I don't think we'd give a shit about him if he was alive, but because he croaked in that bathtub in Paris, he'll always remain a cute, pouty-lipped twenty-something. He wasn't bad to look at; I'll give him that. I just don't want to hear him talk.

DeRo: You could drive by Venice Beach and admire the surfers' or skaters' physiques, but never in a million years would you want to talk to them.

Ali: No; oh my god! There's no quicker turn-off than talking to one of those guys.

DeRo: Morrison is the Ashton Kutcher of his time.

Ali: He's totally the Ashton Kutcher of his time! "Hey, dude— where's my pants, my lyrics, my brain?" But Ashton is at least smart enough to know he's not the Laurence Olivier of his generation. Whereas Morrison thinks he's William Blake, or at least Jack Kerouac.

DeRo: I'm sure that Demi Moore doesn't let Ashton get away with that shit; I saw *G.I. Jane*, and she probably beats the crap out of him when his ego gets out of line.

Ali: To backtrack a bit, I remember when they were filming *The Doors*, and all my friends wanted to be extras. They were filming at the Whiskey, and I asked, "Why do you want to do this?" They were like, "Well, it's eighty bucks a day." And I'd ask, "Do you like the Doors?" And it was, "No, they suck! But I want the eighty bucks a day!"

DeRo: Ray Manzarek perpetrated this con on the punk movement: the Doors as proto-punks. Suddenly X was hiring him as a producer. I never understood that.

Ali: I was so involved in that whole movement, and I did not know anyone who was into the Doors. The Who, maybe. The Stooges, definitely. But *the Doors*? It just didn't make any sense. X was a little confused about things.

DeRo: Well, they were L.A. kids. There's always that thing of being seduced by "the dream factory," isn't there?

Ali: No, here's the difference: They weren't L.A. kids. John Doe and Exene Cervenka were born in frickin' Illinois! They came to L.A. from other places.

DeRo: It's the people who come to a place because of an idea of what that place is "supposed" to be about who are always the worst perpetrators of the fraud.

Ali: And those are the people who love the Doors, O.K.? The real Angelinos—the people who grew up in L.A.—are the people who know the sham. They know it's not just a place where movies and bad poetry are made; it's where millions of people were employed by the aerospace industry, where race riots happened in Watts, and, now, it's the first state where white people—i.e., blondes—are the minority.

DeRo: Growing up in L.A., what was your first exposure to the Doors?

Ali: They were a constant—they were just everywhere. You could not get away from them. By the time I had a musical consciousness, "Light My Fire" was already playing in elevators. As Muzak, it was a natural fit.

DeRo: How about some of the other alleged examples of *The Best of the Doors*? "Break on Through (to the Other Side)"—a William Blake reference, it must be important. But I actually kind of like the music on this song.

Ali: Yeah, it's a little harder, but there are a lot of bluesy bar bands that do it better. *"Dah-dah-dah, do-do-do, dah-dah-dah...."*

DeRo: Who ever thought it was a good idea to have a rock band without a bass? Maybe it was because John Densmore couldn't play a backbeat to save his life. Now, I don't believe that *everything* has to rock—I'll champion Nick Drake, who, by the way, was a better poet and died much more romantically....

Ali: Oh, please, there's no comparison between Nick Drake and Jim Morrison. Nick Drake topped Jim Morrison in every way—better poet, better death, way cuter.

DeRo: What I'm saying is that there's a lot of music that I would consider great rock 'n' roll that doesn't actually rock—everything doesn't have to. But the Doors are *trying* to rock on "Break on Through," and they can't.

Ali: It almost sounds as if the song was written by a real rock band, and then this swingin' cocktail combo, the Doors, adapted it for their Tuesday-night gig at the hotel bar.

DeRo: How about "Love Me Two Times"?

Ali: "Love me two times, *bay-bee*...."

DeRo: It doesn't sound as if he can get it up once, let alone twice.

Ali: Apparently, he couldn't! That was the story: He was impotent.

DeRo: You L.A. people always have the best gossip! Wasn't he fucking witches and all sorts of other women?

Ali: He wasn't fucking *anyone*, DeRo; he couldn't get it up. So that whole "Love me two times, bay-bee" line was a pipe dream.

DeRo: Literally! Forget about "Light My Fire" and "Riders on the Storm" and listen to "Alabama Song (Whiskey Bar)"—isn't this song alone bad enough to end an entire career?

Ali: Oh, it's horribly bad! Why *didn't* that end their career?

DeRo: I have no idea, and it's on the first album. It's a polka tune that they're trying to pass off as a roadhouse song.

Ali: That's an insult to polka enthusiasts everywhere.

DeRo: I love that whole roadhouse trip—"Roadhouse Blues"....

Ali: If you were wearing that poet blouse with the big sleeves and the leather vest and pants, and you walked into the roadhouse, you'd get the shit kicked out of you.

DeRo: Well, all the '60s greats were going "back to the roots" around that time. You had the Stones singing about factory girls and the salt of the earth and drinking to all the hard-working people....

Ali: Yeah, but the Stones were playing blues.

DeRo: The Doors were trying to acquire roots they just didn't have.

Ali: Everybody was, but the Doors' easy-breezy, boardwalk style was similar to something you'd find in my Great Auntie Gert's LP collection, so it just didn't make any sense. You've got to have the strut and the fire and the passion and approach country or blues roots as a rocker, not as a cocktail band. I think the Doors were totally panicked by the explosion of creativity in the late '60s. There was some amazing music coming out of that era, and they probably had a band meeting that went something like this:

Jim: "We have to do something a little extra here. The Beatles, the Stones, and just about everyone else except for the Lovin' Spoonful are kicking our ass!"

Ray: "Hmm. I've got it, Jim: roadhouse!"

DeRo: Oliver Stone and all of those Doors biographers gave us the lowdown on that strategy session, when Manzarek and Morrison sat on the beach, tripping like wildebeests and they had their great psychedelic vision for the band.

Ali: Oh, that's right! Weren't they quoting Carlos Castaneda? What a pack of visionaries.

DeRo: They were breaking through the doors of perception.

Ali: They were drawing circles in the sand, as Belinda Carlisle said.

DeRo: They were riding the crystal ship, and joining the Spanish caravan.

Ali: They were waiting for the sun! Here's the other thing that all the guys who were really into the Doors talked about: "Five to One." Do you remember what the Doors fanatics said it was about?

DeRo: Wasn't it the ratio of African-Americans to whites in Los Angeles?

Ali: Right. Basically, whitey is outnumbered, and no one here gets out alive because "they" are going to turn against us—which is also what Charles Manson believed. That's why he stockpiled food, weapons, and a cult of gals in the desert, because he thought blacks were gonna rise up, kill most of the whites off, and then those who were left would make him their leader.

DeRo: If you're a romantic poet, you need an apocalypse to play against.

Ali: That's a lame apocalypse! It's as old as racism itself. Couldn't Morrison have at least created a new apocalypse for his generation?

DeRo: Morrison was fundamentally conservative; he was born in Florida as the son of a Navy admiral. And he was making music against the backdrop of a genuine apocalypse, when the U.S. was fire-bombing huge stretches of Southeast Asia and killing babies in their mothers' arms. I've never understood why all of the Vietnam movies use the Doors on the soundtrack. If you're crawling through the jungle, are these bad lounge tunes really going through your head?

Ali: They could have been, because you were just saturated with it. Stupid shit goes through your head all the time—the Sealy Posturepedic jingle when you're walking down the street....

DeRo: But the posthumous Vietnam connection gives the Doors' music an added gravitas that it really doesn't have.

Ali: No. If you go back and listen to "Baba O'Riley," it still resonates—the Who was talking specifically about that moment in time, but the song still resonates now, and you still feel that anger and the injustice and the spirit of, "Fuck you, this is not my war." When you listen to the Doors, you don't hear any of that; you hear somebody jumping on the bandwagon.

DeRo: They're reaching for a depth that they simply don't have.

Ali: Exactly.

DeRo: Alright, but answer me this: Despite everything we've just said, I own *The Best of the Doors,* and I won't part with it, and you've got it, too. Why do we feel compelled to have this now-double-CD as part of our music collections?

Ali: The fact that you only have a best-of speaks volumes. You couldn't even be bothered to amass a comprehensive collection of albums by the Doors, and you're a rock critic. You feel compelled to keep it as a reference, but do you ever pull it out to listen to it? You had to pull it out to do this; you've used it for reference, now you'll put it away.

DeRo: So it's like a college textbook or some particular novel I was forced to read that I feel an obligation to keep because it's supposed to be good for me, even though I know that's a crock and I basically hate it.

Ali: That's it. It's like walking down the stairs and having your foot go through every other step—there's just no substance. It's punching a hole through a paper wall—there's nothing there.

PINK FLOYD
The Dark Side of the Moon
Capitol/EMI, 1973
By Burl Gilyard

*N*othing's happening yet. I can't hear anything. What? Am I supposed to be hearing something? Huh? Wait, I hear drumming. At
least, I think it's drumming. Maybe it's footsteps. Nah, it's supposed to sound like a heartbeat. Is that good? I think so. Yeah. It's going to
be all right, man. Be cool. WHATEVER YOU DO, DON'T ACT HIGH!

*Wait, somebody's saying something. I can't understand what he's say-
ing. Turn it up. It's like a subliminal message! This is eerie. You're supposed
to listen to this on headphones, dumbass. Now it sounds like a helicopter.*

*Is this good shit? The guy said it was good shit. He's a friend of mine—
we can trust him. But how do we know if it's good shit? Just relax. Everyone
says it's good shit. Shouldn't something be happening? Shouldn't I be feeling
something? Shouldn't there be song titles on the outside of the CD?*

As recently as 2003, Pink Floyd guitarist David Gilmour told
Rolling Stone, "You don't have to be stoned to enjoy our stuff. But it
can help." Heh, heh. Why do you think they call it Pink Floyd?

But listening to Pink Floyd doesn't really remind me of being
high. Well, maybe it reminds me of being high and wanting to listen
to something else.

💀 💀 💀

Pink Floyd's *The Dark Side of the Moon* was not deemed the most significant release in the May 24, 1973, issue of *Rolling Stone*. The lead
review? A rave for *Heart Food* by Judee Sill. That was followed by a

lukewarm take on Alice Cooper's *Billion Dollar Babies* and a savage, sarcastic broadside on *The Best of Bread* by Lester Bangs, wherein Bangs dismissed David Gates and company as "lowest common denominator Malt-O-Meal." Pink Floyd fell fourth in the review lineup.

In 1973, *The Dark Side of the Moon* was just another album. Solo albums by former Beatles were bigger news at the time. *Rolling Stone* reviewer Loyd Grossman took note of the album's dark themes: "It seems to deal primarily with the fleetingness and depravity of human life," he wrote, "hardly the commonplace subject matter in rock." Grossman concluded, "*The Dark Side of the Moon* is a fine album with a textural and conceptual richness that not only invites, but demands involvement." There was no rating or grade for the album; *Rolling Stone* had not yet instituted a star system.

Naturally, no one—not Grossman nor Jann Wenner nor Pink Floyd itself—could have imagined the cultural nerve that the album ultimately would strike. *The Dark Side of the Moon* proved to be a time-release bombshell, initially staying on the album charts for an unheard-of seven hundred forty-one weeks (that's fourteen years) after its release. It was a career-making record for the band members, who were transformed from avant-garde moody soundtrack artists into mega-selling moody soundtrack artists. If there was a Mount Rushmore for the revered figures of classic rock, Pink Floyd would be there. The minimalist album cover is a pop icon in and of itself.

Judee Sill's two albums were reissued by the online-only collector's label, Rhino Handmade, in 2003 in limited editions of five thousand copies each. More than thirty years after its release, *The Dark Side of the Moon* typically sells more copies in a single week. An advertisement in 2003 touting the new "Surround Sound" CD edition of the album noted that it had then sold more than thirty-five million copies. A *Rolling Stone* article marking the thirtieth anniversary of the disc reported that it had been averaging two hundred fifty thousand copies annually for the last decade. "Money," as band lyricist Roger Waters wrote, "it's a hit."

Naturally, if the songs hadn't become ubiquitous, we'd hear the music differently today. If *Let it Be* by the Replacements had sold thirty-five million copies, you'd hear that album differently, too. But selling a lot of records and/or CDs is neither an indictment nor a vindication of *The Dark Side of the Moon*.

Who can argue with success? Your college logic course may have taught you a little Latin: *argumentum ad populum*, or an appeal to popularity. In philosophic terms, it's a fallacy to argue that something has merit simply because it's popular. *Argumentum ad bonghittum* means it's a fallacy to argue that something has merit simply because it makes a good soundtrack for dope smoking. And *argumentum ad pabulum* ... well, you get the idea.

It's difficult today to remember a time when this wasn't one of the best-selling albums in the history of the planet. *The Rolling Stone Illustrated History of Rock & Roll* (first published in 1976) makes only passing references to Pink Floyd, in a chapter dissecting "Art Rock." Nobody talks much about "Art Rock" anymore, and for that, I am grateful. But by the time the original *Rolling Stone Record Guide* hit the streets in 1979, the album had ascended into the canon of allegedly essential rock music. The book deemed *The Dark Side of the Moon* the band's "masterpiece," while aptly noting that Pink Floyd had become a "cult band with a mass audience."

Some crank named Jim DeRogatis once described the album as "the Floyd's catchiest record." Well, yeah, O.K. In light of the band's oeuvre, I confess that I'm hard pressed to argue the point. But isn't that like talking about the pain that hurts the least?

☠ ☠ ☠

There's an old movie cliché often uttered just before the shit hits the fan. "It's quiet," says a character, pausing for dramatic effect. "Too quiet." Immediately thereafter, the bad guy appears and havoc ensues. *The Dark Side of the Moon* is quiet. Too quiet. It's also too moody, ponderous, torpid, and humorless.

The album tackles the big themes. "Time." "Money." "Brain Damage." Hey, what else is there to this life, huh? Don't get me wrong: I have nothing against pessimism, paranoia, depression, or dystopian philosophy in general. Each can be wonderful, in its own way. It's just that I don't like this particular musical expression of pessimism, paranoia, depression, and dystopianism.

Writers being writers, they are prone to overthink and overanalyze things. Maybe that's why rock critics always seem to have a soft spot for the "concept album." Writers like concepts because they have their own intellectual conceits, and they admire works that seem to have some kind of high-minded intellectual structure. What do you need for a concept album? Have all the songs run together with no breaks, add a few orchestral pretensions and choir-like vocals, and you're all set. Without the "concept album" patina, who's to say what might have become of *The Dark Side of the Moon*?

The album contains nine tracks. Well, maybe ten, because the first cut combines "Speak to Me" and "Breathe." But then "Breathe" is reprised later during "Time." When you get right down to it, it really feels like one endless song. Or suite. Or soundtrack. Or Art-Rock soundscape. Or whatever you want to call it. I call it Muzak, and I'm convinced that there's a connection between *The Dark Side of the Moon* and the eventual dawn of New Age music.

There are vast stretches on the album when nothing much seems to be happening. Compared to the band's previous incarnation as free-form avant-gardists, this is a tidy little pop album, but atmospheric noodling still seems to outweigh the vocal passages. When three out of four band members are credited with playing the synthesizer, and two get credit for "tape effects," I don't take it as a good sign.

It's two minutes and thirty seconds into the album before the lyrics of "Breathe" begin. Similarly, the intro to "Time" drags on for a full two and a half minutes. Many efficient pop songs take less time total than the buildup to these two Floyd tracks. In the end, it feels like all foreplay with no climax. Overall, there's a somnambulant, half-comatose feel to the music. For millions, it's hypnotically beguiling, but to me it brings on acute musical fatigue.

As rock instrumentals go, "On the Run" and "Any Colour You Like" have to rank among the least interesting, but they aren't really meant to stand alone. They're soundtrack segues connecting surrounding songs. "The Great Gig in the Sky" sounds like a scales exercise. Jack Black's character in *School of Rock* directs a student to check out this song as an example of truly soulful singing. Of course, when classic rock is your reference point, "The Great Gig in the Sky" is the apex of soul. Heck, I'll play along: It is easily the album's emotional high point, if for no other reason that it seems to have an emotion other than aloof, resigned detachment. And it's a relief to listen to someone (Clare Torry) other than a member of Pink Floyd sing, even if it feels like a vocal improvisation that doesn't really go anywhere.

The real essence of *The Dark Side of the Moon* is summed up in its joyless lyrics. Consider "You are young and life is long and there is time to kill today," from the song "Time." (And since there's time to kill, you can spare forty-three minutes to listen to this album, right?) Later in the same song, Waters writes, "The sun is the same in a relative way, but you're older / shorter of breath and one day closer to death." Rock 'n' roll is here to stay, baby.

While those lines seem almost comically dire, we've all had our darker, more fatalistic moments when we think, "God, life is so boring and pointless!" It's a common lament, particularly among teenagers and undergraduate college students studying the liberal arts.

Pink Floyd feels your pain.

Take another line, from "Brain Damage": "There's someone in my head, but it's not me." The lyric resonates with anyone who's ever thought of themselves as "crazy," which again—at one time or another—is pretty much everybody. The lyrics are so vague and abstract that they're undeniably universal. If you feel alienated, Pink Floyd is there for you.

Every year, there's a new crop of youngsters throughout the world who find themselves trying to come to grips with boredom and alienation. That's Pink Floyd's bottomless market. Sooner or later, many of them will turn to *The Dark Side of the Moon* for solace. And what better comment on boredom and alienation than to make boring music? Isn't that really the ultimate indictment of this crazy, mixed-up world? Damn. Pink Floyd wins again.

BOB DYLAN
Blood on the Tracks
Columbia, 1975
By Chris Martiniano

At Bob Dylan's induction into the Rock and Roll Hall of Fame in 1989, Bruce Springsteen remarked with the kind of self-importance that only the Boss can muster, "Bob freed the mind the way that Elvis freed the body. He showed us that just because the music was innately physical did not mean that it was anti-intellectual." Springsteen's comparison of Dylan to Presley assumes the belief that rock can (and probably should) be more than mere fun, something that makes you dance—it should "say" something that will endure as "Art." Never has this notion been more evident among rock critics then in their reaction to *Blood on the Tracks*, an all-too-important, semi-autobiographical album that Dylan fans fall on their swords defending, and which media giants consistently rank among his most important.

There are essentially two Bob Dylans. The first is Bob the wayfaring folkie from Hibbing, Minnesota, who waded in the great blues tradition that floated up the Mississippi. This is the same Bob who traveled to the Village and sat at Woody Guthrie's bedside, playing his acoustic guitar and recanting the sick man's own songs to him—the Bob who chummed with Joan Baez and other folkie darlings in cafés, galleries, and at parties all over New York City.

Then there is the other Bob, who turned on his ailing friend, pissed off Baez, plugged in at Newport, and flipped a calloused mid-

146

dle finger to the whole scene. This is the Bob that Springsteen is interested in—Bob Fucking Dylan, the Rock Star Who Says Something, the frontman who took his band on the road and convinced a whole generation of Baby Boomers that rock music is "important." No, wait—it's better than important, because surely Presley was important. It's *meaningful,* with a surreptitiously intellectual quality that somehow allows it to endure beyond the heat and sweat and swagger of the three-minute dance number. Elvis, like our bodies, is temporal, arguably even disposable. You can hide Elvis's hips, but you can't escape Bob's words. Dylan, by being what Springsteen calls "intellectual," is eternal.

The important Dylan albums—*Highway 61 Revisited*, *Blonde on Blonde*, and *Blood on the Tracks*—come from the second Bob, though throughout the Dylan catalog, the first Bob rears his folkie head, either out of boredom, or in an attempt to remain credible and authentic. To those who fall in line with Springsteen, *Blood on the Tracks* is perhaps Dylan's greatest album, if not one of the most important efforts ever committed to tape. But perhaps it's only the context that makes it seem significant. In a review of the 1976 album *Desire*, Lester Bangs pinpointed the only redeeming quality of its predecessor, *Blood on the Tracks*. Bangs noted that he only really played the album after he was half-cocked and had a fight with someone he was falling in love with; then, he'd go home and sit up all night with his misery and Dylan as his soundtrack. The album's "principal utility…was at worst an instrument of self-abuse," he wrote.

Blood on the Tracks is considered Dylan's and arguably rock's most complete and profound exploration of love lost and the search for peace of mind, but it sounds anything but complete and profound. Leaving the Band after a wildly successful tour and live set in 1974, and pulling the plug on his first attempt to record the album in New York, Dylan retreated to Minneapolis to try again with a cast of local session players. Similar in arrangement and instrumentation to the light, country lilt of *Nashville Skyline*, *Blood on the Tracks* is a clichéd, dull, and at times a tragically sloppy album. If the artist's goal was to evoke the shattered fragments of his psyche in the wake of his split with Sara, he didn't share that with his band, or the musicians simply weren't listening. Worse yet, perhaps they didn't care.

The album sounds like the work of a man who has been out of the game for six or seven years, living a relatively quiet, unobtrusive, unimportant life, who has hired a bunch of jingles artists to back him in the wake of a really lousy separation. Bob's brother, David, helped guide the decision to stop the presses on the New York version of *Blood on the Tracks*, and he helped put together the band that would eventually appear on the Minneapolis version. It's been said that the sessions were eerily quiet, that Bob only spoke to the musicians through his brother, with the exception of the mandolin player on "If You See Her, Say Hello," to whom he delivered a vague metaphor about making it sound like "birds' wings flapping in the air." This separation between the artist and the local players provides such a great distance between the vocals and the music that at times it sounds as if Dylan is singing over a karaoke soundtrack.

The opening track, "Tangled Up in Blue," begins the album with a wash of guitars, organ, and an over-assertive bass. The music doesn't propel, define, or accentuate Dylan's words about drifting in an attempt to forget. The drums are a mere pop in the mix, with no bottom or resonance, and the three acoustic guitars create a harmonic quicksand which swallows the lyrics. It's well-known that Dylan shoots from the hip in the studio, preferring light rehearsal and the fewest takes possible in order to capture the "feeling" of a song. This process leads to an emotional vacuum on *Blood on the Tracks* as he attempts to carry the weight of the words with his voice alone, begging the question, "Why did he leave the folkie model in the first place?"

If the lyrics are supposed to be what makes Dylan the paradigm of the modern singer-songwriter, it's plausible that he chose to set the music in a subservient role to the narrative. That muddy bed of sound would then be the neutral foundation upon which he builds his story. But the tale that "Tangled Up in Blue" tells of love lost on a dark, sad night and the time and effort it takes to get over that loss is well-trodden ground. The lyrics follow the narrator from the East Coast to the West, down South, and then home again. For five minutes and forty-two seconds, we follow him from here to there, through seemingly endless shitty jobs and strip clubs and eventually a strange living situation on Montague Street, only to come to the conclusion that he and his estranged partner felt exactly the same, but "we just saw it from a different point of view."

In the liner notes for the *Biograph* box set, Dylan explains that many of the songs on *Blood on the Tracks* were written to evoke past, present, and future simultaneously, an idea he adopted from art teacher Norman Raeben. This narrative playfulness creates a subtext for "Tangled Up in Blue" that cleverly acknowledges the linear limitations of storytelling in song. The resulting tangled mess, however, is a disjointed, cryptic portrait of a past relationship, not a modern, inventive narrative.

The song begins post-breakup as Dylan recounts the reasons why this relationship was doomed from the beginning: "Her folks they said our lives together / Sure was gonna be rough." The second verse begins to move into the past, recalling the "split up on a dark, sad night"; it ends by foreshadowing a future meeting on "the avenue." The third verse reinforces the narrator's drift as he picks up odd jobs, gets fired from them, and finds himself unable to forget the girl. The fourth verse jumps (presumably) way into the past, portraying the girl before they met, while she was working at a strip club. ("She was standing there in back of my chair / Said to me, 'Don't I know your name?'") But here the narrative grows muddled, because the singer never makes it clear whether this is indeed a reference to the past or the introduction of a new girl who relights the flame in his heart with a book of poetry from the thirteenth century, "Like it was written in my soul from me to you."

The second half of the story positions the narrator in the "beautiful" basement on Montague Street, where he's either living with the girl with red hair and her parents, who doomed the relationship in the first place, or the new girl that he met at the strip club. Or maybe it represents a play on first- and third-person narration, and the narrator is the main character, with the basement serving as a trite metaphor for his memory, where all the characters eventually blur together as one—"All the people we used to know / They're an illusion to me now."

The shifting points of view, blurred sense of time and place, and Dylan's metaphorical relationships to the girl—the daughter of a disapproving family, a married woman well on the way to divorce that he meddles in with "a little too much force," a stripper on stage as a performer and as a slave to her customers, and finally an illusion among illusions—result in an oblique and pretentious portrayal of aimlessness. For all of its cleverness, the lyrical structure of "Tangled Up in Blue" isn't new: Poets and novelists such as Henry James and Gustave Flaubert had been toying with temporal structure since the mid-nineteenth century, and they did it much, much better. Does Dylan's song really "free the mind," or does it simply boggle it?

One of the enduring compliments for *Blood on the Tracks* is that it's the most consistent of Dylan's albums: All of the songs in one way or another address the longing, the regret, and the search for peace of mind after a failed relationship. But the totality of the vision is disjointed and hardly consistent. The songs fall into three very distinct categories of rationalization and regret.

"Tangled Up in Blue," "If You See Her, Say Hello," "Buckets of Rain," and "Meet Me in the Morning" reflect the narrator's bad choices and how the couple came to the same intersection but took separate paths. The resolution in each track is that the girl still lives on in his heart—as regret, memory, and imagination—and all he is left with is to keep on getting on. The characters are in limbo, passing each other or separated by a great space, whether it's the dark side of the road, the different points of view in "Tangled Up in Blue," the intersection of 56th and Wabasha in "Meet Me in the Morning," or the great expanse of the Atlantic in "If You See Her, Say Hello."

"You're Gonna Make Me Lonesome When You Go," "A Simple Twist of Fate," "Shelter from the Storm," and "You're a Big Girl

Now" ascribe the relationship to destiny or a metaphysical world that the lovers can't control. Neither can take responsibility for what is ultimately going to come of their coupling; all they can do is hope that each still listens to the other. "A Simple Twist of Fate" tells how the lovers ignore obvious signs of their impending break-up, the relationship in "You're A Big Girl Now" is subservient to time, nature, and the rules of love, and "You're Gonna Make Me Lonesome When You Go" and "Shelter from the Storm" portray a love that is overruled by the post-Edenic law of mortal error and weakness.

In "Idiot Wind" and "Lily, Rosemary and the Jack of Hearts," the narrator falls prey to backstage scheming and conspirators who won't allow the relationship to exist in peace. The girl in "Idiot Wind" becomes the bad mouth which conspires to smear the narrator's good name. The Jack of Hearts, presumably Dylan, is unable to see his wishes through with Lily because of the jealousy of Big Jim, the unhappiness and regret of Rosemary, the incidental bank robbing at the theatre, and the drunkenness of the hanging judge. What was supposed to be profound and moving suddenly seems to have spiraled into a trite, B-grade screenplay.

These three very distinct narrative approaches to rationalizing the ultimate failure of the relationship leave the album without a conclusion; it ends without having said anything about what really killed this epic love—fate, bad choices, or the meddling of third parties. We're left where we started, somewhere between dark and light, law and chance, hopelessly tangled up in ambiguities. The pretentious exercise of presenting the present, past, and future simultaneously, coupled with the seemingly random reasoning that each narrative suggests, ultimately leaves *Blood on the Tracks* in an infinite loop that devours itself. There is no singular artistic vision, only the aimless ponderings of a second-rate poet and philosopher.

So what then has Bob "freed" with this allegedly great album? If it is the possibility of rock music to be intellectual, somehow more than just a physical force, then his music has failed. The music is at best a background sketch, the narrative a poorly executed exercise, and the vision an incoherent mess. The album is ultimately neither physically moving nor intellectually inspiring. And if Dylan, as Jon Landau suggests in his 1975 review of the album for *Rolling Stone*, "is the best of the lot," who does that leave in second place?

Landau's soon-to-be client, Springsteen, of course.

What Springsteen ignored—or simply forgot somewhere between *Romeo and Juliet* and *Philadelphia*—is what happens to rock music when it is over-intellectualized, when it's treated as "Important Art": It becomes lifeless, meandering, and aimless. The very physicality of rock music is what places it in the moment, where it stirs the passions and the intellect of the listener. Because music exists in the present, it can't be read like literature or poetry—it's the culmination of sound, rhythm, melody, and words that create something great, timeless, and maybe even important.

To his credit, Dylan never claimed to be important—only those who worship him do. Maybe the title *Blood on the Tracks* isn't a visual metaphor for what was left of his broken relationship with Sara, but for the grotesque end of his great experiment, the notion of rock as Art—and that is better left for dead.

Patti Smith Horses

PATTI SMITH
Horses
Arista, 1975
By Melanie Haupt

I want to like Patti Smith's music. Really I do. I'm thinking, though, that I missed the boat—was born a few years too late or something. Whatever it is, I am just not down with the *Horses* aesthetic, or any of Smith's music.

To not like *Horses*, it seems, is a crime among rock critics, especially if you're a woman. Someone actually suggested that I am retarded because I don't care for this album, or any of Smith's musical output. It's ironic, actually, because I admire Smith from a feminist perspective. Here is a woman who broke—or at least significantly bent—gender-performance roles; took many rock-star-*artiste* lovers (including photographer Robert Mapplethorpe, playwright Sam Shepard, and, of course, her eventual husband, Fred "Sonic" Smith of the MC5); wrote an entire album based on Rimbaud's poetry, and, more than thirty years into her career, continues to draw acclaim not only for her songwriting, but for her poetry and artwork.

All of these things appeal to me on an intellectual, theoretical level, but the fact remains that when it comes right down to it, Patti Smith the artist does not speak to or for me. In fact, Smith's music is the clichéd fingernails on the chalkboard—good primarily for inciting rolled eyes and annoyed groans from the safety of my critical couch.

This is an issue that pains me greatly, because one of my main gripes during this crazy stint as one of the few girl (or should that be

153

"grrl"?) rock writers is that I don't get to critique or profile many women in rock. Sure, there are some, but they're either aimed at a younger demographic or aren't smart or sassy enough to hold my attention for long. This has been a theme throughout my life, since I was raised by music-loving hippie parents. Apart from naming me after Melanie Safka (who's got a new pair of rollerskates to go with that brand-new key, cutie), they didn't really feed me a diet of rockin' '70s chicks. Think Rush; think Journey. On hipper days, think the Beatles and Led Zeppelin. My dad's admittedly drool-worthy vinyl collection should have a crudely drawn sign on it that says, "No Girlz Aloud." Hell, I can't even remember Dad playing any Joni Mitchell when I was growing up, despite the fact that he loves her.

In addition to the seeming dearth of women in rotation, there was certainly no New York punk in the Texas home of my childhood. No Ramones, no Talking Heads, no Television. There was no Blondie or Patti Smith. (But, to Dad's credit, there was no Bruce Springsteen, either.)

I've had a lot of time to think about this since finishing grad school, where I was afforded the chance to cultivate some truly righteous feminist outrage, which is why when I trawl through my CD collection searching for strong female voices to provide the accompaniment to my own barbaric *yawp,* Patti Smith is always left behind in favor of younger, sassier artists, women less prone to artsy-fartsy wankery. While I agree that there can be no Sleater-Kinney (or Kathleen Hannah and Karen O) without Smith (and Debbie Harry and Siouxsie Sioux), I will always turn to the daughters first. They speak my language with the cleanly articulated white-hot fury of a generation weaned on television, imagining our lives as sitcoms of which we were the stars. There was no Summer of Love for us, no ERA, no Ed Sullivan, no British Invasion, no Kennedy assassination. We had Boy George, Madonna, Ronald Reagan, "Three's Company," and an endless assault of Victoria's Secret advertisements. We've been there, done that with the free play of gender roles, sexual freedom, bawdiness, and camp. We need someone to talk about what's important to us. At some point, those old inroads begin to grow mossy and unused because, well, the view from there just isn't that spectacular or relevant anymore.

I think that's the central problem with considering *Horses* a "classic" album. I prefer to think of it more as a disc that captured the spirit of a particular cultural moment (and connected with a heck of a lot of critics along the way), like *OK Computer* did back in the late '90s. Just as Radiohead perfectly articulated the anxiety of an increasingly digitized age, Smith ensnared the zeitgeist of the late-'70s postmodern moment, with its tensions between punk and not-punk, music and not-music, poetry and not-poetry. She tackled religion and lesbianism, as well as "performing" gender, and she attempted to link the lyric genius of Rimbaud to the youthful free play of the Ramones, all in an effort to make *art* with a capital "A." But is it really Art, or is it just bad music?

The thing is, music is a miracle. When I listen to truly incredible music, I'm filled with the kind of awe people reserve for sunrises and sunsets, rainbows, babies, and what have you. It can come courtesy of Mozart or Coldplay, it doesn't matter, as long as it blows my hair back and makes me wonder, *"How the fuck did they figure that out?"* There's a fine line between pushing boundaries, experimenting in an attempt to find that rhapsodic combination of mathematical precision and raw emotion, and just plain jerking off. When it works, you get *Astral Weeks*. You get "Flight of the Bumblebee." You get the appropriately named *Grace* by Jeff Buckley. When it doesn't work, you get *Horses*. I could give my year-old nephew, my arthritic grandmother, and my tone-deaf best friend some guitars and a piano and they'd far outshine the steaming pile of poo dropped by the Patti Smith Band as led by producer John Cale.

Rolling Stone's recent egregious and outright infuriating special issue enumerating the "five hundred greatest albums of all time" (really just another sorry attempt to sell ads, as well as further proof that the magazine is now floating, bloated belly distended and stinking, in a pool of rock-star vomit) rates *Horses* at number forty-four, claiming that Smith was backed by a "killing band" on the record. Let's unpack that, shall we?

There is Richard Sohl (rest in peace) on piano, who also worked with Iggy Pop and folk singer Elliott Murphy. Then there's Lenny Kaye, who has a resume as long as...well, it's fucking long. He has contributed his mad guitar skillz to the Jim Carroll Band, those chart-busters, Gabrielle Roth and the Mirrors, and countless others in between. Sohl and Kaye are the two criminals responsible for perpetrating the horrendous faux-reggae rhythm of "Redondo Beach," its rinky-dink two-step a far cry from anything remotely resembling "irie." It is puerile playing ranking in sophistication somewhere around "Chopsticks," and anyone who would consider this "classic" musicianship should probably consult a dictionary for the definitions of "classic" ("serving as a standard of excellence") and "deluded" ("deceived, tricked"). Kaye, a former record-store clerk and rock critic, told Billy Altman in a 1979 *Creem* interview that "all of us essentially learned how to play within this group." That should speak to the quality of the playing on this album. It's a bad case of one of those *High Fidelity* geeks inexplicably making good on his pipe dreams, despite being bereft of talent. Kaye's writing isn't much better than his playing: As he has aged, his scribblings have grown increasingly incomprehensible. But he and Smith were both friends with all the right critics—Altman, Nick Tosches, Lester Bangs, Richard Meltzer—which is always a privileged position for the aspiring *artiste*.

Next under the microscope is bassist Ivan Kral, another Iggy alum who also worked with Cale on several other projects. It's hard to fuck up playing the bass, but there are only two bassists out there who "kill," and neither one of them is Ivan Kral. The only musician on this record I can't find fault with is drummer Jay Dee Daugherty, whose credentials are damn near impeccable, including stints with the Indigo Girls, the Waterboys, and the Church (one of my personal late-'80s favorites). His drumming on "Free Money" helps drive the rest of the band to heights it seems unwilling to strive for elsewhere on the album. Not that the drumming is going to win any contests—

it's pretty straightforward timekeeping, with the exception of "Free Money," and not in the least bit busy. In fact, it's got very few frills to speak of, but that's O.K. Mr. Daugherty, I hereby acquit you of the charge of "hack" leveled against you earlier in this essay (but hang on—why are you holding a knife in the liner-note photo?). The rest of your colleagues can suck on it, though. Which brings us to Patti herself.

While I think it's all well and good to investigate the possibilities of poetry in rock—indeed, there are many poets out there masquerading as rock stars, Bob Dylan chief among them—I do take exception to the affectation of urbanity that seems to go hand in hand with Smith's prosaic explorations. The wildness and rebellion, the anger and sensuality that make up the undercurrent of these songs all seem so mannered, so staged. Then again, that's the thing about the postmodern moment—*any* postmodern moment—it's all artifice. Why else would Smith's floppy, bizarre delivery ("Heeaooooowww," she howls in "Birdland"—what the fuck word is that?) come off sounding so phony-baloney (or, if you'll forgive the anachronism, like a bad Cher impersonation)? But there's no excuse for it. Sure, she was untrained as a vocalist, but she was also an aspiring rock critic before embarking on her musical career—surely she would have recognized that impersonating a cat in heat wouldn't exactly bring the folks flocking to the "S" section of the record-store bins. That, paired with the alternating breathless little girl-cum-guttural-sex mama smatterings of spoken-word just screams art-school pretension, and, if given the choice between taking it or leaving it, I'd just as soon leave it for something more sincere, more *felt*.

Smith's cover of Van Morrison's "Gloria" is perhaps the most problematic song on the record. The vocal and musical thrusts punctuate her feral declarations to "make [Gloria] mine." Smith fantasizes about taking the nubile Gloria on her couch in the middle of the night. What's she doing here? A woman voicing a rape fantasy toward another woman certainly breaks the rules, but why does she do this via a Van Morrison cover? Is it an attempt to revise the musical canon?

It's a pretty cool song to listen to, and I don't think it's an accident that one of the stronger songs on the album is one that Smith and company just tweaked and made their own. The intensity was already there; Smith just borrowed it and stretched it out to suit her needs, something she and her band prove incapable of doing within their originals.

The evidence is right there in the next track, "Birdland." What a snoozer. It rambles and shambles and reeks of crappy poetry: "His father died and left him a little farm in New England / All the long black funeral cars left the scene / And the boy was just standing there alone / Looking at the shiny red tractor / Him and his daddy used to sit inside / And circle the blue fields and grease the night. / It was if someone had spread butter on all the fine points of the stars / 'Cause when he looked up they started to slip. / Then he put his head in the crux of his arm / And he started to drift, drift to the belly of a ship / Let the ship slide open, and he went inside of it / And saw his daddy 'hind the control board streamin' beads of light / He saw his daddy 'hind the control board / And he was very different tonight / 'Cause he was not human, he was not human."

Is the voice intentionally childlike, or has Smith just pulled a fast one on all those New York boho-punks who (apparently) wouldn't know good poetry if it came up and said, "Hello, I'm good poetry." The song itself clocks in at just over nine minutes, which is about six minutes too long to endure the minimalist guitar-and-keyboard noodling in the background while Smith breathes her junior high-school musings. Go back and listen to "Gloria" again and compare the borrowed piece to the original. Which one are you going to want to listen to more than once?

The same thing goes for "Kimberly," which, when it comes down to it, is just dull, dull, dull. Smith's apocalyptic vision might be an interesting bit of storytelling if the music weren't so drab and unimaginative. One might argue that the music shouldn't overtake or overshadow the poetry, but the music has to be interesting enough to keep the listener from tuning out altogether and completely missing

Smith's daymare of the sky splitting apart. Same goes for the musical triptych of "Land." The instrumentation tries to evoke the driving urgency of Smith's lyrics (which are not so much poetry as an extended string of word associations interspersed with absurdisms such as, "I fill my nose with snow and go Rimbaud"), but it just falls flat.

The CD issue of the album ends with a bonus track, a cover of the Who's "My Generation." Simply put, it rocks balls. Gone is the overly simplistic drone of the guitars—the gloves are off and the players are screaming. Smith emits a passionate growl not heard anywhere else on the record. It's the most satisfying song on the entire album, and is it any surprise that, once again, it's borrowed from someone else? Someone who knows how to *rock*?

Here's my theory about why people love Smith so much—or claim to, anyway. I think that no one really finds her music palatable, but one's hipster cred goes through the roof when partygoers do the CD-scan in their host's home and see something as inaccessible as Smith in the collection. It's kind of like going through Navy SEAL training—it's hard as shit, not everyone makes it through, and those who do are considered badasses by the rest of us, even though they're not really able to talk about the experience. Don't you feel a little bit cooler for having a friend who's a Navy SEAL? Same thing with Smith—your hipster profile goes up, thanks to the associations with the Velvet Underground and all those purveyors of New York attitude of a certain era, but you can't really talk about the music (despite your proclaimed love for it) *because it's so fucking painful to experience*. Dammit, though, your friends think you're cool and it makes them want to hang out with you that much more! You must, therefore, make an uneasy peace with this screaming, twirling person of indeterminate gender who makes your ears bleed.

This is a cycle that was created and is perpetuated by Smith. Just look at Cale's involvement in this project: In hiring a Velvet, Smith bought herself the credibility she and her "babelogues" lacked. *Horses*, and, by extension, Smith's career itself, is an exercise in borrowed cool, from that famous album cover photo by Robert

Mapplethorpe, to her brief partnership with Sam Shepard, to her marriage to a (semi-)famous rock star. She claims Rimbaud and the Beats as influences, but her work lacks both the acidity of the former's infernal bridegroom and the élan of the tea-fueled quest for transcendence of Ginsberg or Kerouac. It's just…blah, inspiring neither passion (unless it's passionate hatred) nor admiration. Smith is cool only by association. I won't go so far as to call her a fraud, but I will say that there is no *there* there—at least not on *Horses*.

But that's the great thing about being a postmodern *artiste*: Everything is fake and unrealistic, so much so that you can slap a title on a pile of shit and get an installation at MoMA. Nearly two years ago, I was nursing a fairly serious broken heart at the hands of one of the great loves of my life. My friend told me about a long, juicy profile of Smith in *The New Yorker* that she found inspirational. She thought that I might see it that way, too, seeing as how Ms. Smith has endured so much heartache in her own life. I read it and I cried and I fell in love with Smith and her incredible strength and incomparable intellect. Then I went home and listened to *Horses* again, and I just got annoyed. I popped in her 1996 album, *Gone Again* (which I'd bought because of Jeff Buckley's contributions), a superior effort compared to *Horses* but still grating, and I turned it off three tracks in. *Gah!* Then I put in Sleater-Kinney's *All Hands on the Bad One* and threw my fucking fist in the air and screamed until my throat was sore and bopped around in my bedroom and felt so much better about being a girl.

There is definitely a place for feral, unrestrained female anger and emotion in rock 'n' roll—for performances in which the players retain their femininity without going all pink and fluffy-bunny (Sarah McLachlan, I'm looking at you), unselfconsciously losing control because it's the only thing they *can* do. That's the kind of performance today's women need—art that is sincere and heartfelt. What women don't need is the musical equivalent of a disheveled little girl bent on destruction, a whirling dervish in a tattered dress who keeps checking to make sure the grown-ups are watching while she smashes the good china.

BOB MARLEY &
THE WAILERS
Exodus
Island, 1977
By Dave Chamberlain

o you think that when Bob Marley wrote the delightfully superfluous sex homage, "Jamming," from his critically acclaimed album *Exodus*, he envisioned the track's one-drop one day being synchronized to an alligator-riding frog peddling Budweiser to shallow-headed football fans during the Super Bowl? Me neither. Revisionist history is the first thing to avoid during any discussion of Marley. Music fans, and especially die-hard reggae fans, have a lot to dislike about Robert Nesta Marley: Budweiser commercials, frat houses with the poster of Marley smoking a zeppelin-sized joint, coffee shops in Amsterdam that play nothing but Marley songs, *High Times* magazine, head shops bedecked in red, gold, and green. None of the above has anything to do with Marley, because all of them were the product of marketing after Marley died in 1981. To hate a man—or an album—for what became of the music after he departed smacks of revisionist history at its worst, and we'll make no attempts at that here.

But we will tear down an album that has somehow become hallowed since its release in 1977. How *Exodus* ever took on "classic" status is a mystery more shrouded in darkness than the building of the pyramids, crop circles, or the drafting of Sam Bowie in front of Michael Jordan. If sales and critical applause mean anything, then *Exodus* was a keeper—but we know they don't, and it isn't. In fact, the album is crap, hardly worth one listen, and to any serious reggae fan, it borders on painful. Worse yet, it's just plain boring. Sure, it was the first of Marley's recordings to hit the Top Ten in the U.K., and seven out of its ten tracks became Top Forty hits—in fact, the album stayed on the charts for more than a year. And in the United States, despite not achieving the same kind of success, both the title track and "Waiting in Vain" cracked the R&B charts and went gold. Musical historians will generally agree that *Exodus* was the album that turned Marley into a bona fide rock star, so to speak, the first to call a Third World country home. To this day, the weak-minded can't stop sucking this album's dick, a point driven home in 1999, when *Time* magazine went so far as to name *Exodus* the "Album of the Century."

Judged against the backdrop of other albums released in 1977, and, for argument's sake, the year before, *Exodus* not only stands as a piss-poor version of its own genre, but as an uncreative pop record that signified Marley's unwavering lock on a formula designed to promote sales. And that's just in comparison to other artists' recordings; held up against his own discography, *Exodus* marks a low point in his career, highlighted by his worst vocal performance at a time when his home-country fans needed more.

Exodus lacks fire. The tracks—even those that weren't later hijacked for use in commercials—are too long, dull, repetitive, and formulaic. Side one begins with the tragically Rasta-cliché-ridden "Natural Mystic," which includes the so-insightful line, "Things aren't the way they used to be," and it ends with the never-ending title track. One listen makes it clear that Marley is working with a money-making formula that borders on being mathematical: a one-drop rhythm plus a stabbing blast of brass every fifty seconds equals reggae; toss in some organ to solidify the groove, and keep the vocals steeped in *Patois*. "So Much Things to Say" and "The Heathen" might as well be the same song, especially in terms of the vocals, which could be described as whining. Worst of all, Marley doesn't say a damn thing worth hearing.

Side two of the old vinyl LP is equally embarrassing. Even if you accept "Jamming" and "One Love / People Get Ready" as well-textured reggae tracks, Marley obliterates the entire second half of the album with "Turn Your Lights Down Low," a song so sappy and low-key that it has more in common with James Taylor or Lawrence Welk than Jamaican music. By the time Marley and the Wailers get to "Three Little Birds" (for the non-obsessed, that's the "Every little t'ing gonna be alright" song you've heard overplayed everywhere between here and Amsterdam), he's already made a mockery of virtually everything he'd accomplished in his career up to that point. And three sex songs on one side of an album, an album called *Exodus*, no less? Shameful, Bob. Shameful.

The absolute flat-line of *Exodus* is nothing short of astonishing when you consider the context in which the album was written and recorded. Marley's much-publicized political involvement led to an assassination attempt when masked gunmen stormed his home in Jamaica amid a hail of bullets not six months before he entered the studio to begin recording. Jamaica in 1977 was in the process of life-shattering political unrest, with its two main parties—the Jamaican Labour Party and the People's National Party—literally arming their supporters and sending them into the streets of Kingston. The "official" Jamaican Army had just committed what became known as the Green Bay Massacre, the murder of ten Jamaican gang members, five of whom happened to be Rastafarians. It was a country marked by extreme poverty and low employment, and it was ripe for protest music, especially while the United States—through the Drug Enforcement Agency's "Operation Buccaneer"—was attempting to eradicate the island nation's only viable cash crop, marijuana, which brought in an estimated two billion dollars a year. With many doing their best to take money from a group of people who didn't have any in the first place, Jamaica became a creative melting pot for some of the greatest anti-oppression, anti-Capitalist songs ever written in any genre.

Some of that music came out within months of *Exodus*. Peter Tosh's *Equal Rights* is an album of scathing political commentary saturated with uncompromising anger about the situation his country had been subjected to by its own government. A former member of the original Wailers—that is to say, a former partner of Marley's—Tosh laid it out the way you might have expected Marley to. Set against intricate and pointed bass lines, Tosh, whose voice was admittedly much rougher on the ears than Marley's, took on not only Jamaican issues, but issues for Africans everywhere; little is made of it, but his "Apartheid" pre-dated the white-guilt awareness of South Africa's racist regime by ten years. His anger, set against a backdrop of genuine oppression, still reverberates.

You'd never know a thing about Marley's life or the life of those around him by listening to *Exodus*, except perhaps sensing some implied fear. Is he trying to convince himself that "Every little t'ing gonna be alright"? If he believes that, why don't I? Does he feel sorry for his would-be assassins in "Guiltiness" when he laments that his "downpressers will eat the bread of sorrow"? If so, why don't we feel that? The expression in his singing voice was its strength. As far back as the Wailers' earliest rocksteady material, Marley could evoke tears with the silliest of love songs; when he breathed out, "Do you remember that first night we met / That was a moment, I never will forget" in "How Many Times" (a 1968 single collected on the excellent *Rock to the Rock*), his voice was so wrapped in soul, it could make a grown music fan cry. Not because of what he was singing, but because of the sheer beauty of *how* he was singing it. The same goes for the rest of his pre-*Exodus* material, from his Lee Perry-produced recordings ("Soul Rebels," "Soul Shakedown") to the classic Wailers' albums (*Burnin'*, *Natty Dread*), Marley not only sang with emotion, he imparted it. Then came the assassination attempt, and the emotion ended? It has never made sense. Maybe Marley was afraid—afraid enough to stop singing for Jamaicans and start trying to glean cash from the Western world in an attempt to distance himself from the all too real violence at home. Even the more astute reviewers at the time noticed a lack of verve in his voice. Reviewing *Exodus* for *Rolling Stone*, Greil Marcus concluded, "The complete lack of extremes on *Exodus*, of deep emotion, intensely drawn situations, or memorable arrangements and melodies, does not mean Marley is playing it safe, but it does imply some sort of paralysis that must be broken before he can strike again with real power." Considering that he would strike with real power again on his final album, *Uprising*, and also, to a lesser extent, on 1979's *Survival*, Marcus clearly was on to something with his paralysis theory.

Or maybe Marley was just checking out for one album in order to regroup, making *Exodus* to fulfill contractual obligations. But even if Marley was interested in taking a breather from overly mystical, serious, and political material, *Exodus* still ranks as one of the lesser efforts of the three-year block from 1975 to 1978, considered the golden age of roots reggae. If he had listened to the artists around him, he might have noticed that the vocal harmonies and joyful expressions from the Mighty Diamonds' "I Need a Roof" make him sound like an amateur dancehall singer. In terms of straight reggae with reverberating rhythms and no vocals, 1977 saw Augustus Pablo release the five-star *East of the River Nile*, which smoked every bar on *Exodus*. Two other musicians, King Tubby and Lee Perry, were busy creating a new sub-genre, dub reggae, that would go on to have a lasting influence nearly forty years later. (Which leads to the question: Why not just do—as was already in vogue in the day—a dub version of *Natty Dread*?) And all of this was just two years removed from Winston Rodney's (a.k.a. Burning Spear's) classic protest album, *Marcus Garvey*. These examples are merely the mainstream reggae efforts; brilliant albums were also made in the same time period by Dr. Alimantado, the Melodians, Errol Dunkley, Dennis Brown, Pablo Moses, and the Abysinnians, to name a very few.

That's the real nitty-gritty of the situation: *Exodus* just doesn't hold up, whether you're comparing it to Marley's own work, or the work of contemporary geniuses. Every time you play "Jamming," there's another song by a lesser known artist that outdoes Marley's lame effort in every way, from soul to sex. Every time you associate "One Love" with the friendly Jamaican man at his all-inclusive best, remember how that song was a cop-out to the people in Jamaica who only ate one meal every two days.

What could possibly be behind *Time* naming *Exodus* the best album of the century? Take a look at those posters hanging on the walls of the Kappa Omega Kappa house, and spy what Bob's got in his hand.

FLEETWOOD MAC
Rumours
Reprise, 1977
By Jim Walsh

igh above the fray, up near the rafters and the American and Canadian flags, I am guided by voices, the ones singing, "You can go your own way." Hundreds of feet below me, the sheep are standing and singing along, but they are not going their own way. Not like me. They are wearing fanny packs, Izod shirts, Dockers, and the combo cologne scent of the Great Washed, out for a night on the town. I am wearing jeans and the same Ramones/ C.B.G.B.-O.M.F.U.G. T-shirt that I wore under my high school graduation gown in 1977, and a leather strap-pad to cushion the blow when the rifle pops into my shoulder.

It was easy getting the gun in here. Easier than it should have been, and a lot easier than everything I'd heard about post-9/11 arena security. But the Target Center in Minneapolis is like any other basketball arena in North America that slums as a concert venue. The sound is bad, the concession prices are high, and expectations for musical epiphanies are low. It's classic institutional inertia: People don't ask tough questions when they're doped up on nostalgia and overpriced drinks, and all that comfort fuel trickles down to the security guards, who don't frisk you or look too closely into your laptop backpack when they're middle-aged and happy and the crowd is middle-aged and happy, too.

Everybody knows my name at the Target Center. I've reviewed

concerts here for the daily newspaper for years. Along with too many forgettable nights, I've had a few mind-tripping experiences in this press box, all of which escape me at the moment, but believe me, it's not as glamorous as it sounds. Sportswriters get the free food and the buddy-buddy camaraderie and the TV monitors and the stat sheets that basically write their stories for them. Daily newspaper rock critics might get a nod from the pariah at the other paper, a single phone-line to file from, and early deadlines that dictate that the review is written before the concert is over.

They sit up here, in a small section over the second deck, with a view of the stage that's "above it all," which is perfect for how some of these fuckers write about music, and the sightline is akin to Lee Harvey Oswald's over Elm Street.

Oswald used a 6.5 mm Mannlicher-Carcano bolt-action. Mine is a Remington 700 ADL, a deer rifle. I got it from my cousin, who taught me how to shoot. He was surprised. He knows I'm a pussy, a pacifist, whatever, and that I'd never shot a gun in my life, but I told him I was thinking about writing something about violence and rock. He bought it. We drove up to some land he owns near Benson, and I practiced on some tin cans and hay-bale archery targets that he's got set up. I got pretty good over two days of shooting and drinking, and after that I practiced in the garage at night after the kids went to bed. The truth is, I developed my trigger-finger on *Doom* and *Grand Theft Auto 3*, both of which I knew would be more challenging than the project at hand, because my targets, who made a record called *Tusk*, for God's sake, wouldn't be moving nearly as fast as anything on the family PlayStation.

It took me two months to get the gun in. I took it apart and, one dreadful concert after another, packed it all—scope, silencer, shaft, magazine—into my backpack. Most nights, the security guards— "Hello, Bud! Bobby! Army! Drew! Nice job, fellas!"—would greet me, give me shit or shinola about my last review, and wave me through. Some nights, there'd be a newbie who took his or her job too seriously (the only ones more power-hungry than rock critics are rock concert security guards), and make me unzip every pocket. Upon which I'd look at my watch, do my Harried Journalist on Deadline routine, and hope they wouldn't dig too deep.

One night, the night I brought the scope, this overzealous bitch made me lay everything out on the table near the press gate and explain to her exactly what everything was. AC cord. Keyboard. Cell phone. Notebooks. Pens. Printouts of other papers' reviews. It took ten minutes, and I was sweating. The scope was the final piece to my masterpiece, which I'd need the following night. When she picked it up and peered through it, I cooked up something about my eyes going bad, and binoculars not being strong enough to see sexy Rod Stewart shake his ass from the press box. She said her mom has the same problem, and I was on my way to the escalator, where I first got the idea.

Night after soul-numbing night, I'd go up that escalator, take the elevator up to the second level, walk past the unguarded door marked only by a small "Media Entrance" sign, and take the back elevator up to the press box, which was always empty, always unguarded, always dark. In all my years, not a single, "Where are you going?," "Who are you?," or "Do you have any identification?" It was up here, during a bad modern country-rock show, that I first felt the urge, first squinted at the stage through sniper's eyes, first thought I could get away with it.

I unzipped my backpack, took out the scope and my trusty roll of duct tape, and taped it underneath the long table-top desk that runs the length of the press box. I checked to make sure that the other pieces were still there, and they were, safe and snug as eggs in a bird's nest. I went down to my seat in the arena, watched Rod shake his ass, came back up during the encore, and wrote and filed my review ("Does Rod the Mod still have it? Well, eight thousand mostly middle-aged female fans at the Target Center obviously thought so Sunday night…"), and waited.

You have to be patient if you're going to pull off something like this, if you've decided that rock criticism isn't enough, that the pen isn't mightier than the sword, and that, in the end, there really is only one way to make a stand against all the bored, lonely nights you spent up here, raining on everyone's parade and suffering all the fool editors who hired you as market research bait for "younger readers." Every night I came here for shows like this, shows where I knew that nothing remotely spontaneous or unscripted could happen, shows with an audience that sees one concert every two years, and I muttered the same thing: *Welcome to another night of music for people who hate music.*

I picked my targets carefully. Any number of symbolic sacrifices would have sufficed, but long ago this one had sold me, a Midwestern kid, a bill of goods about California, and their singer was one of those out-of-reach witchy women who would never have had anything to do with someone like me. They represented a softness in this country, a complacency, a world dulled by mellowness and Muzak and neo-mysticism. Their biggest record came out in 1977, the year that changed my life, the year punk broke, the year of *Rocket to Russia, Never Mind the Bollocks... Here's the Sex Pistols, No More Heroes, New York Dolls,* and *The Clash*; the year Joe Strummer sang, "No more Beatles and Rolling Stones in 1977," nevermind Fleetwood Mac, still alive and pirouetting after all these years, still hawking the soap-opera marriage hooey that everybody in my high school senior class gobbled up. But not me. I never gave a shit.

I told my editor I was going on vacation and that she'd need to have a freelancer review the show. Besides, I'd had my say. I wrote a pithy preview, something about the Dixie Chicks' real crime not being dissing the president, but covering "Landslide," and I punched out. The night of my masterpiece, I kissed the wife and kids goodbye, grabbed a baseball cap and sunglasses, and drove downtown. I found a meter a couple blocks from Target Center, and walked into First Avenue, the legendary nightclub where I grew up, which sits across the street from the arena.

The guy at the door recognized me, which is exactly what I wanted, and he crossed my name off the media guest list. Documentation. I sat at the bar for an hour, looking out the big second-floor window at the thousands of suckers streaming past First Avenue and into the Hard Rock Café and the Target Center. I had a cup of coffee, watched a good loud local band, the Idle Hands, heard a few songs from a good Chicago band, the Redwalls, then slipped out the side door, where bands bring in their equipment, and strolled over to the Target Center.

I put on the baseball cap and sunglasses, went up to the box office, and bought a cheap-seat ticket with cash. No credit card. No press pass. No trace. No cops rifling through receipts and putting two and two together a couple months from now, and certainly no answer to tomorrow morning's first canvassing question of, "Who has access to this press box?"

I found an empty seat in the back of the arena and waited for the lights to go down. When they did, I went up to the press box. It was empty, and I was relieved. Some nights, I'd come up here to write my review and the place would be crawling with drunks—radio winners basking in their fifteen minutes of media celebrity, or pot-smoking DJs doing a live feed and entertaining their entourage. But now I was alone, just like I'd planned.

I crawled under the press box desk and, one beautiful piece by one beautiful piece, peeled off the duct tape and put the Remington together. It took three minutes. I lay down on my back, cradled the rifle to my chest, and listened to the throng who couldn't stop thinking about tomorrow. I crawled out when the voices guided me to go my own way.

I dragged a chair to the back of the press box, to where I was sure I'd be out of sight—no witnesses claiming to have seen a rifle disappearing into the shadows above section 233—and got up on it. I propped the rifle up on a plastic garbage can, turned my baseball cap backwards, looked through the scope, found the singer, and waited for the song to finish. When it did, she backed away from the microphone, went to the back of the stage, and took a drink out of her plastic water bottle. As she tossed her hair and dabbed at her cheeks with a towel, I squeezed the trigger.

She fell in a heap by the drum riser. Just like I'd imagined, the guitarist, keyboard player, bass player, and drummer gathered around her. I waited until they were all crouched over her and waving for help. Then I picked them off, too, turning them into one big pile of sundresses and bell-bottoms. The between-song lights were down, so the only people who realized that something was wrong were the roadies and the people who'd paid two hundred and fifty dollars a piece to sit in the "Golden Circle." I think I gave them their money's worth.

I took the Remington apart, packed it in a garbage bag I'd stuffed in my pocket, and got in the elevator. By the time the lights were up and the screams were starting to roll through the arena, I was down the stairs and out the door. By the time the cops were radioing all points to secure the venue, the Remington was in the trunk of my car. By the time the local newscasts were setting up in front of the Target Center, I was back at First Avenue drinking a beer, having slipped back in the band door.

A few minutes later, my cell phone rang. Right on cue.

"Where are you?," she said. My editor.

"Well, hello to you, too, Cathy," I said, trying my best to sound vexed and interrupted. "Where am I? I'm on vacation is where I am. Meaning vacation from *you*."

"I need you," she said. "Now. I hear music. Where are you?"

"I'm at First Avenue, watching a band," I said. More faux-vexation. "Cathy, let me repeat: I'm on vacation. Listening to music I actually LIKE. If this is about Fleetwood Mac, I told you . . ."

"First Avenue? Perfect," she said. "I need you to get over to the Target Center. Somebody shot Fleetwood Mac. Give me thirty inches by 11:30."

She hung up before I could do the feigned horror act that I'd practiced so hard. It was 10:30. I ran out the door, past a couple of bouncers I know, and shouted, "Someone shot Fleetwood Mac!" I went to Bud at the security gate and told him I had to get in and report. He gave me an all-access laminate (*Rumours Revisited: The Together Forever Tour*), and I started interviewing fans who were waiting to be frisked before leaving. None looked horrified, most looked inconvenienced. They all came through with the learned art of the sound bite.

"Who would do something like this? I've waited all my life to see them, and it has to be this night," said a woman my age from Brooklyn Park. "This has to be the worst moment in the history of rock 'n' roll."

"This was her first concert," said a mom from Edina with her arm around her school-age daughter. "Can you imagine? I feel like I'm living through my own personal *Behind the Music*."

"I'm gonna hang onto this ticket stub forever," said a guy wearing a Weezer T-shirt.

"I'm gonna put mine on eBay," said his friend.

I wrote down every word. I interviewed Bud, who defended the arena's security. I interviewed the road crew, who talked about the personal and professional joys of working with the band for so many years. I interviewed the road manager, who called the band "visionaries" and "true artists that verged on spiritualists." I called the hospital, but discovered that one of our cop reporters was already on that angle.

I took the elevator up to the press box. Like most concert reviews, I could have written the whole thing before it even happened. I ended it like this: "Fleetwood Mac's heyday was 1977. Their album from that year was *Rumours*, which readers and critics of *Rolling Stone* magazine voted as one of the top rock albums of all time, on the strength of hit singles such as, 'Don't Stop,' 'Dreams,' 'Songbird,' and 'Go Your Own Way.' At press time, police had no suspects in the shooting."

I plugged my laptop into the phone line and filed. I waited a few minutes for the copy desk to call back and give me the all clear. Then I took the elevator down, talked with Bud for a minute, went home, and slept like a baby while the printing presses and carriers cranked up to deliver the secondhand news.

PAUL & LINDA McCARTNEY
Ram
Capitol, 1971
By Tom Phalen

Dear Paul...
Oh, Paul ...
Hey, Paul ...

What the fuck happened to you?

It's not like you didn't write precious, cute, or even silly stuff when you were part of the Fab Four, but at least you had John Lennon and the rest of the band to temper your corny excesses back then. Left to your own devices, as soon as you cut loose, beginning with the self-aggrandizing *McCartney*, you went overboard, and you got lazy, or possibly too stoned, or both. Suddenly, barely cogent snippets of songs ("The Lovely Linda"), unpolished, unfinished ideas ("Oo You"), and amateurish instrumental performances (sorry, but you're no Ringo) were acceptable.

The critics slammed you for your under-produced, homemade record, probably in part because you dared to leave the Beatles. In hindsight, especially in comparison with much of your remaining body of work, it was probably your best-realized effort. *McCartney* was certainly a stronger album than the follow-up, *Ram*, with which you tried to appease the critics with bombastic, massively over-produced material. The recording that should have rectified your weaknesses only magnified them, bringing up the question that would

174

haunt your entire post-Beatles career: Are you a true artist, or simply a clever craftsman?

Not that you were alone in the doing; there was also the lovely Linda. In fact, *Ram* is credited to "Paul & Linda McCartney," the only post-Beatles, pre-Wings recording to be so identified. I've long held, both from personal experience and ongoing observation, that the greatest danger to bands is significant others. It's not ego, not creative differences, not money, but girlfriends. Worse yet: wives. Sorry, this is nothing personal or sexist or misogynistic. I'm really not like that, and I'm not pointing any fingers, especially not at my first wife. But when you start taking the opinions and contributions of people who only get a say in matters because you're sleeping with them, trying to keep them happy, or making them feel involved with something they very likely didn't have anything to do with creating, you only screw yourself. John had Yoko; you had Linda. Yoko, Linda, Linda, Yoko, Uma, Oprah—it doesn't work. And when your mate has a tendency to be as corny as you are, well, you're doubly doomed. I mean, Linda developed a British accent to match yours. And it didn't work for her anymore than it works for Madonna.

But the biggest disappointment is that your music on *Ram* made promises that it couldn't keep. For all the big production values and overblown musical constructions, the songs fall flat. "Too Many People," the opening track, is a perfect example: Right from the start it's vague and confused. It begins with the interesting but undecipherable melodic reference to the song's chorus; I don't know what you're saying and I've listened to this opening hundreds of times. I've even looked up the lyrics on Google, and although there is no shortage of people—too many of them, really—who are driven to post your words online, it seems as if no one else can understand your opening lines, either. No one, and I mean no one, has made sense of them. The best I've found is: "This I blay-ay-ay-ay-ay-ay." What is that? It doesn't bode well for the rest of the album—like "Monkberry Moon Delight"—but we'll get to that later.

The attempt in "Too Many People" to address social injustice is also weak—the Marie Antoinette, common people, cake-and-break reference, for instance. Yep, it's rough out there, but how rough is it for you? Surely those hardscrabble days in Liverpool must have faded by 1971. Personally, I'm always going to have problems with rich guys singing about the rest of us have-nots. You aren't quite as offensive as, say, Sting, telling us in "If You Love Somebody (Set Them Free)" that, "Forever conditioned to believe that we can't live, we can't live here and be happy with less." Be happy with less? This is the guy that led his second wife around on a horse at their million-dollar wedding. Hey, Gordon, for Christ's sake, come on! You've already had like fifty kids with Trudy, what do you need with a giant wedding? The Chapel of Love, in Vegas, with Elvis officiating—we would have been alright with that.

Not that you maintain the social commentary for very long, Paul. "Too Many People" quickly becomes another love song—love as revenge—before ambling off into an extended lead. And is that you on lead? It sounds like it. Unlike your bass playing, which has always been spot-on, your lead guitar has always been less immediate, as if you're always trying to catch up with the rest of the band, which is especially funny when you *are* the rest of the band. You're always running just behind the train, much like Mick Fleetwood's drumming—a dollar short and a day late. It drags down what is otherwise a respectable melody.

"3 Legs" follows. A blues? Granted, it has a couple of changes not usually found in a twelve-bar construction, but that doesn't save it. The song is about… what? A three-legged dog; a dog with no legs at all? Jerry Cantrell once told me that the cover of Alice in Chains' fourth album, the one with a three-legged dog, had to be changed in Japan; it seems the Japanese are highly offended by pictures of deformed animals, and the record company rejected the image. I think the Japanese have something there, and it should be applied to all songs about all short-changed mutts. Except, perhaps, "Hound Dog."

"Ram On"—I'm guessing this is sort of the title tune—is even more irritating. George Harrison's fascination with the ukulele—I know in his final days he was reportedly giving them to all of his friends (a sure sign that his days were, indeed, final)—doesn't justify its place on any album that claims to be rock, or, for that matter, anything else. God! *"Twink-a, twink-a, twink-a, twink-a, twink-a, twink-a-twink-a, twink!"* Maybe, just maybe, that's alright for "Tiny Bubbles," but that's it. And again—a paucity of lyrics. "Ram on; give your heart to somebody, soon right away." That's it? And then you have the balls to reprise it as track eleven? It's not just filler, but bad filler, and bad filler positioned as the title tune. Filler, filler, filler—not unlike this sentence.

"Dear Boy" is sort of pretty, I guess. It does ramble on, though. You blew it, boy, and now I have the girl. Isn't that story line addressed on the Beatles' "You're Gonna Lose that Girl"? And, now that I think about it, at least half the Beatles' catalogue? Only better?

"Uncle Albert/Admiral Halsey" is Ram's first ungainly musical construction. Lots of special effects (did you borrow that ringing bell from "A Day in the Life" and the whistling from "Blackbird"?), lots of thematic and melodic changes that really don't add up. The supposed "dichotomy" of two different characters? Well, the Admiral and Albert are little more than caricatures, and barely drawn ones at that. Then there's that lame-ass voice you do in the second verse—that officious English cup-of-tea singing style. It's so music hall, Paul, so *veddy* old school. But then you've always been music hall. I fully expect at any moment you'll break into "We'll Meet Again," a whole pub-load of you and yours, pints lifted, red-faced, rose-blossomed, teeth failing, singing to those boys over there; stiff upper lip and all that. Oh the Empire, oh the Empire. It's dead Paul, like you supposedly were, only more so. Get over it.

Though I've avoided it up until now, out of respect, I must address the shrill, brittle, over-reverberated background vocals here, there, and everywhere. Did you guys record this in the Chunnel? No, there was no Chunnel in 1971. How about a wind tunnel? Wherever you did it, it's the stamp you put on every post-Beatles recording. You and Linda, overdubbed over Linda and you, overdubbed over you and Linda, and on, and on, and on. No matter how many times you multi-track yourselves, it still sounds as thin and dishonest as the President's last promise. Poor Linda was chastised throughout her musical career with you for having no voice, no chops, no sense of rhythm, and ultimately no business being in a band, other than the fact that she was your girl. (See, it's the girlfriend thing again—bad ju-ju.) But you're really the one to blame, Paul. If you couldn't fix her in the mix, you should have slipped in a vocal double and told Linda later that it was her. She would have believed you; she believed that story about being jailed in Japan, didn't she?

And then comes "Smile Away," without a doubt the most horribly annoying track on *Ram*, and that's saying something. You once said that if you'd have known that "Smile Away" was going to get so much radio play as a single, you would have written more hooks. It wouldn't have helped. If you had known it was going to get that much radio play, you should have put it to sleep, and put us out of your misery. From that tired rock 'n' roll opening vamp, to the really horrible lyrics, this tune is a drag. Your friend can "smell your feet … smell your breath … smell your *teeth* / A mile away"? Fuck you. I personally believe "Smile Away" was the olfactory precursor to the proliferation of fart jokes in Farrelly Brothers movies. It just gets dumber and dumber, and you really need to be held accountable.

"Heart of the Country"—once again, you're plagiarizing yourself here, Paul. I think this song was called "Mother Nature's Son" on "The White Album." The same lilting acoustic guitar, same peaceful easy feeling, same head full of straw, same one with the animals and-or God vibe—I have this image of you sitting naked in a stream, and it's not a pretty picture.

"Monkberry Moon Delight" works as *Ram*'s only musically cohesive piece, the only overly ambitious attempt that does. But you completely throw it away with these nonsensical lyrics. Ironically, of all the songs on this recording, this is the only one where the lyrics are actually understandable on first listen. Except, perhaps, for the title. For years, I thought it was "Moonberry," not "Monkberry," but then I really thought that Jimi Hendrix was singing, "'Scuse me while I kiss this guy" on "Purple Haze." (I'm not proud.) Oh, and is that piano "*up*

your nose," "*on* your nose," or "*at* your nose"? I found it referenced three different ways. Personally, I like the image of the piano up your nose (that's how I heard it); it's a picture I've been carrying around for days now, and it's much better than the one of you naked in a stream. For one thing, you're dressed; for another, you have a baby grand stuffed up your nostril! This vision is usually accompanied by lethal headaches and out of place odors. Those aren't your feet, are they?

"Eat at Home" and the following "Long Haired Lady" are about sex. If you didn't get that from the former's title and its usage in the first verse, surely "Lady let's eat in bed" in the second verse will set you straight. In "Long Haired Lady," Linda opens the song (it's her drum solo) with, "Do you love me like you know you ought to / Or is this the only thing you want me for?" I don't think she was talking about her photographs. These, by the way, are two of six songs Linda coauthored, so the sex really was a joint effort.

You guys seemed to be singing about sex in order to convince us that you were actually having sex, because the idea of Paul and Linda having sex was almost as unbelievable (and uncomfortable) for us as the notion of our parents having sex. Anyway, together you wrote much more about sex than you ever did with the Beatles. There was "Why Don't We Do It in the Road," sure, but we were never really sure exactly what you were doing in the road, Paul. It could have been anything. Unfortunately, you and Linda—unlike John and Yoko, or even Ringo and Barbara—had a way of making sex sound pedestrian, or vanilla at best. I can't help but think of occasional groupie and writer Francie Schwartz's book, *Body Count*, in which she described sex with you as good but not great. I remember Linda's defensive "She got a great lay!" response at a subsequent news conference. But getting back to "Eat at Home," I don't know that I ever needed to know that you two practiced oral sex, at home or in bed (or even in the road). It really hadn't crossed my mind before.

As for "Long Haired Lady," what's with the "bells are buzzing" because Linda is your "sweet delectable baby" line? Hey, buddy: Bells ring; buzzers buzz. What else were you getting wrong? But forget

179

that, because no sooner do you get in the last "Win or lose it" at the "Hey Jude"-like finish then you segue in to that damnable reprise of "Ram On." I know, I've cursed this earlier, but that's how irritating this rerun is. Fortunately, it's a little shorter this time than it is in the track-three position.

Finally comes the finish: the overly long and convoluted "Back Seat of My Car." As auto-erotica goes, this is no "Paradise by the Dashboard Light." You and Linda may have been better-looking than Meat Loaf, but the Loaf was always so much more about the sweating and rutting. His opus has a lakeside location, barely dressed seventeen year olds, and an absolute slew of hot and heavy baseball metaphors. He slides headfirst and *then* gets around to wondering if it's safe. You and Linda only sit in the backseat (like the Beatles only wanted to hold her hand), all hung up about what dad would think about you two "making love." Even in a car, your sex is pedestrian!

Ultimately, *Ram*, rather than a break-through, was a let-down, and unfortunately the first of many. Perhaps we all suffered from over-expectation; we anticipated so much more from you, you had done such amazing work with your former band, and we assumed you would do the same solo. I mean, it isn't that you've been without successes over the many, many, many years; certainly *Band On the Run* was a shining moment, as were parts of *Venus and Mars*. And, remarkably, more recent works such as *Flaming Pie*, *Run Devil Run*, and *Driving Rain* have proven that you've still got it, despite the loss of Linda, another marriage, knighthood, fatherhood, and the fact that you're damn near sixty-four. It's just that there's been so much chaff between the kernels, how can any of us not be critical? How could you not listen and fail to take note?

After all, Paul, in the end, the crap you take is equal to the crap you make.

JOHN LENNON /
YOKO ONO
Double Fantasy
Geffen, 1980
By Allison Stewart

It's okay to hate *Double Fantasy*. Before the fog of grief and instant nostalgia set in, plenty of other people didn't like it either, and they said so, in public. But after John Lennon's death, three weeks after its release, impending critical reviews of *Double Fantasy* were pulled, already published negative reviews were atoned for, and people throughout the world went about pretending to like it. Out of a sense of decorum (respect for the dead), they tried to emphasize the good things about the album—like its relative brevity, or the fact that it wasn't as bad as *Two Virgins*.

In the intervening years, it became impossible to separate *Double Fantasy* from the horrors of the circumstances surrounding its release—impossible, in other words, to hear "Woman" without envisioning those black and white photos of Lennon and Yoko Ono walking in Central Park. But the album's reissue in 2000, re-mastered and with several new tracks, served as a sobering reminder that it is possible to be moved by the inadvertent, after-the-fact poignancy of *Double Fantasy* and still think it's a pretty awful album. The passage of time, it turns out, hasn't done it any favors. Bad to begin with, it has aged particularly poorly, in the way that albums from the early '80s often do.

Double Fantasy wasn't the first time Ono and Lennon collaborated. That was on 1968's indelibly dreadful *Unfinished Music, No. 1: Two*

Virgins, the one with the nude portrait on the front and back covers, the one recorded the night Lennon and Ono consummated their relationship. It is little more than an experimental collection of bird calls, yelling, and indiscriminate tape loops. Things couldn't help but improve from there. *John Lennon / Plastic Ono Band*, which stands with *Imagine* as his best solo work, demonstrated that Ono and Lennon could come together to produce music that wasn't horrifying, and *Plastic Ono Band* had the added virtue of being divided into his and hers discs, making Ono's contributions easier to avoid.

But *Double Fantasy*, which is billed in the liner notes as "A Heart Play, by John Lennon and Yoko Ono," is essentially a call-and-response album, with each Lennon track followed by an Ono track. The disc's primary flaws lay in its failure to discriminate between the two, and its insistence on giving each set of contributions equal weight.

Much has been said throughout the years about the baffling, incomprehensible atonality of the average Ono album, and it's all true. While *Double Fantasy* finds Ono at her most accessible (there's an attempt at melody, in other words, and you can occasionally understand the lyrics), this isn't saying much. Taken alone, Lennon's contributions to *Double Fantasy* would have served as a moving if slightly cloying testament to his allegedly happy "househusband" phase. Not great, but not thuddingly, teeth-grindingly awful. But Ono's tracks are inserted with little thought to the album's flow, which means that mild, mid-tempo pop tracks are frequently followed by... well, whatever it is that Yoko does. This makes listening to the album a frustrating, disjointed experience. The average fan, given a choice, would likely have preferred not to share Lennon's last recorded moments with Ono in her disco phase (though Lennon, artistic pervert that he was, probably wouldn't have changed a thing).

Critic Stephen Holden famously called *Double Fantasy* "an exemplary portrait of a perfect heterosexual union" (as opposed to what, he didn't say: An imperfect heterosexual union, which it clearly was? A perfect homosexual union? The ideal coupling of owner and pet?). To her everlasting credit, Ono spends much of the album dispelling that myth, however inadvertently. There's an arch, brittle quality to many of her tracks, and more than the faintest whiff of narcissism: With the exception of the best song, "Beautiful Boy," all of John's contributions are about Yoko, and all of Yoko's songs are about Yoko, too.

The majority of the personal criticism directed at Ono, much of which had to do with her assumption of the male breadwinner role in her marriage, was misogynistic twaddle; anyone listening to, say, "Kiss Kiss Kiss" will find plenty of genuine reasons to dislike her. But *Double Fantasy* laid bare what *The Village Voice* referred to as the "infantilization of John Lennon" ("the little child inside the man"). The marriage—more specifically Lennon's utter dependence on Ono, a distant and mystifying figure then and now—could have been the basis for one of the deepest, most devastatingly good relationship albums of all time, the kind that gets dragged out in a crisis and played over and over again, like Bruce Springsteen's *Tunnel of Love* or Richard and Linda Thompson's *Shoot Out the Lights*. But the couple's relationship—with Lennon the needy, grasping son and Ono the imperious mother—is so strange, so *sui generis*, that to hear it is to be occasionally fascinated and frequently repelled, without ever really understanding. The album's better tracks shed no light about what this relationship means to the larger world, and the lesser tracks make listeners feel as if they're gazing into a black hole. "The marriage seems as self-contained as a tautology, and as useless; it trivializes a great artist and deifies a dubious one," wrote *Village Voice* critic Robert Christgau (and he *liked* the album).

Lennon's conversion from the pithy crank of "How Do You Sleep" and "Working Class Hero" to the needy, mostly affable husband and father of "Watching the Wheels" is the beating heart of *Double Fantasy*, and the primary public rationale ("at least he was happy at the end") behind any real failure to analyze it critically. To hate the album was, somehow, to appear ungrateful for his happiness.

By the time *Double Fantasy* was released, Lennon hadn't made a truly good album since 1973's *Mind Games,* and that's if you're feeling charitable; if you're not, you'd probably say *Imagine* in 1971. The

183

drunken Lost Weekend-era *Walls and Bridges* was wildly uneven, and *Rock and Roll*, a pleasant enough 1975 collection of early rock covers, was remarkable mostly for the lengthy feud with Phil Spector that marked its birth.

Imagine excepted, after twelve years of making solo albums, Lennon had yet to find a balance between the humorless treatises on Attica and Northern Ireland found on *Sometime in New York City*, and the gummy, simplistic love songs that characterized his *Double Fantasy* offerings. (Interestingly, these latter tracks resembled Paul McCartney's more uxorious '70s tracks to a greater degree than either artist probably found comfortable, though McCartney's love songs have an irresistible cheesiness—and a universality—that Lennon's don't.)

Lennon's albums, in other words, were notorious for what they *weren't*: Nuanced. Innovative (musical adventurism was something he left, for better or worse, up to Yoko). In a *Playboy* interview given shortly before his death, he expressed a fondness for the B-52's (who had previously cited Yoko as an influence) and punk, but his *Double Fantasy* tracks are distressingly—though not, at that point, surprisingly—conventional. Intended as Lennon's comeback album after years shut up in the Dakota, the glossy, overproduced effort was the first of his solo albums ever to provide a wealth of potential singles (and was, even before his death, shaping up to be an impressive hit). It's certainly the safest album he ever made, to such an extent that several of his tracks, which have a sax-heavy sound typical of the M.O.R. pop of the time, are oddly reminiscent of Huey Lewis and the News, though, this being 1980, Huey Lewis and the News had yet to be invented. It's both distinctly of its era (it's impossible to listen to Lennon's contributions to *Double Fantasy* and think that they were recorded at any time other than the early 1980s) and hopelessly staid, a reflection of the most pedestrian musical trends of the period.

For her part, Ono reigned in her more avant-garde leanings for the occasion, dabbling vaguely in New Wave pop. The more mainstream the track, the more constrained and uncomfortable she sounds: The worst offender, "Yes, I'm Your Angel," is a "Makin'

Whoopie" simulation on which she coos and trills in an alarming imitation of a horny coquette ("Yes I'm so pretty / You're so dizzy / And we're so happy every day"). Like much of *Double Fantasy*, it manages to be both heartbreaking and nauseating at the same time.

The jazz-rock-lite of "I'm Moving On" makes one long for Ono's previous dabblings in primal scream, which, while frequently unlistenable, were at least sincere. It's is preceded by Lennon's raw, faux-funky "I'm Losing You" ("I know I hurt you then.... Do you still have to carry that cross?"), which offers a rare glimpse of his old contentiousness. Much has been made of the juxtaposition of the two songs, with their absolute, in-a-nutshell crystallization of the couple's marital roles—Lennon reaching, Ono remote. It's one of the few times the interplay on *Double Fantasy*, which is, after all, intended as a conversation, actually works as it's supposed to, though the effect is more awkward than provocative.

The "I'm Losing You"/"I'm Moving On" couplet offers a rare moment of both levity and awareness of the outside world from a couple whose joint self-absorption would have seemed to preclude either. But the disc's one-two opening shot, a pairing of Lennon's "(Just Like) Starting Over," an amiable tale of reclaimed love, with its unholy flipside twin, "Kiss Kiss Kiss," is less a wink than a call to arms. Some of Ono's *Double Fantasy* songs border on traditional in structure; that she chose as her opening salvo one of her most patience-testing tracks is saying something—not necessarily something good, but something. Both perky and atonal, "Kiss Kiss Kiss" features, among other things, the sound of Ono having an orgasm (whether real or simulated, it's better not to know). In the Lennon-Ono *Playboy* interview, she explained it thusly: "There is the sound of a woman coming to a climax on it, and she is crying out to be held, to be touched. It will be controversial, because people still feel it's less natural to hear the sounds of a woman's lovemaking than, say, the sound of a Concorde, killing the atmosphere and polluting nature. But the lovemaking is the sound that will make us survive. You see, I believe we will blossom in the Eighties."

As everyone now knows, the '80s only got worse from that point out, but *Double Fantasy* is less a reflection of its time than a testament to the almost-impressive insularity of its makers. Released in 1984, *Milk And Honey*, which contained tracks recorded during the *Double Fantasy* sessions as well as the same alternating his-and-hers song structure, is equally blinkered. Essentially a sequel to *Double Fantasy*, it's stuffed with filler. The inclusion of Lennon's demo version of his wistful "Grow Old With Me" seems almost perversely, intentionally depressing, particularly in comparison with *Double Fantasy*'s countless accidental poignancies.

Ono, who compiled *Milk And Honey*, has spent the decades since Lennon's death serving as an admirable protector of her husband's legacy (and, less admirably, as an energetic burnisher of her own). She has largely avoided the open-the-vaults approach that has marred the posthumous career of artists such as Jeff Buckley, concentrating mostly on compilations like 1998's highly recommended *Lennon Legend*, a greatest-hits package that's virtually Ono-free. Though not the most exhaustive collection (completists will be better served by *Anthology*, a box set released that same year), *Lennon Legend* has virtually every song that matters, and it's the best way to hear his *Double Fantasy* tracks without having to endure hers. (Ironically, this is precisely what Ono feared back in 1980 when, it's rumored, she proposed the he-said, she-said format of *Double Fantasy* as an alternative to the original plan of one artist per side, believing that listeners would simply skip her tracks.)

Double Fantasy was re-mastered in 2000 and reissued with several new songs. Though it's a vast sonic improvement over the occasionally murky original, the bonus tracks don't add much in the way of artistic value. A demo of Lennon singing "Help Me to Help Myself" has a stark simplicity the rest of the album lacks, though it's an awkward fit with Ono's "Walking on Thin Ice," the track Lennon was tinkering with the night he was murdered, and an eventual club hit.

Interestingly, neither the passage of time nor the release of the reissue has occasioned any meaningful critical reconsideration of

Double Fantasy, which may be due more to the slightness of the work itself than to any misplaced sense of critical delicacy. Lennon himself has been left largely unexamined, his controversial biographer Albert Goldman excepted, but Ono's reputation has undergone a seismic shift. Thanks to her noted influence on artists such as Sonic Youth and Björk and the release of 1981's agonizing *Season of Glass*, Ono has been publicly transformed from the reviled defiler of the Beatles, to pitiable widow, to one of those artists that hipsters pretend to listen to (but really don't), much like John Cage.

Equally instrumental in Ono's rehabilitation was the release of the 1984 tribute album *Every Man Has a Woman* (its title derived from her *Double Fantasy* track, "Every Man Has a Woman Who Loves Him"). Alongside contributions from Roberta Flack and Harry Nilsson, there's a not-bad Elvis Costello cover of "Walking on Thin Ice" and an improbably hard-rocking version of "I'm Moving On" by Eddie Money (yes, Eddie Money).

Though Money deserves credit for being the only contributor brave enough to tackle any of Ono's *Double Fantasy* tracks, he nevertheless manages to single-handedly disprove the theory that her songs are better when she isn't doing them. Note to Yoko: The next time Eddie Money offers to help restore your credibility, it's okay to say no.

THE SEX PISTOLS
Never Mind the Bollocks... Here's the Sex Pistols
Warner Bros., 1977
By Jim Testa

ver get the feeling you've been cheated?

You're fifteen years old. You hate your parents, you hate your school, you hate the music all the cool kids listen to (*Dave fucking Matthews?* No way!), and you're desperate to find a way out. Then one day, you hear it, that magic word: PUNK. The music of misfits, the soundtrack to adolescent rebellion, a screeching torrent of pent-up aggression and resentment. But the crap that the kids at school consider "punk" just doesn't cut it for you. Simple Plan? All-American Rejects? Good Charlotte? Blink-182? It's all sissy-boy pop tunes dressed up in a pair of tight black jeans. Where is the *real* stuff? So you ask around, you read some books, you—God help us all—thumb through *Rolling Stone* and *Spin* in search of the answers. And then, you find it, the *ne-plus-ultra* of punk, the mother lode of anti-social behavior, the avatar of adolescent acting-out: the Sex Pistols.

You mow some lawns, set aside your allowance, steal a couple of bucks from mom's pocketbook, whatever, and you score your very own copy of *Never Mind the Bollocks... Here's the Sex Pistols*. You throw it into your CD player and you play it through for the first time. Yeah, man. "Anarchy in the U.K." *rocks*. And "God Save the Queen," well, you're not sure who the queen is or what any of that has to do with you, but that guy with the scurvy voice screaming, "No future, no future, no future for youuuuu"—that's *punk rock*. But the rest of it, well, it doesn't leave much of an impression. So you go back and play it again. "Uh, wait," you think. "I must have missed something. Shit, it's only about forty minutes long, lemme give it *another* spin." And then it hits you, a feeling that knots your stomach and slams you in the face like a coiled fist. And you know, you just *know.*

Cheated.

Congratulations, kid. You're the victim of the great rock 'n' roll swindle, a con that was perpetrated over twenty-five years ago and which still hustles suckers today. The Sex Pistols didn't invent punk. They certainly don't define punk. And you could easily make the argument that they aren't now—and never were—punk, not if you define punk as something other than a desperate attempt at making a lot of money by selling a lot of records to a lot of suckers.

So what's all the friggin' fuss about?

I'm not going to lie to you: When I heard "Anarchy in the U.K." for the first time, it blew my mind. Ditto with "God Save the Queen." And I'm not ashamed to admit that I heard them back when those singles first trickled into the record bins of the Lower East Side. Those two singles, along with the first couple of Ramones albums and some intensive late night debauchery at various clubs in late-'70s New York City, literally changed my life. I had never even thought about writing about music until punk happened; my eyes were set on becoming the new Rex Reed, a celebrity interviewer tossing off tasty *bon mots* about film and theater for bourgeois newspaper readers. Then punk happened, and it was all over. I was a rock critic for life, like it or not.

But back to our story. The Sex Pistols came to America as a rumor before they were a reality for us fans. The British music press—the *New Musical Express, Melody Maker, Sounds*, all readily available in New York and pretty cheap back in those days—trumpeted the band's historic magnificence on their covers every week. *Rolling Stone* and *Creem* dispatched reporters to England to check out the madness firsthand. We read about the Pistols, but we couldn't hear them on American radio; even really cool DJs such as WNEW-FM's Vin Scelsa didn't play punk at that point. The band's only TV appearances were on the BBC, and the records simply weren't available here.

I bought both "God Save the Queen" (which I found first, even though it was released second) and "Anarchy in the U.K." as pricey import singles; each cost more than a full domestic LP at the time. They were great songs, and totally of the moment. The United States and Great Britain both wallowed in the throes of an ugly economic recession. Kids got out of school in England and went on the dole—that's welfare to us—and they had little chance of ever finding a decent job, much less starting a meaningful career. "No future, no future for you"—that was the state of Queen Elizabeth's faded empire in the year of her silver jubilee (marking twenty-five years since she ascended to the throne).

The twisted story of how *Never Mind the Bollocks... Here's the Sex Pistols* eventually reached the public is a *grand guignol* tale of Machevellian cleverness, driven by the Sex Pistols' Svengali and manager, Malcolm McLaren, and coupled with an almost unbelievable level of record-industry temerity and stupidity. The band managed to sign with—and collect large checks from—EMI and A&M, but both labels chickened out and cut the band loose before releasing its debut album. Virgin became the third label to sign the Pistols, and the album finally was released in October 1977. A short time later, Warner Bros. released it in the United States, and Americans could finally hear the Sex Pistols on a reasonably-priced domestic LP instead of an expensive import.

And I, for one, felt cheated.

The purpose of this book, according to its editors, is to reconsider the classic albums of rock 'n' roll with a fresh perspective. But I'm not even sure that *Never Mind the Bollocks... Here's the Sex Pistols* qualifies as a classic. Let's look at the band's claims to greatness and see if the group measures up.

Clearly, there's a short list of requirements that qualify a band for immortality: Longevity. Influence. Originality. And, finally, musical achievement. The Sex Pistols fall short on nearly all fronts.

Longevity? Bah! Although dozens of bootlegs, demos, and live recordings bear the Sex Pistols' name, the group only released two official albums—*Never Mind the Bollocks... Here's the Sex Pistols* and the soundtrack to *The Great Rock 'n' Roll Swindle*. But the latter double album doesn't do much more than regurgitate the best songs from the debut and pad the release with a lot of filler (unless the likes of "Friggin' in the Riggin'" and Sid Vicious croaking his way through "My Way" earn a place in your particular rock 'n' roll pantheon—I think not). Name one other band considered to be iconic that only released one album. Derek and the Dominos, maybe? Puh-leeze.

Okay, how about influence? That's a good one. Just compare the Sex Pistols to the Ramones. Starting with pop-punk mainstays such as Screeching Weasel and the Queers, and continuing through a long, long list of pop, punk, and even metal bands, most fans can tick off a dozen different acts that were clearly influenced by da bruddahs from Queens. But go ahead, name one band you'd consider as having been influenced by the Sex Pistols.

Can't do it, right?

Let's look at originality. No less an authority than *The Rolling Stone Record Guide* cites the Sex Pistols as "unquestionably the most radical new rock band of the Seventies," but with typical *Rolling Stone* mush-headedness, it never explains why. Reliable historical reports tell us that guitarist Steve Jones and drummer Paul Cook were mucking around with a band that would eventually morph into the Pistols as early as 1972. But by the time the group played its first gig with Johnny Rotten (Lydon) on vocals in late 1975, the Ramones had not only established a presence in New York City, but had been signed by Sire Records. Richard Hell and Patti Smith had already cornered the market on nihilism long before the Pistols got around to "Holidays in the Sun," and let's not forget that Hell takes credit for the spiky-haired, safety-pinned look that McLaren appropriated as the *sine qua non* of punk fashion.

The Sex Pistols wallowed in obscurity for a while, playing shit gigs and one or two music festivals, but they couldn't find an audience. Then came the fateful night of December 1, 1976, when they appeared on Thames TV's "Today" show and flabbergasted host Bill

Grundy by unleashing a tirade of four-letter words live on the air. That appearance made the Sex Pistols a *cause célèbre* in Great Britain and kick-started their career. But by then, *The Ramones* had already been released in the U.S.

What made the Sex Pistols radical? Surely it wasn't stripping the wretched excesses of '70s arena-rock down to a raw, basic rock 'n' roll sound; the Ramones had already taken that concept to the extremes, and even they were working on a foundation laid down by earlier bands such as the Stooges and the New York Dolls (whom McLaren had also briefly managed, pre-Pistols). And while the Sex Pistols did throw a nose-thumbing dose of political agitprop into its lyrics, "God Save the Queen" didn't even scratch the surface of the radical left-wing agenda of Detroit's MC5. More to the point, the MC5 lived its lyrics (and saw a key member thrown in jail because of his beliefs). The self-proclaimed "anarchists" in the Sex Pistols not only cashed in for every dime they could wrench out of the corporate bankers of the music industry, but were "exiled" to a lush resort in the Bahamas after the band crashed and burned. There, they consorted with McLaren and felon Ronnie Biggs (of "the Great Train Robbery" fame) to put together *The Great Rock 'n' Roll Swindle* film and cash in even more.

Finally, we come to the question of musical achievement. No one—not even an old curmudgeon like me—can deny the fist-pumping exhilaration of "Anarchy in the U.K." or "God Save the Queen." I'll even give you "Pretty Vacant" (which was written by bassist Glen Matlock, who was kicked out of the band before the debut album was released for the alleged crime of liking the Beatles). That's three great singles, granted, but they were all released before *Never Mind the Bollocks… Here's the Sex Pistols.* Ira Robbins, writing in *The Trouser Press Record Guide,* notes that when people finally got to hear the rest of the album, it was largely considered a disappointment, even back in 1977. Today, it sounds crudely dated and more than a bit clunky.

"Holidays in the Sun" kicks off with a series of corny guitar flourishes and a four-four backbeat appropriated almost wholesale from the Bay City Rollers, while the descending guitar riff at the core of the song could have been lifted from almost any hit single by the Sweet or Thin Lizzie. Rotten rants about wanting to visit "the new Belsen"—shock horror! A Nazi reference!—before the declamatory chorus about wanting to jump over the Berlin Wall takes the song... nowhere.

"Bodies" enjoys a certain notoriety as perhaps the only anti-abortion anthem ever recorded by a band proclaiming to be anarchists. Fortunately, the band's unsavory reputation has prevented it from being adopted by the pro-life movement. (What an embarrassment that would be to punks everywhere!) The verse recycles the chord progression for "Anarchy in the U.K." (a recurrent theme throughout the album), while the "I'm not an animal" chorus has the cliched catchiness of a British football chant.

More evidence of the band's paucity of musical ideas comes on "No Feelings," which pretty much rips off "God Save the Queen." (The Pistols should have never kicked Matlock out of the band; they never wrote another decent song after he was replaced by Sid Vicious.)

Does "Liar" sound a little like "Anarchy in the U.K." too? Well, yes, it does. Case closed.

"Problems" may be good cause for me to retract some of what I said about the Sex Pistols never influencing any other bands. The vapid lyrics are echoed today in the tiresome drivel of a thousand adolescent pop-punk bands. To wit: "Eat your heart out on a plastic tray / You don't do what you want / Then you'll fade away / You won't find me working / Nine to five / It's too much fun being alive." Unfortunately, it's just not much fun listening to this song more than once a decade.

"Seventeen" makes so little sense that it's not even worth analyzing. The chorus, "I'm a lazy sod," apparently refers to Rotten's refusal to spend much time on lyrics, although the three-chord melody also sounds as if it was patched together in about ten minutes. I suppose, if you want to be generous, you can credit the track with being some sort of Dadaist commentary on the barren worthlessness of the adolescent mind.

"Submission," a bonus track on the album's U.S. release, qualifies as almost pure filler, a simple blues progression coupled with a ridiculous lyric that uses the metaphor of a submarine mission to describe the travails of love. If Led Zeppelin had recorded the same song, it would not only have been played much better, it would have been cited as an example of exactly the sort of arena-rock vapidity that the Pistols were allegedly trying to destroy.

"New York" takes a cheap shot at Johnny Thunders of the New York Dolls, or someone from New York City very much like him: "Think it is well playing Max's Kansas / You're looking bored / And you're acting flash / With nothing in your gut / You better keep yer mouth shut… Still out on those pills / Do the samba." I guess we're not supposed to notice that the band is regurgitating the verse to "Anarchy in the U.K." for the third or fourth time on the album, and I won't even get into the sad irony of a band ranking on a drug-addicted wannabe rock star when it has the likes of Vicious in its own ranks.

"E.M.I" finishes the album with a swipe at the label that signed the Sex Pistols and released "Anarchy in the U.K." as a single, but then dropped the group like a hot potato when the company's corporate elders got a good look at what they were in for publicity-wise. Here's Rotten doing what he does best, being snotty and self-aggrandizing: "And you thought that we were faking / That we were all just money-making / You do not believe we're for real / Or you would lose your cheap appeal." Musically, the song sounds like any other Sex Pistols track, and the lyrics pale compared to much more witty and vitriolic anti-record label songs such as the Clash's "Complete Control" or Graham Parker's "Mercury Poisoning." Even Elvis Costello's "I want to bite the hand that feeds me" from "Radio Radio" resonates with a lot more truth and genuine sarcasm than Rotten's shallow backbiting.

Some bands just come along at the right time. Others are lucky enough to be remembered as far more than what they actually were, simply because they came to epitomize a certain point in history. I'm sorry, *Rolling Stone*, but the most radical rock band of the '70s was the Ramones; the Sex Pistols don't even finish a distant third. They were a media creation largely invented by the press, remembered far more for their haircuts and clothing and repugnant personal habits than for their music. In that respect, they're a lot like disco, another manifestation of that decade's flair for extravagant bad taste.

Although the Sex Pistols had several hit singles in the U.K., the ultimate irony is that they turned out not to be the "money-making" proposition that Rotten bragged about at all. It took twenty-five years for *Never Mind the Bollocks... Here's the Sex Pistols* to go gold in the U.S. Not only was it all a big con job, but it wasn't even a particularly lucrative one. That's still half a million suckers, granted, but at the rate of only twenty thousand a year. Avril Lavigne sells that many CDs in twenty-five minutes.

As for the rest of the story, we all know what happened to Vicious. Cook and Jones have enjoyed long, undistinguished careers in a myriad of forgettable projects. Rotten had fifteen more minutes of justified fame with Public Image, Ltd., but eventually found himself reduced to shaving his thinning hair into a Mohawk and going back on the road with the Sex Pistols, a fifty year old self-parody desperately trying to cash in on half-remembered glories from a quarter-century ago. That brief reunion with the limelight must have inspired Lydon's next career move—a much-ballyhooed guest spot on the British reality TV show, "I'm A Celebrity... Get Me Out Of Here." The American version of the show, you might recall, included such dubious "stars" as Melissa Rivers, "Stuttering John" Melendez, and "Downtown" Julie Brown. Lydon found himself sharing airtime on the crueler and far more humiliating British edition with a disgraced aristocrat, a topless model, and '80s teen idol Peter Andre, but he walked off the show after only a few episodes. Next stop: "Hollywood Squares"?

Never mind the Sex Pistols. Punk rock continues to do quite well without them. But can I interest you in buying a used Strokes CD?

DEAD KENNEDYS
Fresh Fruit for
Rotting Vegetables
Alternative Tentacles, 1980
By Marco Leavitt

I used to wonder why those skin-headed little jerks did it, but here we are, more than twenty years on, and don't you wish you could beat the shit out of Jello Biafra, if only to keep him from releasing those sanctimonious spoken-word albums?

Jello was always the most distinctive but ultimately the most irritating feature of Dead Kennedys. You can't deny the band's legacy: Musically, it was the bridge for a generation of longhairs out of metal, and an inspiration to a host of speedcore bands that followed. But under Jello's stewardship, the group managed to sound both tongue-in-cheek *and* pompous—not an easy thing to do.

At a time when most bands have abdicated the social outrage that was the hallmark of the glory days of punk rock, I suppose poor Biafra can be forgiven for taking Jerry Brown seriously, even though he gets equally worked up over crossword puzzles on "Drug Me." This isn't a guy who's tolerant of very much, but over the years, his grandiose pronouncements and petulant griping have lost a lot of their charm. In a typically serious announcement on his Web site, he earnestly declared that he wasn't running for governor during California's tumultuous political freak show of 2003 (Gary Coleman must have been too much competition).

It's as if after all these years, Jello still thinks that his infamous run for mayor of San Francisco in 1979 was more than a juvenile stunt.

More troubling is Jello's constant sidestepping of the issue of why he needed to rip off his own band. This is what alternative music in the United States has come down to—the defrocked icon of all of American punk making increasingly predictable rants against Capitalism while screwing his former comrades out of the right to sell their songs to commercials for dishwasher detergent. Who do you root for in that fight?

Maybe it's unfair, but it's hard to listen to Dead Kennedys today without thinking of that awful lawsuit. For those who don't already know, the other band members sued Jello, claiming they weren't being paid royalties that they were owed. A judge eventually ruled in their favor, and Jello's Alternative Tentacles record label lost control of the band's albums.

Listening to a freshly pressed CD of *Fresh Fruit for Rotting Vegetables* that was difficult to obtain, thanks to that stupid lawsuit, I'm trying to recapture the feelings I had when I was in high school, sporting the worst haircut imaginable. (Kids today seem to be a little more creative, but for me at the time, a mohawk was all I could come up with—no points for originality.) All of my friends love this album, but nobody seems to have owned a copy in the last fifteen years.

There's Jello bellowing "Kill the Poor" again, but it just doesn't sound right—the mix is flat. Most everything from the '80s was produced pretty poorly, so that shouldn't be a surprise. I try turning up the bass and the treble, just like I always used to, and all I get is mud. Then I turn the treble up three quarters and move the bass down, and that sounds better, but still not quite what I remembered. Maybe it's because it's digital.

I suppose I'm an asshole for trying to adjust my Harman Kardon receiver to get the sound I remember from the eighty-dollar stereo I had when I was fifteen, a big square box with a hard plastic turntable on top. But I just want to be fair. I want to conjure up the state of mind when I actually took all of this seriously.

It's no use. I'm just an old fart who didn't start out as much more than a middle-class poser—the sort of person Jello would have hated.

Except that he would have tried to preach to me, which he did. I lapped up every word back then as I lay on my bed trying to find the picture of the guy about to cut off his own finger amid the crudely cut montage of photos from the nifty black-and-white poster that came with *Fresh Fruit for Rotting Vegetables*. I wish they'd included a second picture. Did he really go through with it? Does anybody know?

Now here's Jello simplifying the debate over welfare reform into a rant on "Kill the Poor" that "the man" would really just wipe out the ghettoes with the neutron bomb if they had the chance. Maybe so, but is that really a very thought-provoking observation? And what is with that voice? It sounds like he's giving head to a kazoo. He hadn't refined his trademark quiver into something distinctive yet, and he alternates between an awkward growl and a nasal mock-operatic tone that comes across like a clichéd attempt to ape Feargal Sharkey or Howard Devoto.

Fresh Fruit for Rotting Vegetables isn't a terrible album. It's hard not to like a song—"Stealing People's Mail"—that makes mail fraud sound like a harmless night of yucks. That's a felony, kiddies; just ask Roky Erickson. But the best songs—"Your Emotions," "When Ya Get Drafted," "Drug Me"—are among the least famous, and they're all on the first side. The rest of it… Well, let's just say that "Kill the Poor" no longer seems like the biting social satire that it once did.

For a band that is revered for delivering scathing indictments against the established order, a lot of Jello's attacks were just a lot of bluster. For all of his rage and occasional vicious humor, he doesn't seem to have been able to focus his diatribes into very compelling arguments. It wouldn't be such a problem with another group, but Dead Kennedys aren't a band that can be separated from its message. It was more prominent than the music.

We also get "Lynch the Landlord," which was a lot more unnerving and subversive when Eddie Murphy did it on *Saturday Night Live*.

Musically, the album shows flashes of the brilliance that would emerge later on. East Bay Ray was pretty handy with those effects pedals, especially on "Holiday in Cambodia," which may be a pretty dumb song, but damn if it ain't catchy, even if that's not supposed to be much of a selling point for a punk song. Same for a number of the group's other famous cuts. Unfortunately, a good deal of the time, this promising material is derailed by Jello's vocalizing (yes, I'm bitching about that again), with a foreshadowing of the hammy delivery that, by 1985's *Frankenchrist*, would evolve into a pompously bombastic spectacle as embarrassing as anything Queen ever recorded. And at least with Queen, you couldn't help but smile at the audacity of it all, not to mention Freddie Mercury's puzzling inability to tell how stupid he looked in that mustache.

Dead Kennedys are hard to take because they're just so serious about everything, even when they're trying to be humorous. Any good preacher knows that sometimes understatement has more power than fire and brimstone. This is a lesson Jello never learned. It's not hard to imagine him in the early days, living in a squalid, crumbling apartment swatting at cockroaches with a hammer and grumbling how he was going to fix the landlord.

Who exactly is the target of "Holiday in Cambodia," anyway? People who like jazz? Sure, this country is lousy with white liberals feigning empathy for black culture. I won't claim it isn't annoying, but I don't see the unforgivable hypocrisy that warrants shipping these people off to Pol Pot's work gangs. Anyway, if that's his point, doesn't he have the wrong continent? Shouldn't it have been "Holiday in Zaire"?

Sensitive white people will never genuinely understand the suffering of poor repressed minorities, because by and large, life isn't that tough for them. That's not their fault. At least some of them have the decency to feel bad about it, even if it doesn't come off as all that sincere. Are we to assume that Jello alone has attained this level of enlightenment through an arduous dedication to gluing together montages from newspaper clippings? Talk about hypocrisy. If anything, his snide dismissals trivialize the horrors of the Khmer Rouge.

My family actually adopted a family of Cambodian refugees around the time that *Fresh Fruit for Rotting Vegetables* came out. We didn't take them in or anything; our church just wanted us to teach them about Christmas, which they diligently attempted to master. Mostly, I think they wanted to prove to the mirrored-sunglasses crowd that they were American enough to stay. I've always wondered what they would have thought about that song.

As with just about every tune on the album, it's difficult to tell whether Jello is serious or trying to be ironic. "I Kill Children" would turn into a real problem for me when my parents were shocked over the title in a way that only could happen twenty years ago. "It's meant to be a satire," I calmly reassured them, although looking back, that doesn't seem to be quite right. In any case, it didn't work, and to this day I'm convinced my mom still believes me when I told her I destroyed my copy of the album.

What about "Forward to Death," which isn't really in keeping with the band's usual constructive message? To their credit, Dead Kennedys didn't just want you to buy their albums, they wanted you to go out and try to make things better. "This world brings me down / I'm looking forward to death," Jello sings, more in keeping with the sentiments of his goth-rock contemporaries than fellow punks. On a lot of these songs, Jello still seems to be struggling to refine his vision as a lyricist.

I also don't know where he's coming from on "Chemical Warfare." Is this role-playing again? Urging someone to break into a weapons depot and run amok spraying nerve gas is pretty inconsistent with his later lyrics. He also sounds genuinely gleeful about the poor little kiddies who get splattered on the amusement park ride on "Funland at the Beach."

Maybe this was my attraction to this music all along: It was basically a new way to stick a poker in the ass of my parents, who were as undeserving as the hapless progenitors of the irritating, pimpled shits who insist on embracing hollow shock-rockers like Marilyn Manson. There's a guy whose repugnant obsession with deliberately offensive antics would be amusing if he weren't so stultifyingly boring.

Jello and Manson aren't so unexpected: Using obnoxious rock 'n' roll to piss off your parents is a time-honored tradition for American teens. But in becoming a tool to pacify the frustrations of suburban adolescents with meaningless gestures in the same way that Manson now does, wasn't Jello the embodiment of everything he's made a life's work reviling against? Unless that's what he wanted to do all along. Like I said, I'm still not sure, at least not on this first album.

I was living in San Francisco at the time of the band's other infamous legal contretemps, when it was charged with distributing harmful material to minors because it had included an H.R. Giger poster featuring repeated images of a penis penetrating somebody's ass as part of the packaging for *Frankenchrist*. Jello, who has practically been deified in the underground in the years since, owes much of his reputation to this incident, in which he admirably fought for freedom of speech. The band eventually beat the charges, but it went broke in the process. The turmoil was supposedly the reason that it broke up, but maybe the group just realized that it found Jello as annoying as the prosecutors did.

In the midst of all this, Jello appeared on a local rock station, and I was one of the callers lucky enough to get through to him. I told him that the poster from my copy of *Plastic Surgery Disasters* was missing when I bought it, and I asked him if it had been censored, too. There was a conversation in the background that I couldn't quite understand—some kind of sputtering from Jello that sounded as if his head was about to pop. Then the deejay came on and explained that I probably had an Italian bootleg. "Don't buy those!" Jello barked, and I was promptly disconnected. So ended my minor brush with the great one.

The contradiction of how Jello could disparage Capitalism at every turn on the one hand, then ferociously defend his own need to sell albums—and not even give his bandmates their fair share of the cut—didn't occur to me at the time. What about all those pictures and newspaper articles he relentlessly cut and pasted into posters like the one I didn't get? It's impossible to believe he secured the rights for all of them, so regardless of how "fair use" laws work, morally, wasn't he doing essentially the same thing as the bootleggers that so enraged him? He used the poster as a selling point for buying his record, after all.

There's also the picture of the hapless cowboy band on the back cover of *Fresh Fruit for Rotting Vegetables*, which was apparently used without its permission, prompting yet another lawsuit. Dead Kennedys just couldn't seem to stay out of court.

The truth is, the rigid, black-and-white worldview that most of the hardcore punk bands espoused in the early '80s seems increasingly quaint as you get older. Maybe that's why so many bands today steer clear of politics. Punk ideology isn't really that workable as a lifelong philosophy. Most punks eventually figure out that's it's basically just music—about as thrilling and dangerous as the acid rock or folk or whatever geezer sounds their parents listened to. That doesn't have to be a letdown, because your parents' music (assuming that they weren't mean rednecks who liked to beat on longhairs), had seemed just as new and exciting once, before it, too, was exposed as being ultimately meaningless.

Yes, the world is as fucked-up as you thought it was. In fact, it's worse—far worse than anybody said. As you get older, the angst-riddled clichés you once trusted as insightful critiques of the world at large (the world that only people with credit cards could actually experience, unlike you with your band T-shirts and disheveled bedroom) begins to lose their impact as you gain a deeper appreciation of just what a soul-deadening, dishonest, selfish place the universe can be. You know now, because you have a credit card and a college degree and are about to do unspeakable things to pay the damn things off.

Except now, all those unspeakable things—the same hypocritical, dishonest acts you watched suck the joy out of the lives of your parents when they were scrounging to buy you blue hair dye and spray paint—somehow don't seem so bad. Maybe along the way you'll even be able to get a car that starts in the winter. That's when the soul of every punk dies. Or maybe another way of looking at it is that that's just what it means to grow up.

BRUCE SPRINGSTEEN
Born to Run
Columbia, 1975
By David Sprague

The *Physician's Desk Reference* doesn't make any mention of a particularly potent strain of hallucinogens sweeping America in 1974, but the anecdotal evidence is unmistakable. By now, just about everyone who's dipped a toe into the slipstream of pop culture has heard of Jon Landau's Ebenezer Scrooge-like vision of Bruce Springsteen as "rock and roll future," but just as important, if less well-woven into rock's rich tapestry, is the months-earlier revelation experienced by Asbury Park's favorite son himself. "*I* saw rock and roll future," the artist later known as Broooooooooce mumbled, likely within earshot of drummer Vini "Mad Dog" Lopez, who had to be fired as a result of his eavesdropping, "and it is Andrew Lloyd Webber."

With that thought in mind, the shuffling wanna-beat—a likeable enough guy who'd cranked out a pair of albums that had enough charm to overcome his insistence on whipping out his big ten-inch thesaurus every few minutes—reinvented himself as the Messiah of Melisma, the Oracle of Overkill, the Pope of Pomp. In short, the man behind *Born to Run*.

It's hard to discern exactly where Springsteen went off the rails. Perhaps it had something to do with that celebrated show that he opened for schmaltz queen Anne Murray. Then again, the Canadian songbird had a firmer grasp on subtlety—and, judging by her version of "Daydream Believer," better choice in covers—than Springsteen

203

ever manifested. Yeah, he'd already been saddled with the "new Dylan" baggage—an honor he deserved more than, say, Roderick Falconer, if considerably less than Elliott Murphy—but if Springsteen had really bought into that, he'd have started dashing off neo-Biblical allegories about Spiro Agnew (or, at the very least, Hank Aaron's knocking that old drunk, Babe Ruth, off his pedestal, despite the best efforts of the KKK). Instead, he hopped on his motorcycle and—taking care not to wipe out in the Holland Tunnel, thus necessitating one of those recuperative retreats that'd involve a stay in Nashville and some duets with Olivia Newton-John—headed straight for the Great White Way.

I guess my ambivalence towards this particular part of rock history has something to do with the fact that I came of musical age in Cleveland, Ohio, around the time *Born to Run* emerged. That might sound like a non sequitur, but a quick trip in the wayback machine reveals the slavish Bruce-worship that afflicted the media in what was then known as the Mistake by the Lake circa 1974-'76. Bruce's chief champion was a disc jockey who, like one of Springsteen's greaser wannabes, used a Laverne and Shirley-style pseudonym, Kid Leo. Leo—a.k.a, Lawrence Travagliante—made it his mission to ensure that Cleveland adopted this Jersey guy as one of its own. He raved, he proselytized, he did everything but set up a miniature Asbury Park boardwalk on the shores of Lake Erie. Eventually, he'd go on to be, with one slim degree of separation, an employee of Springsteen, Inc.; as Vice President of Special Projects at Columbia Records, one of the more uptight entities in the entertainment industry, he'd insist that he be listed in the corporate directory as "Leo, Kid."

Think *Born to Run* was ubiquitous in the rest of America? Thanks to Larry—I mean, Leo—WMMS-FM, the only remotely rock-oriented station in Cleveland at the time, put every single song on the freakin' record into heavy rotation six full months before the damn thing was even released. Nobody in the Springsteen camp even blinked at the, wink-wink, "unauthorized" leak, particularly since each spin was preceded by the intro—repeated like a Hare Krishna mantra—"Ladies and gentlemen, the main event, round for round, pound for pound, there ain't no finer band around." About the only thing that broke the wall-to-wall, spring-to-fall saturation was (and for this to seem like a relief only underscores the ennui that welled up in my twelve-year-old soul) demo tapes from Southside Johnny and the Asbury Jukes, which stayed on the airwaves for months, even after that band piggybacked its way onto Bruce's label. (Okay, technically the Jukes were on Epic, while Brooooce was on Columbia, but let's not nit-pick.)

It took years for me to muster up the gumption to toss the thing on of my own volition, but when a freebie CD crossed my path, I figured that cracking the shrink-wrap—despite the inherent devaluation such an act would cause come time to trade it in at the local music purveyor—was something of a duty. If anything, the new technology only highlighted the Wizard of Oz-like aspects of *Born to Run*—the emptiness that lurks behind the impressive-at-first-blush shell.

Springsteen supporters have long pointed to this windier-than-Mount-Washington collection of songs as evidence that the Boss was capable of channeling the spirit of Phil Spector, a claim that only holds water if one believes that all walls of sound are created equal. Ronnie's gunplay-prone ex layered his productions with gossamer-like sonic leaf spun so intricately that Byzantine gold-spinners would no doubt nod their heads in approval. *Born to Run*, on the other hand, sounds as if it were slapped together by a gaggle of Ethel Merman-mad drama queens playing a game of pile-on. The schmaltz level peaks whenever the spotlight falls on Roy Bittan, perhaps the fussiest bar-band ivory-tinkler to make it out of the tip-jar circuit.

The treacle that oozes from the melodies of "Backstreets" and "Night," however, only gets Springsteen more jazzed up. Presaging Howard Dean, who, like Springsteen, simultaneously hit the covers of *Time* and *Newsweek* under wildly inflated headlines, he attacks the synapses with a shudder-inducing howl that's obviously intended to, you know, convey passion, but ends up begging for an out-of-context edit that emphasizes the Cuckoo's Nest nuttiness of the whole shebang.

For all Springsteen's insistence on playing up the healing power of rock 'n' roll, *Born to Run* relies primarily on instrumentation and arrangements that are broader than Broadway; there's nary a guitar riff, not a single pelvic-directed bassline to be ferreted out. You could lay blame for the latter omission squarely at the feet of the ironically named Gary Tallent, but the complete lack of what Lester Bangs—in his dismissal of the similarly pompous Jethro Tull—called "rebop" is unforgivable. Even Mary Lou Lord, who jimmied a solo version of "Thunder Road" onto one of her karaoke collections, managed to swing with more authority than the umpteen-piece E Street crew.

Ingested in toto, the eight songs that make up *Born to Run* constitute an unwelcome flashback to an amorphous toppermost of the poppermost rundown of the post-Elvis, pre-Beatles era. Over the course of forty-odd minutes, we get squealing car tires, priapic swells of piano and sax, mist-shrouded protagonists who consistently write checks with their mouth that their asses can't cash, and more melodrama than a year's worth of *Peyton Place*. At least the writers of "Last Kiss" and "Tell Laura I Love Her" delivered payoffs, and managed to do so in under three minutes each.

Bloat is only the most obvious of *Born to Run*'s sins. Having mastered the trick of stuffing ten minutes worth of lyrics into five-minute songs on his earlier releases, Springsteen chose to reverse course and stretch three minutes worth of ideas into somewhere between six and ten minutes of music on each of his new songs. Naturally, that makes room for crescendo after crescendo, false endings and stop-on-a-dime theatrics, the sort of thing that labelmate Mariah Carey would borrow to better effect some years later. The one bright spot in the morass is that the disc's most overwrought numbers—"Jungleland," for instance, and maybe "Thunder Road"—lend themselves quite well to a late-night drinking game in which contestants—preferably pre-lubricated, of course—pound down shots whenever Springsteen goes from a whisper to a scream.

Even if it was possible to create a parallel-universe version of the album, something akin to *Born to Run: Naked*, the songs here simply wouldn't stand up to scrutiny. Ostensibly a conceptually driven examination of hardscrabble lower-middle-class life in a dying town, *Born to Run* ends up going nowhere. Yeah, that could be a clever bit of meta-rock tomfoolery on Springsteen's part, but frankly, it all boils down to a paucity of melodic ideas. He would go on to create even-toned collections that do stand up—*Nebraska*, for instance—but here, the sound of wheels spinning is deafening.

At its conceptual core, *Born to Run* doesn't depart drastically from *Greetings from Asbury Park, New Jersey* or *The Wild, the Innocent and the E-Street Shuffle*. If anything, the characters devolve. There are rebels who may have a cause, but who draw the line at, you know, *actually rebelling*, and guys who rail against "cages on Highway 9" while happily returning to lock-up at the appointed hour, just like work-release convicts jonesing for a good-conduct medal. They blow off steam by driving from exit to exit, stopping every once in a while to moon over the bright lights of the big city looming across the Hudson, without having a real clue about what might lurk there.

Those are the guys. The gals, of course, are mere window dressing. They're there to gussy up the back end of a hog or the shotgun seat of a muscle car, smiling prettily with the wind blowing through a helmet of teased, peroxided hair. And they'd better be willing to put out—"the door's open but the ride ain't free" cagily avoids the Spencer's Gifts cheesiness of "grass, gas, or ass, no one rides for free," but the message is clear enough to be understood in any Hell's Angels chapter.

Taking advantage of starry-eyed innocents has been part and parcel of rock 'n' roll since Chuck Berry's first Mann Act violation, so there's nothing all that shameful in Springsteen's unabashed dry-humping. The ignominy stems from the quasi-Steinbeckian veneer the guy uses to mask his horndoggery: "Wendy, let me in / I want to be your friend"? Gene Simmons couldn't say it any more unctuously.

The thing is, the creeping creepiness isn't even all that well-disguised. Leonard Cohen injected the notion of the beautiful loser into the bloodstream of the well-read rock songwriter; Springsteen ham-fistedly excised the beauty entirely, leaving characters that are all but impossible to empathize with. The whining protagonist in "Meeting Across the River" has delusions, not so much of grandeur, but of impending adequacy—he's a character who's supposed to resound with some sort of mythos, but ends up seeming like one of the inter-changeable C-list background thugs on "The Sopranos." He's not a genuine tough guy, not a charismatic guy, not a man with a plan. He's a petty thief who'd heist household goods from his own gal, then pout because she won't wrap her legs 'round his velvet rims anymore.

It'd be a while before Springsteen tapped into the allure of the working man—interestingly enough, the whole dead-end job shtick didn't really occur to him until he was ensconced in a gated commu-nity—so we're left with a series of interchangeable connect-the-dots losers and, naturally enough, a presciently post-modern degree of self-reference. We're talking the missing link between the Monkees and Pavement: Dropped allusions to the Big Man abound, and since this isn't even a revival meeting, you know Springsteen is referring to his saxophonist, who invariably responds by playing the one solo he knows... again... and again... and again.

While subtlety is hard to come by here, Springsteen and compa-ny reach the nadir on "Jungleland," a nine-plus-minutes "epic" that's inflated to ridiculous proportions by one of Clarence Clemons' most purposefully ostentatious sax solos, a distraction that can't quite divert attention from the fact that the song itself is little more than a Cliffs Notes take on *West Side Story*, replete with neo-Sharks and demi-Jets duking it out in the shadows of the Pulaski Skyway: "Kids flash guitars just like switchblades hustling for the record machine / The hungry and the hunted explode into rock 'n' roll bands that face off against each other out in the street down in Jungleland." Leonard Bernstein wouldn't exactly be green with envy, particularly seeing as how Springsteen can't even get his meteorological elements in sync: The street's on fire, even though raindrops are falling on the head of the obligatory eye-candy as she sips her Rheingold.

After positing that head-scratcher (not to mention the notion of the Rangers having a homecoming in Harlem, which is not exactly the hockey capital of the tri-state area), Springsteen revved off into the sunset, leaving his characters "wounded, not even dead." Not long after the album's release, the Boss traded the Technicolor glamour of cherry-top lit blacktop runs for grey-flannel legal battles that kept him in limbo for the better part of three years. It's telling that Springsteen's enforced hiatus after the release of *Born to Run* didn't create much of a cultural vacuum. Sure, his supporters bemoaned the sidetracking of rock's one true prophet, but the world as a whole didn't notice all that much, and for good reason: As with all Broadway productions, there was an understudy waiting in the wings, one who actually admitted he was simply playing a rock 'n' roll singer on TV.

Before you could say, "Do you promise to tell the whole truth, Mister Appel?," Meat Loaf had supplanted Cousin Brucie, matching him bellow for bellow, and, thanks to Jim Steinman, gust for sonic gust. Yeah, it took a hand from Todd Rundgren, and some other body parts from future "Night Court" honey Ellen Foley, but *Bat Out of Hell* ultimately left *Born to Run* in the dust in terms of sales (nearly tripling Bruce's showing on the platinum-ometer) and sheer spectacle.

Bruce's rejoinder? In a perfect world, he'd have joined a touring company of *The Rocky Horror Picture Show* to show Mister Loaf how it really oughta be done. But as we all know, the world is far from perfect, and tramps just have to tread water until that bitchin' Camaro finally comes rolling onto the used car lot, undercoating—and Wendy—included.

BRUCE SPRINGSTEEN
Born in the U.S.A.
Columbia, 1984
By Rob O'Connor

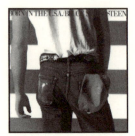

I lived in New Jersey for the first thirty years of my life and survived to tell the tale. I never met a girl named Janie or drove a '69 Chevy with a three-ninety-six, fuelie heads, and a Hurst on the floor. Then again, maybe I have, since I have no fucking idea what one might be. I currently drive a Toyota (very fuel efficient), and would seriously consider—for my girlfriend Lora's sake—driving all night, but not to buy shoes.

I expect a certain amount of romance in my music, and as I grow older, I no longer lash out at excessive poetic license like I used to. However, much of Bruce Springsteen's music steps over the line. Why the same critics who lampoon Meat Loaf get positively misty-eyed when writing about the Boss is one of rock criticism's great mysteries. In many ways, this essay is more about them and their response to Springsteen than it is about the man himself, who has always seemed to be a likable, if slightly boring, guy.

Deep down, I love much of Springsteen's work. I own nearly all of his official albums (I gave up on *Greatest Hits* and a few live discs), and I have about a dozen bootlegs that range from fascinating to horrible. The acoustic version of "Thunder Road," a slow piano rendition of "For You," and any recording of "The Promise" remain among my favorite songs by any artist. And my dislike of *Born in the U.S.A.* is not a slam dunk.

Born in the U.S.A.

I was not happy with the album when it came out in the summer of 1984, as I turned sixteen, but when I recently took out my vinyl copy—with the receipt that says 6/6/84, my mother's birthday and two days after the album's official release date—I noticed that the grooves were all bled white. This just wasn't the album that I wanted from Springsteen at that point in time. I was an awkward adolescent looking for introspection, not a flag-waving American icon and massive promotional machine. But I played it endlessly, anyway, hoping to once again experience the same chills I got while listening to "Backstreets" or "The River," when I was the perfect sucker for the question, "Is a dream a lie if it don't come true or is it something worse?" I nearly got there with "Downbound Train," but most of the rest of *Born in the U.S.A.* left me searching.

At his best, Springsteen creates a dramatic aura around the lives of people who aren't doing much more than surviving. He visualizes their unspoken dreams. However, his weakest work turns mundane rituals into monumental struggles where innocent people do battle with the grip of death to emerge as winners and losers instead of just one lumpen mass of downtrodden souls. You can tell he never had a real job because you have to be fairly disconnected with the ins and outs of the working life to romanticize it so. As the son of a rubber-stamp manufacturer who spent summers working alongside his old man, believe me, I can tell you there is absolutely nothing heroic in such work. Some may consider it honorable, but it's really just boring. I could regale you with tales of what it was like, sweeping up that sawdust and cutting up the ol' rubber, but even I don't have the heart to participate in so dull an exercise.

Critic Tom Carson once wrote that Springsteen "thought rock 'n' roll was basically wholesome. It was an alternative, an escape—but not a rebellion, either as a route to forbidden sexual or social fruit, or, by extension, as a rejection of conventional society. To him rock redeemed conventional society." In other words, he's corny. And just as walking around with a Dave Matthews record or a Douglas Coupland book under your arm announces your own incredible lameness, buying into Springsteen's modern day street-life mythology makes you gullible, if not a fool.

It's been said that Generation X understands irony first and foremost, with sincerity being the least trusted tool. This is true. With Springsteen, what they're offered goes beyond mere sincerity into patronizing slap-ya-on-the back camaraderie. For us X'ers, at least this was good for a laugh. What Generation Y thinks of it is beyond me. Embracing supersized pre-fab hype is sad, but I only had to climb over mountains of hair-sprayed heads and Bon Jovi worshippers. They've got the entire Disney Army to take out.

Throughout the writing of this piece, I've wrestled with what it is that annoyed me so greatly about *Born in the U.S.A.* upon first listen, and what it is to this day that makes it such an appalling piece of work. Springsteen's strong suit is his introspective melancholia, his sense of things falling apart. The album is his grandest gesture. With it, the subtleties of his anxiety disperse, the party-guy aura of "Glory Days" takes over, and the existential despair is securely hidden under the car seat. Much of Springsteen's work is uneven—from the bumbling Dylan-isms of *Greetings from Asbury Park New Jersey* (1973), to the *West Side Story*-mawkishness of *Born to Run* (1975); from the endless John Ford struggles of *The River* (1980) to the Charlie Starkweather blues of *Nebraska* (1982), which is probably his best album. Bruce has always been less a rambling spirit stumbling on personal reinvention than a quick study of American archetypes, a control freak obsessed with recreating a sense of "average" to the point where it's all high-contrast black-and-white photography, darkness and light. Gray area is insignificant in Springsteen's world because it works against his sense of drama. People must sink or swim, they never just float.

At the time of *Born in the U.S.A.*'s release, you'd swear the rock critic union had signed a pact with Columbia Records to never utter a discouraging word. There was this joke that said something along the lines of, "If Bruce Springsteen hadn't come along, rock critics would've invented him." Well, I'm not so sure he did come along. From *Born to Run* onward, he's been produced and managed by Jon Landau, the rock critic who wrote, "I saw rock 'n' roll future and its name is Bruce Springsteen." (Which, if he were being honest, should have read, "I saw Jon Landau's future and its name is Bruce Springsteen.") Between Landau, Springsteen's official "unauthorized" biographer, Dave Marsh (whose wife Barbara Carr has shared management duties with Landau), and the cabal of critics at "serious" rock publications, the manner in which Springsteen is written about is nearly uniform, and the conspiracy of tone is downright weird. The Boss is likened to F. Scott Fitzgerald, Thomas Wolfe, and Elvis Presley, but never Andy Griffith. You don't read a lot of jokes about him; for that, you should check out Billy Altman's review of *The River* in the January 1981 issue of *Creem*, where he likens Bruce not to Theodore Dreiser, but to Ted Baxter of "The Mary Tyler Moore Show."

In the reviews at the time, no one seemed to notice how badly *Born in the U.S.A.* was produced. *Village Voice* rock critic Robert Christgau said it reminded him that what teenagers loved about rock 'n' roll was that "it just plain sounded good." Jeff Nesin in *Creem* noted the five men involved in the album's recording and decided that the *Totally '80s* production gave it a "sense of pop currency." As a teenager in those doldrum days, I thought it sounded like crap. Listening today, it still sounds pretty lame and hopelessly dated, yet with distance, it's quaint in much the same way that all that insipid '70s music is, now that it's lost its context. The big gated snare drum obliterates any chance of subtlety. The mix is typical of '80s records aimed at radio, with an emphasis on mid-range frequencies that sound O.K. on a cheap car stereo but tinny and crass on today's average home system. And the synthesizer! That Yamaha DX-7 has a clunky, unattractive, and fake sound that smoothes over all of the rough edges, a definite non-rock 'n' roll trait. But good taste was not really applicable in the buy-now, pay-later decade.

If you catch a Springsteen video of this vintage, you can almost see the chalk marks blocking his every move as he smiles through each song and dances like a fifth-grade student in Miss Armando's Dance Studio. Comic Bob Goldthwait said Bruce seemed like a member of Up With People. He looks lobotomized, but amazingly, he's capable of singing words completely at odds with his mouth's movements. He's clean-scrubbed and well-built, having spent more time with the Nautilus equipment than he spent in the studio checking on this album. But, hey, it sold. Like McDonald's and Coca-Cola, *Born in the U.S.A.* connected with the masses, except that fast food is not good for you, and with Springsteen, you get the hard line that these songs were created for your moral uplift.

Personally, I could not care less, moral uplift being low on my list of aesthetic priorities. But if you can make it through *Glory Days*, Marsh's second Springsteen biography, you can read one soul-deadening paragraph after another about how these songs connect with others in the Springsteen canon, thematic unity apparently being uplifting as hell.

It's funny how huffy Springsteen fans got over how the song "Born in the U.S.A." was allegedly "misread" by the fist-pumping masses. You see, the red, white, and blue iconography of the album's cover, the flag used as the stage set's backdrop, Springsteen's uncanny resemblance to Rambo, and his own fist in the air while screaming, "Born in the U.S.A.!" were—get this—*ironic*. If you listened to the verses—you know, the shit mumbled between the catchy choruses—you learned that this was a song about a Vietnam vet who got shafted by this country, and the jingoist chorus was a send-up of all the patriotic pomp. Well, Springsteen may understand irony better than Alanis Morissette, but like U2 and R.E.M., he's trying to have it both ways. Crowds understand grand gestures; they don't read the fine print.

It wasn't until *The Ghost of Tom Joad* tour in 1995 that he offered up the title track of his most successful album without the theatrics; he wouldn't speak out against Reagan in the '80s for fear of alienating his audience. In the '90s, with Republican revolutionary Newt Gingrich losing favor, he finally got around to formally letting us know that a lot of people (mostly Republicans) had misinterpreted the tune. By then, even his demeanor was different.

Back in the day, the Boss spoke to his audience like one of them "regular guys" who asked if he should check under your hood to see if you needed some oil. By 1995, he sounded more like a stern high school principal admonishing his audience for speaking out of turn, because his new tunes (and I use that term ever so loosely) required the silence they were written in to be heard correctly. Bruce seemed to know that his own glory days had come and gone.

Back in the '80s, though, hot damn, he was as big as Michael Jackson, Madonna, and Prince! There he was, always smiling, loving people, picking girls out of the audience to dance, while his red, white, and blue album just sold and sold. Times were good. Springsteen's brand of three-chord retro-rock emphasized normalcy: There wasn't a jock in my high school who didn't respect that. The whole family could go to one of his concerts. You didn't have to worry about songs about perverts in a hotel lobby jacking off to a magazine—Bruce came parentally approved. Everybody thought he was even better than Huey Lewis (though this is debatable; Huey's band, the News, weren't nearly as clunky as the E-Streeters, whose sole charm is that of a unionized New Jersey bar band where every member must play on every song or else management gets fined. Someone get Clarence a tambourine so at least it looks like he's working!) His was a world where white people who grew up on *Big Chill* '60s rock could mingle within the cozy folds of nostalgia, and the music never dared to challenge anyone.

Back to the album itself: All fourteen cuts, all written by B. Springsteen. If some of the titles sound a bit familiar, it's probably because they are. If you don't believe me, here, real names be proof: "Cover Me," a hit for Percy Sledge; "Downbound Train," a song by Chuck Berry; "I'm on Fire," a hit by Dwight Twilley; "Dancing in the Dark," an old standard popularized by Fred Astaire, Tony Bennett, and Cannonball Adderly. These "borrowings" are allegedly designed to lend scope to Springsteen's vision, but it's just further proof of the grandiose aspirations that his detractors decry. Amazed at how he grabbed "Wreck on the Highway" from Roy Acuff, "Mansion on the Hill" from Hank Williams, "Reason to Believe" from Tim Hardin—all top-drawer songwriters at that—friends of mine used to imagine how much further Bruce would dare to go. "Why, here's a little ditty I wrote late one night called 'Stairway to Heaven!'" We'd even make up lyrics: "Why, I told Kelly that night at the 7-11 / One day I'll buy you, pretty baby / A stairway to heaven!"

Aside from the title track, *Born in the U.S.A.* consists of a bunch of sad-sack songs about a bunch of guys that no one would ever really want to know. In theory, everyone's a populist—that is, until Cousin Kevin comes over, drinks all the good booze, and pukes on the carpet, and then it's time to start screening those phone calls. Listen to "Darlington County." You've got a guy named Wayne and the narrator allegedly coming from New York City to pick up girls and have a good time. They "sha-la-la" to all hell in the choruses and say stuff like, "Our pa's each own one of the World Trade Centers / For a kiss and a smile I'll give mine all to you." Even when he's attempting to be lighthearted, his characters talk like transplanted Okies.

My favorite line has always been, "Why, the world don't know what me and Wayne might do." Trust me, fellas, the world doesn't give a shit. And how about "Working on the Highway," where, over a rockabilly groove that even the Stray Cats wouldn't bother pinching, Bruce tells us about guys who go "down to Stovall's wearing trouble on their shirts." It's just this kind of romanticized cheese that allows me to imagine that what Springsteen was actually describing were a bunch of guys who were into the heavy-metal band Trouble going to the local biker bar to head-bang—which is probably what the real characters in Springsteen's songs would do. They wouldn't be caught dead listening to a record with such prominent synthesizer.

"Cover Me" has always sounded like great David Bowie, which means a lot coming from me, since I've always hated that insincere jerk-off. "No Surrender" and "Bobby Jean" are the kind of wretched sentimentality that ends up being quoted in senior-class yearbooks, as my high school proved. But the crown jewel at the album's center has always been "Glory Days." The synthesizer riff is as catchy as the clap but half as much fun, and the sentiment is painfully wretched. I tell you, it must really suck being, um, thirty-five and unable to hit those "speed balls." (And are we on the baseball diamond or partying with John Belushi? Like the rest of America, my friends in Jersey always called them "fast balls.") You can just picture Bruce sitting around with his advisors when someone speaks up: "What the album really needs is something with a bit of 'Bud Light' to it. Maybe something 'Michelobian.'" What's good for Eric Clapton is good for the Boss.

Far more insidious than the lite-rock sound—and indeed, the album's crucial flaw—is the fact that it panders to its audience. Rather than expressing Springsteen's ideas, it expresses what Springsteen believes his audience's ideas are. Viewed as common-folk rock—Woody Guthrie in a hall of mirrors—*Born in the U.S.A.*'s seven hit singles would make Ralph Nader proud: Consumer value was never higher. But these ditties are as much fun as spending a weekend with your grandparents. The artists whose music I've most admired—from Mick Jagger, to Iggy Pop, to Ian Curtis, to Nick Drake, to Mark Kozelek—have always been people for whom community meant nothing. For better or worse, they were outsiders who created worlds that previously did not exist. They were individualists. If they ever participated in an Adopt-a-Highway clean-up crew, they didn't advertise it. The message is "Dirt," "Isolation," and "Wish the World Away," not, "I'm calling from the March of Dimes, can you help us?"

I'm not knocking a good cause. Good art, however, transcends the temporary. It need not be cheapened with an ulterior motive such as a "message." That's just insulting, both to the art and to the audience. As Brian Eno said, "To require of art that it gives political direction strikes me as rather like asking Albert Einstein to tell you the four times table." Look what it's done to Bruce: You get the feeling that as much as he may understand and admire the tossed-off quality of much great rock 'n' roll, he's become far too self-conscious to free himself enough to make any. *Born in the U.S.A.* is Springsteen's community service; he even got out there and visited a few food banks and gave some money to charity. But the question remains: Who gives a shit? Did he?

He returned with *Tunnel of Love* (1987), his "introspective album." The audience scaled down their expectations, and Springsteen's sense of obligation to them lessened. He tried to strike back with two albums at once in 1992, *Human Touch* and *Lucky Town*, but by then, his previously immaculate sense of timing was lost. His audience resented him firing the E-Street Band and replacing them with the blandest session hacks imaginable. He tried to hit the multicultural '90s with the most politically correct set-up he could, but upon failing, he turned once again to his enormous cult and the old gang in the E-Street Band, and everyone welcomed him back with open arms.

💀💀💀

Seven years ago, I wrote the following to end this chapter: "Hopefully, the Boss's delusions of grandeur will be over; modesty and irrelevancy can only help his music. As a has-been, he'll have his ups and downs, and maybe even score a hit here and there. He can take his place next to Barry McGuire, Don McLean, Janis Ian, Sting, and Don Henley—others who've attempted to inject rock with 'social consciousness.' Then again, seeing how it usually goes with him, he'll probably run for President. Bill Clinton would be the perfect advisor."

Well, instead, Bruce's delusions of grandeur led to *The Rising*, the quickest album he's ever written, and a musical tribute to the aftermath of September 11, 2001. I count three and a half decent songs, and applaud and chide Brendan O'Brien's production (he makes the group sound less clunky, but also completely anonymous). To promote it, Springsteen granted a million self-serving interviews, including a dreadful chat with Ted Koppel where it was difficult to determine who was putting whom to sleep. Typically, he played it both ways, humbly offering himself up as a "link in the chain" of American songwriters while simultaneously placing himself among Woody Guthrie and Robert Johnson instead of Elvis Costello and Warren Zevon, two songwriters who regularly outwrote Bruce in their sleep.

What's key here, however, is that Bruce took a national tragedy, personalized it, and in the process somehow managed to make it feel impersonal. But then maybe I'm just a cynical Generation X prick. I'm not a fan of the gospel-inspired "My City of Ruins," or the wishful, "Countin' On a Miracle"; I'm more energized by the deep cynicism of Bob Dylan's "Not Dark Yet" and "Things Have Changed" or Randy Newman's "The World Isn't Fair" when I need a veteran musical presence in my life. Truth be told, every time I hear "The Rising," I can't help but change the words to "Step on up to Verizon," and I wonder just how long it will be before the cellular phone company meets Springsteen's price and secures the tune for its next big ad campaign.

VARIOUS ARTISTS
My Greatest Exes
By Carmél Carrillo

*"No Springsteen is leaving this house!...
You can have all the Carly Simons."*
—**Alec (Judd Nelson) to Leslie (Ally Sheedy)
in** *St. Elmo's Fire,* **1985**

At the end of every relationship, tears may be shed, insults may be hurled, accusations may be leveled. Perhaps no words at all will be exchanged; maybe you'll just shrug at each other and simply *know.* If one of you is a real gutless wonder, you might e-mail or telephone the news. (Ah, the crutches of technology!) Angst, guilt, or even relief may ensue.

One task, however, shall remain: the division of property. More importantly: the division of vinyl, cassettes, and CDs. Most important is the destruction and/or disposal of any cassette or CD given to you during the relationship, or, even worse, mixed expressly for you by your now less-than-pignut-significant other. I never got the whole "this-tape's-for-you" concept. Inevitably, I dated priapic boys whose musical tastes fell under the genres of somnolent, caterwauling, cacophonous pabulum. There was a certain unnamed thrill in taking a hammer—and, later, my '88 Toyota Corolla FX—to said custom-made tapes.

My question is: Why doesn't anyone ever make break-up tapes?

220

Now, here's a notion that makes perfect sense. In fact, it's pretty surprising that some marketing genius at Apple hasn't already created this scheme. An iTunes-in-reverse program would make kajillions off of the bitter, the heartbroken, and the lovelorn. Take every song that was once an "our" song, burn it onto a CD, and digitally retire it forever. Never again would you have to hear the Beach Boys' "Wouldn't It Be Nice." *Never.*

And so, gentle reader, I present to you my fictional break-up tape, *My Greatest Exes*, dedicated to the relationships that failed me. It is, in effect, my day to kill *their* idols.

💀 💀 💀

1. Sting, "Russians"

In high school, it's easy: No real estate, no kids, no stock portfolios to squabble over. Pretty much all you have is music—give or take a class ring and a letterman's jacket. The tough part was telling my parents that I had a date in the first place. My *first* date. My father, who was a cop, ran a license-plate check on the poor schmuck. I did my best mortified-princess act and accused him of not trusting my judgment. (I guess we all know better now, don't we?)

The summer between my sophomore and junior years, I struck a deal with my mother: She'd allow me to take the summer off from flute lessons if I found something "educational" to occupy my time. I was way ahead of her—back in the spring, I had secretly applied for an internship program for minorities at Fermi National Accelerator Laboratory. I never dreamed they'd actually pick me. Because it was a paying internship, I'd even be excused from working in my family's pizzeria—bonus!

Getting to the ultrahygenic Fermilab took nearly two hours from the gritty, industrialized neighborhood on Chicago's South Side where I grew up. Once at Superconductor Central (complete with a meadow of grazing buffalo), we spent half the day in the classroom and the other half with a mentor in our chosen field. Mine was astronomy. Somehow this meant I was qualified to measure things. It was about as thrilling as helping my mother in the kitchen.

At lunchtime, the boys played basketball on the outdoor court, and the girls sat in the shade, gossiping. "Who's the white guy?" I innocently asked my friend Martha one day. And the rest was herstory.

Evan wasn't bused in from the city every day, like Martha and I and the rest of the class; he drove his '81 VW Rabbit from his home in a leafy suburb. For the life of me, I can't tell you where he took me on our first date, but I can tell you he popped Sting's *Dream of the Blue Turtles* into the car's cassette player.

"'Russians,'" Evan said, noting the single.

Sting sniveled, "How can I save my little boy/From Oppenheimer's deadly toy?"

It was merely coincidental, I suppose, that we were studying Oppenheimer's toys at Fermilab.

"It's Prokofiev," I responded.

"What?" he said, confused.

"This Sting guy you've been talking about for weeks on end? He's totally ripping off the composer Sergei Prokofiev."

"Yeah, it's an *homage*, Carmél; take it easy," he sighed. "And how do you know about Prokofiev, anyway?"

"*Peter and the Wolf*," I mumbled.

"Excuse me?"

"Prokofiev wrote the music, and David Bowie narrated...."

"David Bowie, as in Ziggy Stardust–David Bowie? No way!"

"Yes," I responded, slumping farther down into the bucket seat. "And I have the record at home, if you don't believe me. It has a great flute part."

Sting himself cops to "Russians" being based on Prokofiev's "Romance," from the *Lieutenant Kijè Suite*. Prokofiev composed the piece for the 1933 film, based on a story by Yuri Tynianov, according to Prokofiev.org. But what the Web site doesn't tell you is that the bad lieutenant's story is a commentary "on the absurdity of power—and the vanity of power. [The] underlying philosophy is deep pessimism over human destiny and human capabilities," according to the CD booklet. This seems to fly in the face of Sting's universal peace-and-love poppycock: "What might save us, me, and you / Is that the Russians love their children, too."

I gave Evan one last chance. "So it really doesn't bother you that Sting is just this poseur pretending to care about nuclear war and the children of the world, and basically he's plagiarizing somebody who actually died during the Cold War?"

"Nope," he shrugged, shaking his head. "You wanna get some pizza?"

Note to Sting: You don't have to love somebody to set him free.

💀 💀 💀

Leslie: *"I'm taking* **Thriller** *and* **Mahler's Ninth.**"
Alec: *"Kevin is so fond of Mahler."*

💀 💀 💀

2. Bon Jovi, "Livin' on a Prayer"
3. The Psychedelic Furs, "Pretty in Pink"
4. Orchestral Manoeuvres in the Dark, "If You Leave"

By the time high school started again, the geek scene had definitely soured, thanks to Evan and Oppenheimer. Nevertheless, I found myself the only junior in a seniors-only physics class. My lab partner Dan was a hunky little rebel in a *Top Gun* bomber jacket. I wasn't thrilled about it at first—he was one of the slower kids in class—but he made me laugh a lot. And he listened, too, which was a twist. Desperate to lose my Joanie image, we became fast friends, although my cussing and sarcastic behavior shocked him on occasion.

Dan startled the hell outta me before we even went on our first date. I was working at the pizza joint—waitressing, cashiering, washing dishes, you name it—and I spent a lot of time in the kitchen, with at least a third of my body covered in flour and/or cornmeal.

"Hi," Dan said mischievously one night. He could barely reach the counter.

"Hi," I grimaced, trying to get the flour out of my eyes. Oh, this was a good look for me; Catholic-school uniforms are boring as hell, but at least there's a short skirt involved. My father and Uncle Phil were out back, fifty feet away.

"You want a slice of pizza or something?" I asked nervously. Uncle Phil had returned, and he was trying to see who was at the counter.

"Just a can of RC," Dan said.

Uncle Phil's voice bellowed from the cooler. "I got it, Mel."

I blushed and rolled my eyes.

"Mel?" Dan smiled devilishly.

"Family nickname," I responded.

He nodded, and slid a cassette tape wrapped in lined notebook paper across the counter. "I made this especially for you," he whispered.

Uncle Phil came around. "Who's this?"

"This is Dan, my physics partner," I said.

"Your physical partner?" Phil guffawed.

"*Physics*," I growled. "Physics."

"Oh, my mistake," he said, looking Dan up and down. "Nice to meet ya, Dan. I'm Uncle Phil."

He handed Dan the pop. "It's on the house."

"Thank you, sir. It's a pleasure to meet you, sir." He sounded like Marcy from Peanuts. Christ.

"I'll see you tomorrow, Dan," I not-so-subtly hinted.

"O.K." He grinned widely. "See ya."

That night, deep under my blankets and with the aid of my Hello Kitty flashlight, I unwrapped Dan's tape. He had transcribed the lyrics to every single track. He even wrote out the lyrics to a certain song more than once: "Livin' on a Prayer."

"*This is our song,*" Dan declared at the top of the page, as if I somehow might have missed the magnitude of this sacred ditty. I read Bon Jovi's idyll. The problem was, I didn't really understand what the tune had to with *us*. I mean, we were in freakin' high school. The song is about some dude named Tommy who "used to work on the docks," but "Union's been on strike," so his girlfriend, Gina, is supporting them both by working as a waitress.

Was this Dan's secret plan for us—to live together on a prayer in near-poverty while he fought The Man and his six-string languished in hock? Dan didn't even play guitar. He worked at MusicLand at the River Oaks Mall. What about college? I wasn't taking physics for fun, y'know. Well, O.K., maybe I was, but that's not the point.

I set all of that aside in time for our big first date (after my dad ran another license-plate check, of course): the Molly Ringwald–Andrew McCarthy epic-teen drah-mah, *Pretty in Pink*. Impoverished-yet-stunningly beautiful Andie (Ringwald) is from the wrong side of the tracks (but somehow manages to drive an old pink Porsche—how Barbie!), and she falls in love with oversized-blazer-wearing, stinkin'-rich Blane (McCarthy), whose hair is, what, *glued on* in this film? Andie wears a lot of pink, and looks pretty in the process, probably because it complements her red hair. Other than that, the film and the title track have little in common.

The song by the Psychedelic Furs is about some hag named Caroline whose "lovers walk through in their coats." Caroline might be the one who calls off the joke, but the Furs are laughing at her nonetheless. "And wasn't she easy," Richard Butler croaks.

Meanwhile, '80s teen guru John Hughes bends over backwards to depict how virtuous his muse Molly—I mean Andie—is: She won't screw around with her best friend, Duckie (Jon Cryer), even though he's been in love with her since the fourth grade. And she certainly won't go near that snake Steff, sulkily portrayed by James Spader. (Note to anal-retentive cinéastes: Yes, I know Hughes didn't direct *Pretty in Pink*; Howard Deutch did. But Hughes wrote it, and he was clearly the auteur.)

"She doesn't have anything / You want to steal," Butler and the Furs moan. This we can buy, given the destitute state of both Caroline and Andie. But let us not forget: They're both bodaciously pretty in pink.

That year everything was pink—my prom dress, my homecoming dress, the Swatch watch, and the roses Dan gave me for my birthday.

There was one song from the film that Dan and I heartily avoided; he'd fast-forward over it when it came up on the soundtrack cassette, or change the station if it came on his car stereo. I was going away to college in the fall, and he wasn't. The breakup was inevitable, and we both knew it. Orchestral Manoeuvres in the Dark's "If You Leave" was becoming our very own epic-teen drah-mah.

One day, we were driving in his van and the song came on the radio. He started sobbing so violently that he had to pull over, near 110th and Avenue M. He drew me close and cried, "I don't want you to go away. I know you have to go, but please...."

I turned up the radio and hugged him tightly. The truth was, I wasn't so sure I wanted to go. *Why go?* I was a good girl and always did what was expected of me, with the exception of going out with a guy like Dan. The thing was, he treated me like a princess, and I fell head over heels for him.

"I touch you once, I touch you twice / I won't let go at any price / I need you now like I needed you then / You always said we'd meet again someday."

But what would I do *for the rest of my life?* Work in the pizza place and go to community college? Live on the East Side and marry Dan? I'd die of boredom, or at least from the toxic spew being pumped outta the steel mills.

"Dan, I have to go." Now I was close to tears. "I'm sorry."

"If you leave I won't cry / I won't waste one single day / But if you leave don't look back / I'll be running the other way.... Heaven knows what happens now."

Needless to say, Dan and I didn't make it—on a prayer or otherwise.

About ten years later, out of nowhere, my mother asked me what became of him. I shrugged.

"Your father and I always liked him best out of all the boys you dated," she said.

I groaned and reached for my car keys. "I'm going to the mall," I said.

"For what?" she asked.

"Something pink," I spat.

Alec: *"You can't have the Pretenders' first album. That's mine."*

Leslie: *"I bought it."*

Alec: *"You did not…. You can have all the Billy Joels. Except* **The Stranger.***"*

💀💀💀

5. **Billy Joel, "You May Be Right"**

6. **Billy Joel, "This Night"**

7. **Billy Joel, "C'Etait Toi" ("You Were the One")**

8. **Billy Joel, "Through the Long Night"**

My mother is a Billy Joel freak, so I grew up listening to *The Stranger*. I even made up a gymnastics routine to "Big Shot" (which isn't from *The Stranger,* but it's Billy Joel shmaltz at its best. Or worst. Whatever.).

In any event, I spent three of my college years dating another Billy Joel freak. He didn't have the excuse of being a Baby Boomer; he was a whole four months younger than I was, and he was pretty damn impressed that I knew the Joel catalog in its entirety. We met at a marching band party in the spring of our freshman year. I was sitting on the kitchen countertop, swinging my legs nervously and nursing a bottle of bad beer.

"Carmél"—my friend Therese put her hands on my feet to make my legs stop swinging—"this is my friend Brian."

I barely looked at him. I had been scoping out a cute blond boy named Bill for weeks. Therese and I decided *this* would be the night that I *finally* talked to Bill, if he ever showed up.

"That's a pretty name," Brian said.

"Thank you." People were always saying my name was exotic or unique or unusual, but what they really meant was *different,* out of place, not belonging. It occurred to me that no one had ever said it was pretty. I turned to Therese. "Do you know if Bill's here yet?"

"Who's Bill?" Brian asked. *Nosy.*

"He just walked in," Therese said, pointing the tip of her beer bottle toward the door. He was drunk, and hanging all over some girl—some petite, perfect girl with perfect blonde ringlets down to her perfectly small shoulders.

"Great," I sighed.

"I'm sorry, Carmél." Therese consoled me and pointed to her empty bottle. "Can I get you anything?"

I shook my head. "A paper bag? No. I'm fine, thanks."

"What do you play?" Brian asked as Therese walked away. It sounded as cheesy as, "What's your major?" or "What's your sign?" Like a line from a Billy Joel song.

"Nothing now," I said. "I used to play flute."

"Why flute?"

I shrugged. "My grandmother used to take me to see 'The Nutcracker Suite' every year at the Arie-Crown Theatre. I wanted to take ballet, really, but they told me I was too tall. So the next best thing was the music."

"So why flute?"

"Why not?" I shrugged. "It was the cheapest instrument, so my parents were able to pay for it."

"And what else?" he asked, sensing I was holding something back.

I told him the truth because he had said my name, and new people never said my name—not the right way. "The flute's so quiet compared to all the other instruments in the band that if I made a mistake, no one would ever know. They'd all drown me out."

"Did you make a lot of mistakes?"

"No." I shook my head, smiling.

He smiled back and looked down at my legs. "Maybe you should've been a dancer."

I laughed. "I don't dance."

"Good." He smiled again. "I don't either."

O.K., so Brian the Billy Joel freak cheered me up. He was an excellent kisser, and he was literally one of the few people on campus from out of state, and not some suburban fraternity rat. Nothing pissed me off more than when somebody said he was from Chicago, and it turned out he was really from Buffalo Grove or Schaumburg or Naperville. We spent every waking moment of the remainder of the semester together, and at the end, decided that because we would be so far apart (I was in the *real* Chicago, and he in one of those mitten-shaped states), it would be O.K. to see other people. In the fall, we'd just see what happens—absolutely no expectations.

Yeah, right.

We called and wrote *every day*, and this was in the ancient times before e-mail. When I saw him standing outside the civil courts building on East 111th Street, where I was working that summer, I almost fainted.

"What are you doing here?" I gasped, wrapping my arms around him.

"Taking my girlfriend out for a late lunch," he said, opening the car door.

"You're crazy," I laughed, "but in a good way."

Brian turned on the ignition and blasted "You May Be Right."

"Now think of all the years you tried to / Find someone to satisfy you / I might be as crazy at you say / If I'm crazy then it's true / That it's all because of you / And you wouldn't want me any other way / You may be right / I may be crazy / But it just may be a lunatic / You're looking for."

"Isn't this great?" Brian grinned maniacally and intertwined his fingers with mine. "I left this morning to play golf with some friends, and I thought, 'Fuck it, I wanna see my girlfriend!' And here I am."

"How long can you stay?" I asked.

"I have to be back before midnight," he said.

"So you're going to spend more time driving than you'll actually spend here? That *is* crazy."

"Yeah, it's just like this song." He nodded vigorously. "So cool."

But Brian didn't drive his motorcycle in the rain; he drove his mother's Dodge Omni, and he had to be back before the clock struck midnight. We sent him home with a pizza. No bottle of white, no bottle of red, no bottle of rosé instead.

It was a long summer. I tried to see other people, but it was all about Brian. When we returned to school, there was no question: We picked up right where we left off. Our first night back, we went to the bars on Green Street and got stinkin' drunk (just as good college students should), stumbled back to his tiny dorm room, and…listened to Billy Joel, on tape. We slow-danced in front of his bunk bed to Joel's hang-dog "This Night."

"Didn't I say / I wasn't ready for a romance / Didn't we promise / We would only be friends / And so we danced / Though it was only a slow dance / I started breaking my promises / Right there and then. / …Now that you're here / It's not the same situation / Suddenly I don't remember the rules anymore / …Someone like me should know better / Falling in love / Would be the worst thing / I could do."

Well, maybe not the worst. But close enough.

Two years later, I was deeply restless. Marching-band parties, all-night Euchre tournaments (*didn't they know any other games?*), and especially Billy Joel had drained me of My Life. (I was even *speaking* in Billy Joel songs!) I wasn't Carmél; I was Brian's girlfriend. And, dammit, the arrogant little prick was *always* right; there was no telling him otherwise. He hated my friends and the music we were listening to: Pearl Jam, the Black Crowes, and Nirvana. He hated the flannel we wore. I was sick of it, and I decided to break it off and have an easy, breezy senior year all on my own.

Of course, I eventually missed Brian—desperately, hopelessly, to the point of near-stalking. Now I was the idiot writing out song lyrics: "Here I go again / Looking for your face / and I realize / That I should look for someone else / But you were the one / You were the one."

I think Brian agreed to a reconciliation only to get me to stop pestering him. It lasted less than a year. In the meantime, though, there was lots of making up to do.

"All your past sins / Are since past / You should be sleeping / It's all right / Sleep tight / Through the long night / With me."

In the fall, I went off to law school, and it was my turn to get dumped. Once again, I missed Brian desperately, hopelessly. But I had My Life, and he and Billy had theirs.

💀💀💀

9. Warren Zevon, "Werewolves of London"
10. Aaron Copland, "Hoe-down"

I dated a werewolf, but he wasn't from London—he was from Mississippi.

Jack and I met in grad school, and I couldn't take my eyes off his raven hair or his cobalt eyes. Eudora Welty probably would've told me to run like the wind, but I wouldn't have listened. He seduced me with his Southern accent, telling me stories about growing up there: how his father lived in a house with a dirt floor, and how his mother fed him a spoonful of Vicks VapoRub whenever he had a cold.

Jack survived the South and even lived in Europe for a couple of years, making him that much more exotic to the inner-city kid in me. I grew up on pizza, tortillas and beans, chorizo and eggs, tamales at Christmas, and more typical, bland American fare. Jack loved grits with biscuits and gravy—the latter was magnetically attracted to his dark, bushy beard, and even to his woolly coif—and on the weekends, he made navy bean soup, with the hambone left in it. I had never seen anything like it before, and I lived in terror that our cat was going to end up in the soup pot. You'd have thought she would have been wary of Jack's slightly longer-and-sharper-than-normal teeth, but she loved no one better than the werewolf himself. And I was fascinated with him, too.

Jack's favorite song was—no surprise—"Werewolves of London." Full moon or not, he wailed at full-volume yowl whenever he played Warren Zevon's monstrous hit. Wasn't this sort of song more worthy of Randy Newman, if not Weird Al Yankovic? I mean, this is the guy who brought us the masterful storytelling of *Sentimental Hygiene*, but here he stooped to howling about "hairy-handed gents" sluggin' down piña coladas at Trader Vic's (a nifty bit of product placement). Pretty damn sad, Warren—for you and me both.

There was only one other sound that could soothe the savage beast in Jack. We'd innocently be watching television and the Beef Industry Council commercial would come on. You know the one: A perfectly sunlit panorama of the American West zeroes in on large slabs of Real Meat ready to be consumed by Real Men (after dinner was cooked by Real Women, naturally). Aaron Copland's lively, fiddle-romping "Hoe-down" swells and chassés under actor Robert Mitchum's narration: "Beef: It's what's for dinner."

"Who is that?" Jack demanded.

Jack and I used to play a game with commercials: If I could name the celebrity narrator in five seconds or less, he'd have to cook dinner. Silly thing was, after all those years of working in the pizza place, I still couldn't cook, so if I lost, he'd have to make dinner anyway. But it was fun because I almost never lost. Jack called it my "perfect pitch." I tried to explain to him that identifying celebrities' voices didn't qualify as perfect pitch, but he called it that anyway.

"Robert Mitchum," I responded, without looking up from my newspaper.

"No, I mean, WHAT IS THAT MUSIC?!" Jack exclaimed. He was bouncing up and down on the couch. "It totally *rocks!*"

Now, I like classical music quite a bit, but I don't think I've ever heard anyone say that Aaron Copland *rocks*.

"It's 'Hoe-down,' and it's from Copland's *Rodeo*," I blinked.

"Do you have it?" he asked anxiously.

"Um, yeah, on cassette, I think."

I heard him rip into the cardboard box underneath my bed. "GOT IT!" he proclaimed.

"Great," I sighed.

"I'm going to put some steaks on the grill," he said. "Do you want one?"

I scrunched up my nose. "Nah, I think I'll have a salad."

He took his boom box outside and popped Copland in. I shuddered to think what the neighbors thought.

Maybe "Hoe-down" reminded Jack of growing up in the South, and the barn dances he attended there. It's based on a square-dance tune called "Bonyparte": Copland wrote it as part of the larger *Rodeo* ballet for choreographer Agnes DeMille, whose 1942 technical notes read, "The theme of the ballet is basic. It deals with the problem that has confronted all American women, from earliest pioneer times, and which has never ceased to occupy them throughout the history of the building of our country: how to get a suitable man." Amen, Agnes.

It seemed as if all Jack listened to was "Werewolves of London" and "Hoe-down." Our relationship was souring: I wasn't much of a meat-eater at heart; I preferred gin and tonics to piña coladas, and I just didn't like Aaron Copland that much.

I heard that Jack ended up in Brooklyn, but I suspect he's hanging out in Soho, with the other werewolves. Our cat sat in the window for days, watching and waiting for him to return. I ate a lot of salads.

💀💀💀

11. Barry White, "Can't Get Enough of Your Love, Babe"
12. Donna Summer, "Last Dance"

Bud was a bouncer at a bar where my girlfriends and I went after work sometimes. I was on the rebound from Jack, and I didn't care who knew it, even if he happened to be six-foot-something, two-hundred and seventy-five pounds, and a beer-swilling, meat-eating, cigar-smoking, sports-bar groupie.

Bud had a secret, though: He wanted to be a writer.

He knew I was an editor from the crowd I hung out with, and that I was always looking for something good to read. So what if he worked in a bar?

"Why do you work in a bar?" I asked him one night after I'd had a few too many.

"You never know who you're going to meet," he shrugged, staring at my chest as he spoke, "what kinds of tales they're going to tell you. It can get pretty interesting."

Besides writing, Bud loved disco, and Barry White was his hero. Maybe he could identify with the guy because they were both… big. Barry White was smooth, and Bud *thought* he was, but he was just a drunk bouncer who liked to disco dance and try to pick up chicks.

When he first outed himself to me, I thought he was kidding: I laughed my ass off. Bud got *very serious*. He slammed his fist on the table, pointed the tip of his amber beer bottle at me, and bellowed, "Are you not a disciple of the Round Mound of Sound?"

I stifled a giggle. "I'm more of an apostle of the Reverend Al Green."

"Bitch," he hissed.

"Freak," I barked. "Would your Maestro ever call a woman a bitch? I don't think so." I rose to walk away.

He held up his hands in mock surrender. "You're right. I'm sorry, that was totally out of line. I don't know what I was thinking. I just never met anybody who didn't like Barry White. See, my whole life, I've wanted to *be* Barry White. I know all the words to all his songs. I have every one of his CDs...."

"Uh-huh."

"Will you dance with me?" he asked, all two-hundred and seventy-five pounds of him transformed into a giant, drooling puppy.

I shook my head. "No, thanks. I'm a really terrible dancer."

"I need you by me, beside me, to guide me / To hold me, to scold me / 'Cause when I'm bad I'm so, so bad," he smiled, quoting Donna Freakin' Summer. Was this his way of telling me he was into S & M, too? Gawd.

In lieu of dancing with him, I offered to read some of his work.

Now he was beyond giant drooling puppy dog mode; *down, boy!* He scampered to the back of the bar and returned with a small stack of manuscripts. "Some of them are kind of old, but...."

I put my hand up to his mouth, cutting him off. "Relax," I instructed. "Get a pen, write your phone number on the top page, and I'll give you a call when I've finished reading, O.K.?"

He nodded, my hand still over his mouth.

Like Jack, Bud seduced me with his storytelling. There was a lot of work to be done, and I wasn't afraid to tell him so (which he seemed to enjoy a little too much at times). We had many late-night phone conversations about his writing, and often he'd tell me about his evening at the bar, or a disco CD he'd just picked up.

"Isaac Hayes *jams*," he reported.

"I am *not* having a *ménage á trois* with you," I stated, referring to Hayes's "Moonlight Lovin'."

"O.K., if you have one with someone else, can I watch?" he asked in total seriousness.

"I have to go to sleep now, Bud," I responded. "Send me your rewrites. I think I know some people who might be interested in your work."

"Really? Seriously?"

"Yes, Bud. I'm going to sleep now.… "

A few weeks later, he invited me over for a barbecue. I told him I was a recently converted vegetarian, but he promised to grill some vegetables for me. When I arrived at his apartment, the front door was ajar, and the TV was blaring.

There was Big Bud, sitting cross-legged on the floor, mesmerized by the TV, with his back to me. No stereo or boom box in sight in the little studio apartment. No CDs or cassettes, either—and certainly no complete Barry White discography. But there on the television, swaying gracefully and singing deeply, was Barry White himself, accompanied by the characters of a once-popular sitcom.

"'ALLY McBEAL!'" I shrieked. "You're watching 'Ally McBeal?' All this time, you've been pretending to be some kind of cigar-puffing, beer-chugging, testosterone-loaded, televised-sports-addicted, Barry White disco-love expert, and you've just been sitting on your ass at home watching 'Ally *Freakin'* McBeal!' Do you dream about the Dancing Baby, too, you pussy? Next you're going to tell me you have a thing for anorexic women!"

"No, I'd pretty much do anyone," said the man of no standards.

"UGH!" I threw up my hands, infuriated, and made my way for the door.

"Hey, where're you going?" he asked, in giant, drooling puppy-dog mode.

"I'm tired of being alone," I muttered. "I'm going to find someone who likes Al Green."

"Call me," Bud murmured.

Wouldn't it be nice? *Not likely.*

ELVIS COSTELLO AND THE ATTRACTIONS
Imperial Bedroom
Columbia, 1982
By Michael Corcoran

*I*t opens spectacularly—a jazzy cymbal crash keeping time with a relentless bass drum, and then, coaxed by a wickedly swirling organ, releasing itself into a wild sky ruled by a cautious pilot, a singer who senses an ominous conclusion and therefore delivers his words carefully. "History repeats the old conceits / The glib replies the same defeats." The tension builds, the whole track flies apart, and then it all comes together again. "I've got a feeling," sings the newly forceful voice. "I'm gonna get a lot of grief / Once it seemed so appealing, now I am beyond belief." The chorus becomes a mantra. The bass and drums rumble at full steam; the organ is otherworldly.

When Elvis Costello and the Attractions were on, they were as good as any band in history.

I was there when they unlocked the front door at Strawberry Records in Albany, New York, the day *Imperial Bedroom* came out. I went to work at an antique clothing store two doors down and played the album over and over all day long. I was starved for new Elvis Costello songs the way a country boy is ready for some barbecue after a few months in New England. I was ready to fall in love with the band all over again.

I came to discover Costello's music through other singers. I had heard a few songs on the radio—"Alison" and "Mystery Dance" from the 1977 debut, *My Aim Is True*, and "Pump It Up" from the follow-up,

This Year's Model—but I couldn't get past the sneering, whiny voice that sounded like E.C. was half a swallow from finishing a meal. To tell you the truth, I was more into Joe Jackson circa 1979. Then one night I heard a cover band do "Oliver's Army," and I was so taken with the melody that I went out and bought *Armed Forces*, which was about two years old at the time. I also picked up 1981's just-released *Trust*, which had a duet with Glenn Tilbrook of Squeeze, my favorite singer at the time. I played "From a Whisper to a Scream" and marveled at Tilbrook's gymnastic soul-pop vocals.

Costello's voice was an acquired taste that I eventually came to love with the zeal with which Donald Trump gobbles real estate. Costello was touted for his "inventive wordplay," but to me, lyrics are just something to keep a song from being an instrumental. On the rare occasion that I listened to Costello's words to figure out what they meant, I did come away with some cool lines. "Looking like a figment of somebody else's imagination" especially rang true from my perch behind the counter of the clothing store.

I went back and bought the rest of Costello's albums and listened to little else for the next year. The Attractions—keyboardist Steve Nieve, bassist Bruce Thomas, and drummer Pete Thomas—could carry on brilliant musical conversations, and the front man was that rare intellectual who could swing, man. They had jazz minds and rock 'n' roll hearts.

My girlfriend at the time became equally addicted, and we had a pact that if E.C. and the Attractions came to town, we'd split up inside the arena and meet up after the show. We wanted to have our private religious experiences without having to relate to each other.

My relationship with New Wave's angry young man had never been seriously tested, not even with that almost true 1981 country album. The first "uh-oh" came with Columbia's promotional campaign for *Imperial Bedroom*, Costello's seventh studio album. "Masterpiece?" the ads asked, a question mark never hanging so rhetorically, and never so much resembling a target. The early, pre-release reviews heralded the 1982 album as Costello's "most ambitious project to date" and bounced around words like "expansive," "maturing," "complex," and "grandiose scope." There was talk of cellos and Cole Porter. Uh-oh.

With *Imperial Bedroom*, my beloved Elvis Costello had set out to create an intricately crafted modern masterwork, even hiring Geoff Emerick, the engineer on *Sgt. Pepper's Lonely Hearts Club Band*, to produce. The goal was to dress the merchant of venom in a silk dinner jacket, to relax the punk snarl into a come-hither curl, to sit the guitarist at the piano, where he'd scribble out romantically confessional lyrics and imagine vocal overdubs that would make Dr. Eugene Landy sit up and take notice. Costello's contemporaries would no longer be Joe Jackson and Graham Parker, but Burt Bacharach, Brian Wilson, and Paul McCartney.

Unfortunately, Costello succeeded. He got his French horns and string sections and accordions and *Pet Sounds* harmonies—everything he needed to produce the perfect yawn. "Beyond Belief" is a stirring opener, but too much of the rest of the album reeks of intent over content. One of the greatest rock bands of all time was saddled with syrupy arrangements, melancholy material, and an overall vision of grandeur. *Imperial Bedroom* is an album so proud of its doody that it calls for witnesses before it flushes. "Expansive"? Try "bloated." "Complex"? How about "pretentious"?

The most talented artists are judged not by their highlights, but by their low points, and *Imperial Bedroom* has worn out many a fast-forward button. Costello himself sounds bored with "The Long Honeymoon," a weary tale of marital uncertainty put to bad cabaret music. "...And In Every Home" is an outright disaster—here the snarl is relaxed into a pucker on the fleshy buttocks of high art. "Human Touch," "Boy With a Problem," "Little Savage," "Pidgin English"— this work of self-deluded genius has more padding than a Dolly Parton look-alike contest.

Like the Jewish girls from Long Island who misspend their youths by giving themselves to social outcasts in the Village, but then end up marrying dentists named Cy, Costello seemed desperate to join the class he'd been rebelling against.

The hinge track on the album is "Shabby Doll"; the way you feel about this song will dictate the way you will about the whole recording. The track starts off with such promise—there's a scent of danger in the early verses—but then it dissolves into a sappy, sing-song chorus that makes "Penny Lane" sound like "Gimme Shelter." I have friends who love "Shabby Doll," just as I know some people out there consider *Imperial Bedroom* to be Costello's crowning achievement. But then there are some critics who list *Manhattan* as Woody Allen's best film.

E.C. and the Attractions would rebound artistically the next year with *Punch the Clock* (a better album, though not generally as highly regarded by critics as *Imperial Bedroom*), and in 1986, Costello would make one of his strongest albums, *King of America*, with the other Elvis's old band. But the string of five masterful albums, from 1977's *My Aim Is True* through 1981's *Trust*—the most impressive creative output since Stevie Wonder gave us *Music of My Mind*, *Talking Book*, and *Innervisions* in 1972-'73—was broken.

The albums that hold up best over time seem to be the ones that spring up effortlessly. In the case of Costello and the Attractions, their best album is probably 1980's *Get Happy*, which was reportedly bashed out after the bars closed, with the jukebox echoes of Booker T. and the MGs still ringing.

Many of my all-time favorite albums baffled me on the first few listens. Initially, I thought *Exile on Main St.* was a cluttered mess, but the store wouldn't give me a refund because the postcards that came with the original double album were missing. *Nebraska* was a plodding, boring piece of crap for about a week; *Astral Weeks* was an album to put on when you were doing yoga, and I never did yoga. My first impression of Television's *Marquee Moon* was, "Who told this guy he could sing?"

The fact that *Imperial Bedroom* didn't click with me at the outset only made the challenge more attractive, and potentially more rewarding. I played it twice a day, every day, for two or three weeks, and it still sounded overwrought and under-conceived. It also sounded over-produced, but that wasn't really the main problem. A CD reissue in 2003 containing a bonus disc of alternate takes and early demos of the songs shows that the best versions were the ones that ended up on the album. It seems as if most of these songs just never had a chance—they were doomed from the beginning.

The extra disc also provides a bit of a tease, a cover of the Merseybeats' "Really Mystified" that's more vibrant, soulful, and catchy than anything on *Imperial Bedroom*. It didn't fit on that album any more than Bob Dylan's stunning "Blind Willie McTell" belonged on *Empire Burlesque*.

Somewhere it got out that the role of artists is to constantly challenge themselves and their audiences, to keep evolving creatively, to keep reaching for new peaks of self-discovery. History repeats the old conceits with titles like *Neither Fish nor Flesh*, Terence Trent D'Arby's disastrous reach job, not to mention every second album from the great Brit ska-punk bands of the late '70s. You can't make a true masterpiece on purpose unless you're mentally ill. That should be a rule—the Brian Wilson clause. If you can control your delusions, you don't get to remake *Sgt. Pepper's*.

U2
The Joshua Tree
Island, 1987
By Eric Waggoner
and Bob Mehr

IDS, crack, famine, inner-city unrest, corporate takeovers, recessions, Thatcherism, Iran-Contra, apartheid...the 1980s were a grim decade indeed, haunted from the outset by a sense of impending collapse, even in the proverbial corridors of power. A week before announcing his Presidential candidacy in 1980, Ronald Reagan ominously told author and Papa Bush's White House advisor Doug Wead—the man who later coined the phrase "compassionate conservatism"—that, "We may be the generation that sees Armageddon." As *Creem* magazine was wont to quip: Boy, howdy!

In some ways, it was a great time to be alive, depending on your capacity to be amused by popular delusions and shameless hypocrisy. Famous televangelists were drugging their secretaries and chasing hookers all over the French Quarter in New Orleans; it was that kind of era. But the twitchy end-of-days vibe slopped over, as mass phenomena always do, into the sphere of popular music, and no group with naked aspirations of stardom ever embraced its socio-historical moment with more careerist misery than U2.

Bringing us, perforce, to a telling cultural moment midway through the decade.

It's a long way from lower Galilee to Ireland, and from there to televisions sets the world over. But those tuning into the globally broadcast Live Aid concert on July 13, 1985, could be forgiven for

241

thinking that Christ had suddenly returned in the form of a po'-faced Irish rocker. On that day, near the end of U2's set—appropriately sandwiched between Bryan Adams and Judas Priest—exultant singer Bono leapt from the stage into the crowd. Working his way through a sea of people, he laid his hands on many, holding them close to his bosom and generally acting out what appeared to be a twisted messianic fantasy, attempting everything short of curing lepers and turning water into wine, in front of the entire world. The largest audience to ever view a pop concert—two billion people in one hundred fifty-five countries—had also witnessed the full flowering of one of the most fevered egos in musical history.

This would not be the last, or even most egregious, bit of onstage theatrics from Bono and U2. Just a year later, performing as part of Amnesty International's "Conspiracy of Hope" tour package, they engaged in perhaps the most appalling and arrogant charade ever perpetrated in front of a paying audience.

During the final song of their farewell show, the Police—certainly the most of empty and ambitious of all post-punk outfits—ceremonially handed their instruments to the members of U2 and walked off the stage, grinning priggishly. This carefully orchestrated farce was intended as a rock 'n' roll version of apostolic succession. The torch, ran the impossible-to-miss subtext, officially had been passed. U2 was now The World's Most Important Band.

From the beginning, that was U2's métier—the grand statement, the extravagant gesture—and it was a tactic perfectly suited to the peculiar combination of callow haughtiness and phony, lip-service compassion that characterized the 1980s. Throughout a decade when mainstream rock repeatedly worked itself into a state of smug, ham-fisted piety about what were then called "global issues" (don't bungle the jungle, dudes!), the members of U2 were the era's most devout pilgrims. They *hemorrhaged* sincerity, despite the fact that they looked rather eerily like Kajagoogoo as late as 1984.

This inexhaustible gravitas seemed to work upon contemporary rock writers like syphilis, first clouding their critical faculties, then driving them past simple confusion into madness. Dave "The Edge" Evans's tinny, monotonous guitar work was *epic, echoing,* and *soaring;* Paul "Bono" Hewson's sudden-shriek-of-a-fucked-cat vocals were *anthemic, committed,* and *passionate.* Repetitive hooks and stiff two-four rhythms became *deceptively simple, proto-mythical story-poems about the individual's conflict with society,* or *howls of protest from a raging Everyman pitted against the power elite,* or some such scatterbrained codswallop.

In retrospect, some of this fawning is perhaps understandable, if not exactly forgivable. It was the era of Ray Parker, Jr., and Men Without Hats, after all, and U2's sympathies, worn on its sleeve and lapel and every other exposed piece of fabric, made good copy. But U2's early enshrinement in the pantheon of morally concerned post-punk bands was as much the product of relentless self-mythologizing as of the music itself, and that conceit levied a toll on the band's worshippers as well as the musicians. They had to strike a devil's deal to get the rep they badly wanted.

Hand in hand with the band members' infinite capacity for taking themselves too seriously came an insatiable need to be taken seriously by the rest of the world, and they labored like slaves in the vineyard to attain that *muy serioso* status. In interview after interview, the band brooded over the state of Ireland, Europe, and the planet in general, grousing about rock stars and celebrity and integrity and faith and the ever-present dangers of selling out to corporate interests. The musicians all but wore hair shirts. And once U2's social conscience—make that SOCIAL CONSCIENCE, with a four-color banner and a trumpet flourish—was a matter of faith and fetish among rock journalists, U2 bought its own bill of goods back from the press. It was this self-aggrandizing mindset that carried the group into the recording of what would become *The Joshua Tree.*

Everything about U2's fourth album indicated that it was designed to be its Big Career Statement, the album on which the band's sturdy leftist politics, wild rock 'n' roll heart, and immersion in the orthodox vocabularies of sin and redemption at last achieved a whole greater

243

than the sum of its parts. From spine to grooves, it was a laboriously constructed package, its aesthetic plainly signaled in the austere cover shot: the Frump Four, standing inexplicably in a blasted landscape and looking with morose moo-cow eyes in random directions, as if the bus from the Painted Desert to Death Valley had thrown a rod and they were scanning the horizon for the nearest pisser.

Nearly two decades later, it all sounds precisely and exactly as it did then, as if dipped in amber, every last caterwaul that shaped Gen X's foozle-headed social consciousness: "I Still Haven't Found What I'm Looking For," "With or Without You," "Bullet the Blue Sky," "Running to Stand Still," "Where the Streets Have No Name," and even, God help us, "Mothers of the Disappeared." Newly enlightened undergrads popped it into their Walkmans the way past generations of do-gooders and parlor busybodies schlepped *The Sorrows of Young Werther* and *Zen and the Art of Motorcycle Maintenance* around campus commons, as a badge of pompous sensitivity. If you listened to *The Joshua Tree*, goddammit, you *cared*.

It takes Old Testament-grade vanity to become simultaneously an age's dourest Irishman and its most principled rocker, and by 1987, Bono had scored win, place, and show in the International Furrow-Browed Rock God Derby, beating out such heavy hitters as Sting, Paul Simon, and Sinead O'Connor. Even among his countrymen, Bono was the goods—holier than Van Morrison, wordier than James Joyce, more familiar with hardship's bitter aftertaste than Brendan Behan. And much as he tried to borrow soul by coat-tailing black American music (his injunction to "Play the blues, Edge!," captured in the arena tour documentary, *Rattle and Hum*, stands as one of the most unintentionally hilarious moments in rock history), most of his saintly persona was *papier-mâché* Irish to its hobnail boot-tops. Shane McGowan was content to drink until his liver fell into his left shoe, but Bono milked the old stereotype of the brooding Celtic mystic so relentlessly that its tits bled. And even so, it killed him that he couldn't grow up to be an eighty year old black man from North Mississippi— this, though he hadn't even *heard* of John Lee Hooker until 1985.

U2's late-bloomer fascination with the eternal topics of the blues, coupled with its members' inability to pluck the beam from their own eye while pointing out the mote in their neighbor's, is the key to *The Joshua Tree*—a wonky, ill-fitting marriage of high-minded piety and humorless determination to explore the same stone-simple themes, in exactly the same terminology, until the tape runs out. In a manner akin to the Mad Caucus Race of Lewis Carroll's *Alice Through the Looking Glass*, its songs chase each other in a pointless circle until time is called, then congratulate themselves by awarding first prize to all participants.

Conventional critical wisdom holds that *The Joshua Tree* is the album on which U2 finally combined its Celtic orthodoxy with its longtime adoration of American folk music forms—namely blues, country, and gospel. It isn't. In 1988, the desperately fucked-up *Rattle and Hum* was more ambitious in that regard, shelving traditional Irish melodies ("Van Dieman's Land") alongside rockabilly and Stax soul experiments ("Desire," "Angel of Harlem") without regard for sequence or logic, which is why it all goes so wrong so quickly. Still, though *Rattle and Hum*'s execution mostly falls flat—as on the fawning "Angel of Harlem," the inexplicable Catholic blues (!) of "When Love Comes to Town," or the downright cringe-inducing "God Part II"—it's at least an *honest* failure. We're never more prone to make asses of ourselves than when we love unreservedly. As bloated and self-important as it is, *Rattle and Hum* is the sound of U2's members fumbling to interact with the kind of music they revered, and not giving a damn whether they looked like sycophants or gasbags in the process. In contrast, *The Joshua Tree* takes no risks, rolls no dice, and couches every one of its supposedly deep insights in the broadest, most hackneyed terms possible. As a result, it's not only preachy, it commits Art's cardinal sin: It's boring.

For all its heavy-handed production by studio straw bosses Brian Eno, Daniel Lanois, and mixer Steve Lillywhite—and despite the hype about its distinctive "soundscape"—*The Joshua Tree*'s musical textures are surprisingly unvaried. Of its eleven tracks, six open with an identical slow-crescendo-to-climax intro passage, gardylooed in delay and echo; six are built around conventional-as-mud I-IV chord progressions (frequently overlaid with those twelfth-fret harmonics of which the Edge was so eternally fond); nine are in major keys; four are in the *same* major key (D, with two more in G); and all are delivered, either totally or partially, in first-person narrative voice. As early as the third track, a disorienting déjà vu begins to set in, and not without reason, since what we're hearing is mostly the same song structure reworked in lightly tweaked orders, tempos, and keys.

The album's two operative sonic modes are the drone ("Mothers of the Disappeared," "Bullet the Blue Sky," "With or Without You") and the screech ("Where the Streets Have No Name," "In God's Country," "One Tree Hill")—a clumsy either–or vision, but one perfectly appropriate for an album that sees all of life as an endless Forced March through the Dry Desert Lowlands of the Valley of Fear, where Our Souls Are Scorched and We Hold the Hands of Devils.

And speaking of that, what *about* the album's supposed thematic profundity, borne along on this wave of samey chords and post-production frippery? On this matter, the critics had their say early and often: *CMJ*'s contemporary review called *The Joshua Tree* U2's "most mature LP, with a seething, exquisitely controlled energy. Bono's vocals burn, channeling his emotional excesses into passion rather than exuberance." *Rolling Stone*'s ponderous assessment of the album it recently ranked the twenty-sixth greatest of all time—above entries by Robert Johnson and John Coltrane—ran, "While many of the songs are about spiritual quests, U2 fortify the solemnity with the outright joys of rock & roll." Gushed *All Music Guide*'s Stephen Thomas Erlewine: "Never before have [U2's] messages sounded so direct and personal."

Um, no. On a lyrical level, *The Joshua Tree* is simply one of the most relentlessly banal albums in the pantheon of the greats. Its scrawny nuggets of perfectly commonplace wisdom—life is a pilgrimage; addiction sucks; love hurts; golly, it's barren in the desert— are packed so full of pious oatmeal bulk, bone meal, pencil shavings, and sawdust that any minor insights quickly get buried in an ava-lanche of Old Testament imagery.

There is redundancy of word (from "One Tree Hill": "Raining in your heart / Raining, raining to your heart / Raining, raining, raining / Raining to your heart / Raining, raining in your heart"; from "Exit": "Beating, beating, beating, beating / Oh my love, oh my love, oh my love, oh my love"). There is redundancy of thesis (from "With or Without You": "And you give yourself away / And you give yourself away / And you give / And you give / And you give yourself away"). There is mere gibberish (from "Running to Stand Still": "Singing ha, ah la la la de day / Ah la la la la de day, ah la de day"; from "With or Without You": "Whooaaaaahhhh-ohhhhhh-aaahh-ohhhh / Whooaaa-aaahh-ohhhh / Whooaaa-ohhh-ahh-ohhhh"). And there is out-and-out sermonizing ("Jacob wrestled the angel"—"Bullet the Blue Sky"; "I stand with the sons of Cain"—"In God's Country"; "I believe in the Kingdom Come"—"I Still Haven't Found What I'm Looking For"). And there is an even cross-indexable self-plagiarism ("I'm waiting for you"—"With or Without You"; "I'm waiting for you"— "Trip Through Your Wires"; "I'm still waiting"—"Red Hill Mining Town").

And, dear God, is it dour. There have been many relentlessly depressing albums in rock history—Lou Reed's *Berlin*, Neil Young's *Tonight's the Night*, Nico's *The Marble Index*—but for sheer inexorable gloominess, *The Joshua Tree* beats them all like a rented mule. Its land-scape is peopled exclusively with sufferers and self-flagellants, wailing endless jeremiads to the slate-gray sky. We "turn away to face the cold enduring chill" (as opposed, one assumes, to the warm enduring heat); rivers, wells, and bottles "run dry" with such alarming fre-quency that one wonders why we don't move to well-irrigated Salt Lake City, if we like the goddamned desert so much; we're forever running through alleys, streets, storms, valleys, mountains, deserts, plains, and fields in an attempt to escape fire, rain, demons, locust winds, darkness, heat, cold, dust, and thunder. *The Joshua Tree* is the *Godzilla vs. Mothra* of rock albums: All is cinder, rubble, and death from above.

And with the exception of the *Hair* soundtrack, has there *ever* been as much unasked-for nudity in a rock record? We stand naked, she's holding naked flames, our sons are standing naked in the trees … Jeezis, who's doing the laundry around here? (Oh, wait: The rivers have run dry.) My God, but we're in wretched shape.

Or, rather, Bono is. *The Joshua Tree* is the perfect soundtrack for '80s-era self-absorption—thus accounting for its popularity among eMpTyV hipsters and first-generation yuppies alike—because its endless catalog of bitchery and abomination proceeds from one mouth alone. There are seventy-two instances of first-person pronouns on *The Joshua Tree* (the next most prominent poetic element, water imagery, clocks in a distant twenty-six times; fire comes in third, with nineteen appearances); *I* stand with the sons of Cain, *I* lie on a bed of nails, *I* have climbed the highest mountains, *I'm* thirsty, *I'm* cold, *I'm* bare-ass naked, I, I, I, me, me, me. Bono, honey, come down off the cross. We can use the wood.

Unsurprisingly, considering its socio-historical context, the immediate response to *The Joshua Tree* was massive. Selling some fourteen million copies (a figure the universally panned *Rattle & Hum* would match), the album was feted with awards and honors, earning a pair of Grammys as well as a clean sweep of 1987's *Rolling Stone* critics poll—winning for Best Album, Best Artist, Best Male Singer, Best Songwriter, Best Guitarist, Best Album Cover (ha!), Best Live Performance, Best Bass Player, Best Drummer, Sexiest Male, as well as taking prizes for Best Videos and Best Singles.

In the ensuing years, the album's reputation grew exponentially. In a November, 2001 poll conducted by VH1, gauging the All-Time Greatest Albums, *The Joshua Tree* topped the list in a landslide, besting its nearest competitor, Michael Jackson's *Thriller*, by nearly fifteen percent of the vote, and annihilating everything from *Revolver* and *Pet Sounds* to *The Dark Side of the Moon* and *Nevermind*.

But *The Joshua Tree* has a darker legacy as well. Apart from making vests and bolo ties an unfortunate fashion trend for a time, U2's efforts inspired successive generations of bands to imitate the album's supposedly epic scope and clumsy religious underpinnings. One hears its influence not just on late-'80s contemporaries such as the Alarm, the Cult, and Bon Jovi, but also in the worst kind of modern dreck, from Creed and Incubus to System of a Down, Staind, Linkin Park, and a host of overly emotive, Christ-posing gorgons. In fact, Creed lead singer Scott Stapp has gone on record as citing *The Joshua Tree* as his favorite album and—horrors!—his chief motivation for making music, which alone is enough to require a federal law mandating an immediate and retroactive ban on owning a copy of the disc.

There's no question that rock music can tackle important issues—even heady religious and philosophical ones—and sustain a focused argument over the length of a full album. *Tonight's the Night* says better than any rehab brochure how heroin can fuck you up, quick, two times; the Replacements' *Let it Be* chronicles the brutal, confusing years between adolescence and adulthood so accurately that it's remained timeless. This is the sort of epic narrative arc that the U2 boys seem to have been going for, but in its windy reliance on stock images, *The Joshua Tree* takes the easy way out. The album's oblique imagery supposedly lends it a universal applicability and limitless depth of interpretation. Is "I Still Haven't Found What I'm Looking For" about a spurned lover or a man who's lost his religious faith? Yet that cut might just as plausibly be about a lawyer looking to serve a subpoena, or a celebrity stalker, or a man who's dropped his keys, or some asshole wandering the beach with a metal detector, for all its specificity of language. At all points, *The Joshua Tree* makes us do the legwork and draw the connections, and it doesn't even give us any jarring visuals to work with. "Tongues of angels," my ass; "through the storm we reach the shore," oh, please; "rain pounding on the women and children," are you *kidding* me? This is songwriting done in the style of Fourth Period Study Hall.

The Joshua Tree is an object lesson in what happens when rock decides to look serious—not to any specific purpose, mind you, but simply because looking serious makes you look important. (It also, unsurprisingly, makes you look like a prissy schoolmarm, *viz.* the pickle-pussed cover shot.) In its unelaborated reiteration of theme and content, *The Joshua Tree* gives, gives, gives itself away. It's not a sacred text—it's a religious tract, stuck under your windshield wiper by an acolyte so enamored of thorn and nettle that the message quickly grows tiresome. It's a visit from pamphlet-toting proselytizers determined to badger you into the Kingdom, even if they have to stand on your front porch all day to do it. You sit down quietly and accept the premises of *The Joshua Tree*, or it raps your knuckles. And it is, therefore, bad art.

If we must belabor the Christian metaphor, Bono, the Edge, Clayton, and Mullins would do well to remember that the Old Testament gives us a word for those who neglect good works while touting their own piety in public. They're called Pharisees.

PUBLIC ENEMY
It Takes a Nation of Millions to Hold Us Back
Def Jam / Columbia, 1988
By Arsenio Orteza

everal weeks into the 2003 pro football season, the Reverend Al Sharpton and other notoriously inflammatory avatars of racial demagoguery pressured the conservative radio talk-show titan Rush Limbaugh into resigning from his guest commentator position at ESPN. Limbaugh's sin? Saying that the sports media, in its zeal to see a "black quarterback do well," had over-hyped the accomplishments of the Philadelphia Eagles' Donovan McNabb. Debate over the merits of Limbaugh's contention immediately ensued and, given the self-perpetuating nature of sports arguments, will probably continue for years. It's too bad there's never been—and, given our hypersensitivity to that chimera "hate speech," may never be—an equally public debate about the validity of that notoriously dimwitted genre of aural graffiti known as rap, the artistic merits of which the music media, in its zeal to see young black radicals do well, has been over-hyping for two decades now.

Don't get me wrong, rap can be great fun. At its early best, before it became overrun by gangstas, thugz, pimps, hoez, and other types you wouldn't want to bring home to meet your grandma (or your spelling teacher), rap was the closest thing to a revival of the loose goofiness of Leiber-Stoller-era Coasters that any pop-musical subculture, black or white, had generated in a quarter of a century. As such, early rap was primarily, and ideally, a singles genre, its best albums collections of greatest hits. Like many rock bands in the mid- to-late '60s, however, rappers eventually came to be seen by major record companies as potentially huge moneymakers and, as a result, had a significance thrust upon them replete with the expectation that they would now take what they'd formerly done in fun-sized bits and expand it into full-length masterworks. As was the case with many '60s rock bands (most notably the Beach Boys, but that's another chapter), this fixing of what wasn't broken was the beginning of the end.

Since then many rap albums have had their meager merits exaggerated by the press, but none more so than Public Enemy's *It Takes a Nation of Millions to Hold Us Back*. Released in 1988, it found itself atop many critics' best-of lists at year's end, eventually winning album of the year honors in *The Village Voice*'s annual "Pazz and Jop" critics' poll and establishing Chuck D., Flava Flav, and their DJ, Terminator X, as hip-hop alchemists who would finally bring about rap's transformation from novelty into art. "It's a like-it-or-not, wake-up-and-listen album," wrote Armond White in his "Pazz and Jop" comments, "like Aretha's *I Never Loved a Man* or the Sex Pistols' *Never Mind the Bollocks.*" Added Scott Byron: "It's the first record in ages to rise out of the New York rap scene with enough of that confrontational attitude that alternative programmers love so much. When I say 'confrontational' I'm not just referring to words but to music—[Public Enemy] test their limits at every turn." Eventually, *Rolling Stone* would rank the disc number twelve among the best albums of the '80s: "Virtually every track contains repeated shrill noises that are both irritating and riveting; its agit-prop sound communicates as much rebellion as the lyrics."

In retrospect, the album did no such thing. Both its noise and its lyrics, while an innovation in rap, were hardly new to the music world at large. Non-rappers, for instance, had so established "repeated shrill noises that [were] both irritating and riveting" as sonic staples that as far back as 1981, Lester Bangs could fill a piece titled "A Reasonable Guide to Horrible Noise" with praise for music that he loved primarily for its "wretched squawl." Other than the air-raid siren on "Countdown to Armageddon" with which *It Takes a Nation of Millions to Hold Us Back* begins, most of the album's celebrated "noise" is the result of tightly looped samples repeated over and over. The similarities to Chinese water torture are obvious, but the approach is actually much closer, in both technique and effect, to Philip Glass's minimalist exercises on *Einstein on the Beach* and *Glassworks*. As such, Terminator X's aural assault could be seen as simply the latest example of the sort of cultural cross-fertilization that had been going on between whites and blacks since Europe met Africa in jazz and the blues met country in rock 'n' roll. Clever? Yes. But rebellious? 'Scuse me while I kiss this lie goodbye. If you really want something irritating to clear the guests out, you'd be much better served by Lou Reed's *Metal Machine Music* or the Shaggs' *Philosophy of the World*, albums so rebelliously irritating that even those who love them hate themselves for doing so. (At least one "Pazz and Jop" voter numbered Chuck D.'s voice among Public Enemy's irritating noises. "His vocals are sexless, and always do the same thing," wrote Frank Kogan. "This is boy rock, no girly mush—boys acting IMPORTANT." Kogan was right. With no variation in volume or timbre, with no perceivable vocal texture other than "hard," with absolutely no sense of play, Chuck D. would be utterly unendurable were it not for the commotion going on around him and the comic relief of his foil-jester-sidekick, Flava Flav, whose "Cold Lampin with Flavor" steals the show on this album the way his "Can't Do Nuttin' for Ya Man" did a few years later on *Fear of a Black Planet*.)

Equally over the top were the hosannas heaped upon Public Enemy's "message." Compared to the Black Panther propagandists of the '60s, with whom Chuck D. claimed common ground on the album's most explicitly political track, "Party for Your Right to Fight," Public Enemy's own pugnacious, paranoid, Afrocentric rhetoric came off as both redundant and secondhand. "The community," wrote Panther leader Huey Newton from prison in 1969, "is now seeing that our fight on the campuses is more than just a fight for 'freedom of speech' on the campus, or Blacks gaining a knowledge of our heritage; it's also showing the direct relationship between the reactionary government and the agencies and institutions that are only an arm of these reactionaries. Until we penetrate the community and make them aware and plant the seed of revolution, we will never have freedom at our schools. The community now is being mobilized by the Black revolutionary forces and along with them are our white revolutionary comrades."

Substitute "white rock critics" for "white revolutionary comrades," replace "penetrate the community" with "get widespread radio airplay," work in some rhymes, and add some riveting noise and a smattering of profanities, and you'd have Public Enemy nineteen years before the fact.

Of course, anyone still delivering rants such as Newton's in 1988 would've probably been seen as delusional; instead of ending up behind bars, they'd probably win tenure as a professor of African Studies. Echoing Huey Newton in 1988 required a lot less courage from Chuck D. than *being* Huey Newton required from Huey Newton back in 1969. Besides, Chuck D. was rapping on a major label (Def Jam was a Columbia subsidiary at the time) and was therefore making money from his shtick. Yet critics insisted that in Public Enemy, the world had something innovatively political and socially significant, a genuine musical threat to the hegemony if ever there'd been one. Eventually such opinions hardened into dogma, relegating comparatively lightweight rap pioneers such as Grandmaster Flash, Kurtis Blow, and even Run-DMC to the category of rap known (sometimes affectionately) as "old school," and exposing the likes of Schoolly D and 2 Live Crew for the unsavory lowlifes that they were. From *It Takes a Nation of Millions to Hold Us Back* onward, rappers who wanted to be taken seriously—who wanted to be considered authentically "black"—would need to ratchet up their anger-at-oppression quotient and, thus transported, go for the jugular of the nearest oppressor.

The problem was, Public Enemy's oppressors turned out to be straw men, and straw men *have* no jugulars. For one thing, by 1988, there was no nation of millions trying to hold Public Enemy or any other rap group or black musician or athlete or film star or politician or comedian or plumber back. The now-ubiquitous "white fright" explicit-lyrics parental warning sticker, which many believe has ended up having the unintended effect of boosting rap sales, was not even in use as yet. Perhaps most significantly, the Aerosmith–Run-DMC version of "Walk This Way" had exposed (or forged) the link between rap and metal, officially miscegenating America's two most popular forms of rebellion-oriented youth music.

And it's not as if the country's more conservative citizens—the ones most likely to be rubbed the wrong way by Public Enemy—weren't in a protesting mood. Earlier that year, Martin Scorsese's cinematic interpretation of Nikos Kazantzakis's novel, *The Last Temptation of Christ,* had engendered numerous high-profile protests and boycotts aimed specifically at crippling its box-office success. One year later there would be headline-grabbing controversies over taxpayer-funded displays of the contemporary art of Andres Seranno (whose *Piss Christ* consisted of a crucifix submerged in urine) and Robert Mapplethorpe (whose graphically homoerotic S&M photography remains controversial: Opponents of Arnold Schwarzenegger's 2003 gubernatorial campaign cited Schwarzenegger's past as a Mapplethorpe model as one proof that he wasn't fit for office). Simply put, the album's failure to rise higher than No. 42 on *Billboard*'s Top 200 albums chart and the inability of its four singles to crack the Top Forty were not the result of censorship or of radio's fear of controversy. A nation of millions simply liked Run-DMC better.

Or, to put it another way, while *It Takes a Nation of Millions to Hold Us Back* made itself felt in big East Coast cities (Wrote the Providence, Rhode Island-based Pazz-and-Jopster Jim MacNie: "You couldn't buy ice cream, shoot hoops, or have sex without Terminator X's distillation of racial tension…reverberating down the street"), it barely registered in a whole lot of flyover country. The multi-racial, rock-and-rap-loving Louisiana junior-high-school students to whom I taught English in those days, for instance, who did as much as radio and MTV to keep me musically well-informed, had hardly even heard of the group. "Are they the ones with that guy who wears a big clock around his neck?" one girl responded when I asked her what she thought of them. She had, it turns out, seen pictures of Flava Flav in a magazine and remembered his image, but of his group's music she hadn't heard so much as a beat and was in no hurry to listen. She was a big Tone-Loc fan, and the notion that there could be any rap better than "Wild Thing" and "Funky Cold Medina" struck her as preposterous.

Living in Louisiana, my interest in Public Enemy was not entirely musical. By 1988, the former Ku Klux Klansman and then-Louisiana resident David Duke had exchanged his Grand Wizard's robe and hood for the conservative attire of a serious politician and—first as a Democrat, then as a Republican—begun gaining support among white Louisiana voters. (He was eventually elected as a member of the state legislature, and in 1991 ran an impressive but ultimately unsuccessful gubernatorial campaign.) I was convinced that racial conflicts were about to play a larger role in American society than they had at any time in my twenty-six years, and that an understanding of the complexities involved would be necessary for me to think and act wisely should the need to do so arise. (Public Enemy would later single Duke out as a special nemesis as well, caricaturing him on the cover of their 1994 album, *Muse Sick-n-Hour Mess Age*; ironically, by that time, Duke himself was a straw man, having already ridden out a wave of public support that ended up vanishing almost as quickly as it had appeared. Both he and the man to whom he lost the governorship, Edwin Edwards, are currently in federal prisons.) In retrospect, my crash course in racism awareness was naïve, as if merely by reading Alex Haley's *Autobiography of Malcolm X*, John Howard Griffin's *Black Like Me*, and William Stringfellow's *My People Is the Enemy*, I could develop heroically virtuous sympathies overnight. But I was sincere and open-minded both, and it was in this spirit that I read the aforementioned glowing reviews, bought the hype and a copy of *It Takes a Nation of Millions to Hold Us Back*, put the album on, and awaited revelation.

It never came. What I got instead was David Duke in blackface. Not only was there anti-Semitism once removed, in the form of endorsements for the Nation of Islam's Louis Farrakhan ("Don't tell me that you understand / Until you hear the man… Farrakhan's a prophet and I think you ought to listen to / What he can say to you"), but there was also a crackpot theory of racial superiority, only this time it was blacks who were the Master Race. And "[T]o those that disagree," rapped Chuck D. in "Party for Your Right to Fight," "It causes static / For the original Black Asiatic man / Cream of the earth / And was here first / And some devils prevent this from being known / But you check out the books they own / Even Masons they know it / But refuse to show it—yo / But it's proven and fact."

Really, I don't know whether liberal sports writers exaggerate Donovan McNabb's athletic accomplishments because he's black or not. But I do know that music critics exaggerate Public Enemy's intelligence. Surely many of these critics know that the "original Black Asiatic Man" theory to which Chuck D. was alluding in "Party for Your Right to Fight" is the repugnant and explicitly racist Nation of Islam teaching that a wicked black scientist named Yacub created the white race through biological experimentation that left the newly created "white devils" without pigment and soul. Would the same critics who treated these ideas as harmless eccentricities when coming from Chuck D. have shrugged off equally explicit white racism from a white act? If not, then the toleration of such notions from Chuck D. amounts to nothing more than patronization, a patronization that is itself a form of racism in that its tolerance stems from the assumption that the black man in question is too unsophisticated or downright foolish to know any better. So while it might be stretching things to say that it took the patronization of millions to put Chuck D. forth as an icon of enlightenment, the patronization of a few hundred music critics certainly didn't hurt.

An interesting footnote: In what was almost certainly its version of what's known in sports as the "make-up call," Public Enemy eventually dismissed its most outspokenly Yacubian (and anti-Semitic) the-

257

orist, its "Minister of Information," Professor Griff, shortly before the release of *Fear of a Black Planet*, their 1990 follow-up. (Griff had told *The Washington Post* in 1989 that Jews were responsible for "the majority of the wickedness that goes on across the globe.") That Griff was dismissed in the face of pressure resulting in part from the group's increased visibility suggests not so much a change in Public Enemy's attitude toward white people as its fear of a white boycott. An even more interesting footnote: Griff rejoined Public Enemy in 1997. The group's official Web site currently describes him as "[n]otorious for his uncompromising stances that the media finds offensive." The implication: There's nothing wrong with his manifestly false, unspeakably hateful, and laughably stupid ideas—how can there be, when they're ours and Farrakhan's as well? It's the media that has the problem. Hey, maybe Rush Limbaugh was right about the media after all! Besides, wasn't it T.S. Eliot who once said, "Humankind cannot bear very much reality"? And wasn't Eliot himself a little, you know, suspicious of Jews...?

Besides smuggling the Nation of Islam's harebrained racism into the hip-hop mainstream, *It Takes a Nation of Millions to Hold Us Back* brought into the open a topic that, admittedly, lay just beneath the surface whenever discussions of popular black-identified music styles arose—namely, what does "being black" really mean? Or, perhaps more accurately, in what does genuine "blackness" inhere? The blackness of tormented jazz geniuses such as Charlie Parker and Miles Davis, for example, was never in question. Neither was the blackness of such archetypal bluesmen as Robert Johnson or Muddy Waters. Viscerally affecting soul singers such as Otis Redding and James Brown were definitely black, and so, for that matter, were their refined stylistic opposites at Motown and anyone connected, however tenuously, with the Harlem Renaissance (i.e., Duke Ellington). Eventually, the concept would be stretched to include the likes of Ella Fitzgerald (jazz), Lou Rawls (supper-club soul), Mahalia Jackson (gospel), Paul Robeson (Negro spirituals and Broadway), the Fifth Dimension ('60s AM pop), and Earth, Wind and Fire (all things to all people), leaving blackness far too large and plastic a concept to be useful in any seriously political sense.

Practically speaking, by the time *It Takes a Nation of Millions to Hold Us Back* came out, pop music was arguably more integrated—racially, culturally, and stylistically—than it had ever been. Of the twenty-six performers who scored number-one singles in 1988, only five (Whitney Houston, Michael Jackson, Billy Ocean, Terence Trent D'Arby, and Bobby McFerrin) were black, but in comprising nearly twenty percent of the number-one-hitmaker crowd, they were almost twice as significant, demographically speaking, as blacks in the musical population at large. "Blackness" began to appear even more influential if one took into account unmistakenly black-influenced chart-topping songs such as UB40's "Red Red Wine" (Neil Diamond done reggae), George Harrison's "Got My Mind Set on You" (Rudy Clark done Traveling Wilbury-style), and Steve Winwood's "Roll With It" (blue-eyed soul, yes, but soul all the same). The year's album chart looked similar: Two of the ten number-one albums (twenty percent) were by black musicians (Tracy Chapman's eponymous debut, Anita Baker's *Giving You the Best That I Got*), and another, U2's *Rattle and Hum*, featured high-profile cameos by B.B. King and the New Voices of Freedom, as well as songs honoring Billie Holliday ("Angel of Harlem"), Martin Luther King, Jr. ("Pride [In the Name of Love]"), and the anti-Apartheid struggle in South Africa ("Silver and Gold"). Even MTV, which, prior to Michael Jackson's Jackie Robinson-like breakthrough, had been accused of deliberately "bleaching" its playlists, was scrambling to make room in its heavy rotation for black acts old (Tina Turner), new (DJ Jazzy Jeff and the Fresh Prince), borrowed (Milli Vanilli), and blue (Robert Cray).

None of this "blackness," however, meant anything to Public Enemy. "I declared war on black radio," rapped Chuck D. in "Caught, Can I Get a Witness!" "You singers are spineless / As you sing senseless songs to the mindless / Your general subject, love, is minimal / It's sex for profit." Leaving aside Chuck D.'s anachronistically puritanical attack on sex-commodifying music (cf. Elvis Presley circa 1955 and *The Copulatin' Blues*, circa 1929-1940), what's really hilarious about these lines is that the man calling others "mindless" is the same man who believes that white people are descended from evil mutants created by Yacub and is willing to proclaim as much from the rooftops. Talk about the kettle calling the pot not black.

Worse yet (*far* worse yet), by insisting throughout *It Takes a Nation of Millions to Hold Us Back* that "blackness" is a quantifiable reality, Chuck D. kept alive the very possibility of the racism against which he had allegedly declared war. For only when an undesirable characteristic—the apparently disproportionate propensity of the young black male, say, to join gangs and commit drive-by shootings—can be identified as an ineradicable component of a minority people is it possible to mobilize a nation of millions against them. Convince people, on the other hand, that a black male can become as decent, educated, virtuous, and loving as anyone else, perhaps even more so, and—well, let's just say it's then and only then that hate crimes like "strange fruit" lynchings and James Byrd dragging deaths appear every bit as stupid as hate rhymes like Chuck D.'s.

NIRVANA
Nevermind
Geffen, 1991
By Anders Smith Lindall

I remember middle school like a nineteenth-century sea voyage. From naïve childhood, I shoved off into adolescence; after two or three years of cowering below decks, the shores of sanity slowly crept back into view. I feel lucky I didn't get scurvy.

The midpoint of that trip—the Tuesday morning that I started eighth grade—was September 3, 1991. Exactly three weeks later, Geffen Records gave unto the world Nirvana's *Nevermind*. The disc at first failed to make a ripple on the surface of my adolescent drift, but within months it would hit like a tidal wave.

I hated the goddamned thing.

This did not help my social life.

💀💀💀

In the Rock Bible, *Nevermind* is the sacred text of Saint Kurt. Moreover, it was and remains Exhibit A in the argument that, despite the direst of circumstances or longest of droughts, rock 'n' roll will never die. In my world, though, the album—and especially "Smells Like Teen Spirit," which soon became, like Hammer's "U Can't Touch This" and the Red Hot Chili Peppers' "Under the Bridge," a staple of school-dance DJs—was mostly a good excuse for bullies and jocks to inflict pain and call it a mosh pit.

Outside the dim lunchroom where dances were held, "Smells Like Teen Spirit" fueled the disc's rise up the pop charts. Coasting on a clean, melodic verse that explodes into a roaring chorus, the song introduced the band's soon-to-be familiar formula, as well as some of Kurt Cobain's most pathetic and oft-quoted lyrics. Flog Douglas Coupland raw for the stupid "Generation X" tag, but save some lashes for the man whose shallow, braying complaints ("I feel stupid and contagious") and mumbled shrugs of self-pity ("Oh well, whatever, never mind") gave us the straitjacket stereotype as careless losers.

That's not to say that "Smells Like Teen Spirit" was devoid of value. It neatly showcased drummer Dave Grohl and bassist Krist Novoselic's combined brawn, while Cobain's revered wheedle and his foreboding guitar hook hinted at a creeping sense of dread that the band would evoke more fully elsewhere. Apart from summing up vapid apathy, though, its lyrics—all lame puns and lazy alliteration—lacked specificity and depth.

Spinning it now, it's clear that similar inconsistencies plague *Nevermind* as a whole. Too many good ideas are diluted by a lack of focus, and the band's subtleties are too frequently sacrificed for the sake of noise. Sure, the disc has its attributes—chief among them the unbridled aggression that carries cuts such as "In Bloom" (especially in the breathless run-up to the chorus) and "Breed" (where Grohl sounds as if he's juggling a thousand Hammers of Thor and Novoselic bangs out a fat, rubbery rhythm). The rhythm section scores other points, too, like Novoselic's lean "Lounge Act" bass line, his funky touch and Grohl's cymbal splashes on "Polly," and the moments in "Lithium" when the controlled, slinky groove of the verse bursts into the raw-throated refrain. Cobain, alternately churning and stinging, mostly holds his own on guitar.

His lyrics are another story. Cobain copped to stringing most of his phrases together at random, a Beat-inspired method that made him sound portentous while staying vague enough to let listeners ascribe their own agendas—which mostly meant wallowing in angst and alienation ("I'm so lonely / But that's O.K. / I shaved my head"). I didn't think teenage ennui was particularly fun when I was feeling it, so I never quite understood the attraction of wallowing—and it's not as if a socially engaged band of the time lacked for fodder. When *Nevermind* arrived in late 1991, the Republican grip on the White House was nearly a dozen years old, the Cold War was sputtering in Europe and Asia, and a hot conflict had erupted in the Persian Gulf. At home, the news was ruled by AIDS, a weak economy, serial killer and cannibal Jeffrey Dahmer, and the grainy tape of Los Angeles cops mobbing Rodney King. Cobain's response was to tell the world that things were fucked up, though apparently not so much that he cared to do anything about it. Meanwhile, even Pearl Jam, the supposed anti-Nirvana and symbol of all things careerist and uncool, took a stand against Ticketmaster.

Cobain's personality was no picnic, either. Judging by *Nevermind*, it was tough to tell who he despised more: himself, or the fans he flipped off in the photo on the CD's inlay card and sneered at in his songs ("He's the one who likes all our pretty songs / But he don't know what it means").

The disc's calling card, of course, was the trio's signature mid-song shifts in volume, tempo, and tone: From soft to loud, slow to fast, sweet to scabrous. But on *Nevermind*, those juxtapositions are so frequently deployed that they soon devolve from jarring to formulaic. Some cuts have aged more gracefully; I'm especially moved by "Polly" (a spare, creepy, veiled tale of a kidnapping and rape that Cobain delivers with chilling detachment), "On a Plain" (a melodic achievement that presaged even better things for the band; it's hard-charging, hooky, and hammered home with rhythmic brawn and arc-welder guitar), and "Something in the Way." The latter, a crudely simple but elegant dirge, offers an atypically vivid set of lyrics from Cobain. He sings in a weird, vacant drawl that's echoed by rich cello lines, but the song's grace and subtlety serve mostly to indict the one-note nature of the rest of the album. If you're skilled at such a range of sounds, why be so bleak all the time?

Other songs seem unfinished, overdone, or just so-so. "Territorial Pissings" is a fair enough stab at speedcore, and "In Bloom" is a good melodic idea that would have been better at half the length. "Drain

You" offers succinct lyrics and an appealingly acid guitar hook, but the droning refrain saps its momentum. "Stay Away" suffers partly from context (by the time it arrives, the band's tricks are too obvious) and partly from being half-baked (instead of actually ending, it simply falls apart). And there's the disc's closer, the hidden track, "Endless Nameless," which mutates from vague funk into an exercise in guitar torture—or maybe it's an audiotape of an old car being sawed in half, melted down, and crushed.

Any way you slice it, *Nevermind* doesn't add up to a classic disc. To be fair, though, its stature stems more from its perceived role as The Album That Saved Rock than its track-by-track merits. "No album in recent history had such an overpowering impact on a generation," *Rolling Stone* said in naming it the seventeenth greatest album ever made. The trouble is, that argument doesn't hold water, either. *Nevermind* was the end of something, not the beginning. Just as Altamont snuffed '60s rock idealism, *Nevermind* didn't so much inaugurate a rock revival as toll a death knell for the '80s Amerindie movement. And a sad end it was: Cranked through the corporate wringer, politically neutered, and no fun.

In sound and stance, Nirvana was deeply indebted to its indie-rock forebears—check the taut balance between pop hooks and scabrous sound achieved by the Pixies, the molten righteousness of Hüsker Dü, and the hallucinogenic genre-bending of the Meat Puppets—but *Nevermind* couldn't touch any of those bands. To the contrary, its chart success did more to disembowel the indie underground than anything before or since.

It's an oft-told tale: In the post-*Nevermind* rush to mine similarly profitable diamonds from the grunge-rock rough, major labels signed anyone with a guitar, a flannel shirt, and a pulse. In the short run, this scorched-earth policy effectively drained the talent pool that stocked the indie rosters; in the long run, Nirvana's quick success stoked corporate appetites for the overnight smash, making the majors far less likely to invest money or time in artist development. Instead, they threw crap at the radio, and some of it stuck: Nirvana begat Bush, who begat Everclear, who begat Live, and so on down to Limp Bizkit.

The fact is, *Nevermind*'s commercial legs were always overrated. After selling an impressive six million copies in its first six months, it moved less than two million more in the twelve years that followed, and by the time of this writing, grunge had become an antiquarian blip. To wit: My brother, an avid young rock hound who'll soon be in high school, called recently to ask about a band he'd seen on TV. "The Foo Fighters," he said. "Know anything about them?"

"Sure," I answered. "That's Dave Grohl's band. You know, from Nirvana."

"Oh yeah," he said.

Pause.

"What's Nirvana?"

As noted earlier, the *Nevermind* myth rests largely on its sales figures—which, as with any mass-market product, resulted from the convergence of good luck, good marketing, and a willingness to play the game. (As the widow Cobain, Courtney Love, told this book's editor, Jim DeRogatis: "[Independent record promoter] Jeff McClusky sure as fuck got paid, and so did the rack jobbers, and so did the fucking handlers, and so did the guy in Thailand, and so did that guy, and so did that guy, and so did that guy! It was marketing money!") Forget the helpless baby flailing for a buck on the album cover: Nirvana cut through the corporate waters like Marc Spitz.

Though the band longed to have it both ways—playing to the mainstream while preserving its outsider's purity and Joe Average privacy—its complaints about the burdens of stardom were especially ill-fitting. After all, the group freely signed to a major label, made videos, posed for magazine covers (including corporate *Rolling Stone*), played the awards circuit, and appeared on "MTV Unplugged." And, I might add, they looked good doing so. Sure, Novoselic was a gangly goofball, but Grohl was darkly handsome, and Cobain was a postpunk heartthrob: vulnerable, moody, and possessed of brilliant baby blues.

Neither did the musicians seem overly concerned for the sanctity of their craft. They allowed *Nevermind* to be heavily shaped in the studio by producer Butch Vig (and in post-production by mixing engineer Andy Wallace). They signed off on *Incesticide*, a sloppily assembled collection of leftovers aimed straight at the wallets of newfound fans. And, as if to reinforce the band's contempt for its patrons, *Incesticide*'s notes contained an anti-fan rant written by Cobain.

The contradictions continued with *In Utero*, an album of significantly better songs and musicianship than *Nevermind*. Hyped as Nirvana's abrasive, Steve Albini-abetted affront to the casual listeners whom the band scorned, the disc was nonetheless mixed for maximum radio friendliness by noted mainstream softie and R.E.M. ally Scott Litt. (It's a good thing, too: With "All Apologies," "Heart-Shaped Box" and "Dumb," *In Utero* packs a handful of the best mainstream singles of the early alt-rock era.) At least Cobain copped to having cashed in: "Teenage angst has paid off well," he admits early into *Nevermind*'s follow-up.

Inexplicably, Nirvana was rarely called to account for its inconsistencies. One school of thought holds that critics—most of them grown-up rock geeks—gave the band a pass because the timber-town trio made rock geekdom cool. Another says that critics—most of them white guys who worship guitars—saw the band as rock's last great hope to fend off commercial challenges from rap and electronica. Or maybe they just figured Nirvana was a damn sight better than Michael Jackson, whose album *Dangerous* was knocked off the charts by *Nevermind*. But again, Nirvana's assertion of rock's commercial superiority was short-lived: When Cobain mugged for *Rolling Stone* in January 1994, just months before his death, a collaboration between Bryan Adams, Rod Stewart, and Sting topped the singles chart, and Mariah Carey's latest disc was the nation's best-selling album.

After Cobain's suicide in April 1994, the myth grew exponentially. From Robert Johnson and Jimi Hendrix, to Elvis Presley and John Lennon, untimely death has long been a good career move in popular music. At the very least, it saved Nirvana from the creative missteps and shameless nostalgia that result when rockers grow old gracelessly. If he'd lived, Cobain likely would have made better albums than *Nevermind*, but he probably would have helmed some stinkers, too. He would have made some miscalculations, taken some misunderstood risks, maybe quit the band, then reunited with it for a big payday. (We also might have been spared the endless exhumation of books and movies, the sordid legal squabbles, and the crassly commercial reissues that have sullied his legacy.) We'll never know, of course, but there's no compelling evidence to suggest that today he would be regarded any more highly than, say, Eddie Vedder. Would Nirvana still be seen as more influential than Nine Inch Nails, or would *Nevermind* be deemed more important than *Gish*?

Corporations have profited from selling rebellion (and dead rock stars) for decades now, and *Nevermind* was far from the first great rock 'n' roll swindle. But in terms of making punk safe for the shopping mall, it was a masterstroke. So let's give credit where it's due: Not to Cobain, Grohl, and Krist Novoselic, or to David Geffen, Gary Gersh, or Danny Goldberg, or even to Courtney Love. No, the real heroes of the *Nevermind* story are the anonymous suits, the marketers who executed a truly monumental cultural con job: They took an unexceptional punk-rock record and convinced the world that it was an icon. As for me, all I got was a teenage mosh-pit elbow to the head.

THE SMASHING PUMPKINS
Mellon Collie and the Infinite Sadness
Virgin, 1995
By Rick Reger

A brooding, introspective piano melody. The icy caress of a Mellotron. A delicate unfolding of chamber orchestra strings and reeds. And then, ladies and gentlemen, we're off! Where to, you ask? Why, straight into the heart of one of the grandest, splashiest, most splendiferous rock-taculars ever created, that's where.

Step aside, *Quadrophenia*. Roll over, *The Lamb Lies Down on Broadway*. Hasta la vista, *The Wall*. *Mellon Collie and the Infinite Sadness* has arrived.

That's right, *Mellon Collie and the Infinite Sadness*, the 1995 release from the Smashing Pumpkins that was designed to rank among the most magnum of opuses, an album whose stylistic breadth (metal, art rock, acoustic balladry, melodic pop), lyrical exuberance, and sheer bulk (over two hours) would make it the yardstick by which all future rock genius would be measured.

At least that seemed to be the intention.

There's no question that this is a special album: It sold a shitload, despite carrying a hefty price tag, and it finally gave its creator, Billy Corgan, the rock superstar status he'd so desperately and transparently craved for years. But *Mellon Collie and the Infinite Sadness* is also unique for another, less glorious reason. It may well be rock's first pseudo-masterpiece, a meticulously assembled simulacrum of greatness whose every facet—artwork, lyrics, sound spectrum—was designed to create the impression of "significance" where, in fact, none existed.

That's not to say that it isn't interesting. Just as great forged art demands a forger with real artistic skill and an in-depth knowledge of art history, so *Mellon Collie and the Infinite Sadness* demanded a creator with an intimate knowledge of rock's classic recordings and a real appreciation of its past masters. Corgan clearly possessed that knowledge, and the album is, indeed, effective at evoking the musical heft of a masterpiece. But it ain't the real thing, folks. Not by a long shot.

Now, before laying this leviathan out on the dissecting table, I should state for the record my pre-*Mellon Collie* stance towards the Smashing Pumpkins. I first encountered the band when it opened for Eleventh Dream Day at Metro in Chicago circa 1989. In contrast to the prevailing torn jeans and T-shirt uniform favored by most aspiring indie rockers of that era, the Pumpkins' black leather gear and stylishly coiffed hair made it clear that their sights were set on something bigger than Boho art cred. Fair enough.

I don't remember the specifics of the Pumpkins' music that night, but I do remember not liking what I heard. I vaguely recall a glitzy yet gloomy sort of hard rock that struck me as a tad silly from an artistic standpoint and more than a little misguided from a career-viability standpoint. (I couldn't have been more wrong about the latter.) About two years later, I was in a record store where I found myself tapping my toe to what sounded a bit like a British shoegazer band, but one with better than average melodies and an appealing knack for layering various instrumental textures. When the clerk told me he was playing the Smashing Pumpkins' new CD, *Gish*, I was surprised and impressed. The band had evolved into an effective, appealing purveyor of tuneful, middlebrow pop rock. It's a style that crystallized the group's and Corgan's musical strengths, and it probably should have been the musical approach to which the Pumpkins remained faithful.

But Corgan would have none of that. In a 1993 interview with the Chicago fanzine, *Empire Monthly*, he was quoted as saying that,

"Chicago musicians were only playing for other Chicago people and it seemed really shortsighted in terms of being musically progressive. The way I felt we could move beyond that was to take a much more direct progressive approach to what we were doing. It was a combination of some things I've been influenced by like David Bowie, Bauhaus, things like that—kind of, you know, classic rock structuring... and bringing it up to date... The next album [*Siamese Dream*] will sound way more ambitious than *Gish*. It's gonna be all over the place sonically."

To anyone who was watching and listening to Corgan back then, it was clear that he aspired to be much more than a fairly successful pop tunesmith. He seemed to have his sights set on nothing less than superstar status, and as a diligent student of classic-rock history, he knew that in many cases the key to the rock pantheon was the creation of a no-holds barred, double-album masterstroke. From *Exile on Main St.*, to *Something/Anything?*, to *Trout Mask Replica*, to *Physical Graffiti*, double albums have long been viewed (rightly or wrongly) as rock's most enduring artistic monuments, and as an artist's definitive musical statement. And why not? Back in the '70s, forty minutes of really good music per year was considered a lot to ask of often drunk, semi-junkie musicians neck-deep in groupie sex, so ninety minutes of really good music seemed a feat of superhuman proportions.

Not surprisingly, Corgan opted to erect a musical pyramid to his greatness in the grand manner of the Who's *Tommy* or Pink Floyd's *The Wall*. But he would not simply match rock's past luminaries—he would outdo them! He would transcend Pete Townshend, surpass the Rolling Stones, take precedence over Jimmy Page with a two-hour, two-CD set (that's *three* albums for you old-timers) that would encompass all of the prevalent rock sub-genres of the day while telling the uplifting tale of how an angry outcast could emerge lovestruck and heaven-blessed from the dark night of the soul.

A Herculean task, you say? No! Merely Corganian.

And so it is that we have *Mellon Collie and the Infinite Sadness*. Unfortunately, the album isn't the crowning jewel of Corgan's insatiable musical ambition. It's a sprawling, '90s rock mishmash that's ultimately undone by the very ambition that fueled it. You see, the broad sonic and stylistic scope of *Mellon Collie and the Infinite Sadness* isn't its strength, it's its fatal flaw, and it's attributable to Corgan's fundamental misreading of what made albums such as *Exile on Main St.* and *Quadrophenia* great in the first place. It's true that there's something inherently grand and ambitious and flamboyant about most of rock's legendary double albums. They are indulgent and over the top and, frankly, kind of show-offy, and unapologetically so. The whole "Dr. Jimmy / The Rock / Love, Reign O'er Me" finale to *Quadrophenia* is almost ridiculously melodramatic, and more than a little self-pitying. Hell, just the phrase "Love, Reign O'er Me" is probably too fancy-pants for its own good.

There's no question that *The Wall* inflates its depiction of Western man's collective 20th Century neuroses with such gloomy, Mahler-like grandiosity that by side four, it's arguably crossing the line from morosely gripping spectacle into macabre bombast. And, let's face it, for all its finely-shaded, deftly-crafted art-rock songwriting, the storyline to Genesis' *The Lamb Lies Down on Broadway* is nuttier than a Mr. Peanut skin graft.

But while many of rock's great double albums have a tendency to leave restraint and even sensibility behind when it comes to storytelling and arranging, they all are remarkably disciplined in terms of stylistic coherence. And that's precisely what allows them to pack such a devastating aesthetic punch despite their often-kooky accoutrements.

Sure, the Stones wrapped their drooping, booze-palsied arms around not just rock but country and gospel and the blues over the course of *Exile on Main St.* But those genres were all just facets of the same bedrock Americana that was always the core of the band's sound. (They would thankfully save their more dubious dabbling in reggae and disco for a later day.)

On *Something / Anything?*, Todd Rundgren casually tossed off a slough of utterly brilliant songs that explored every sonic variant of "pop" then known to man (and maybe even invented a few more in the process). But Rundgren never actually ventured outside the relatively well-defined confines of "pop" as he did so.

However, on *Mellon Collie and the Infinite Sadness,* Corgan acts as if little is beyond his ability, and so he ranges freely through quasi-thrash-metal, baroque pop, acoustic balladry, and grunge. Now, if you're determined to create an album that leaves a truly seismic impression, that's not a bad approach to take. The problem is that Corgan just doesn't have much affinity for some of those genres, and the result is a confused effort whose songs fit together about as well as the misshapen miscreants of *The Island of Dr. Moreau.* The basic flaw is that Corgan's talent for melodic mid-tempo pop rock is stretched to the breaking point. Again and again, his songwriting reach exceeds his grasp. While he knows the general sonic attributes of metal and baroque pop, he doesn't really know how to write in these styles, and it shows.

Take "Fuck You (An Ode to No One)." This pounding riposte to unnamed others for unspecified wrongs is delivered in what's supposed to pass for a kind of venomous thrash-metal. Corgan does replicate the clattering, Gatling-gun guitar stammer that's the genre's aural fingerprint, but the song is a formless, hookless tantrum devoid of, say, Metallica's imposing melodic architecture, or Slayer's diabolic intricacy and menace. Basically, the tune delivers little more than the kind of rudimentary jackhammering that makes bands like Deicide such second-rate outfits.

A few songs later, Corgan gives us "Cupid de Locke." (I'll get to these song titles later.) Over a gently bouncing beat, he sets a limpidly lyrical pop tune colored with a sampled harp figure and slurry keyboard harmonies that coalesce to create a mood of gently trippy exotica. It's a lighter example of the kind of spangled psychedelic sound painting that My Bloody Valentine executed so brilliantly before it imploded. But where that band used this approach to produce memorably creepy and mind-altering music, Corgan comes up with the sonic equivalent of a pleasant but largely decorative watercolor.

Much later in the album, Corgan prepares listeners to bid farewell with the penultimate number, "By Starlight," one of those slow, stately rock ballads designed to imply resolution. It's the kind of tune that often pops up near the end of rock masterpieces, such as Spirit's *The Twelve Dreams of Dr. Sardonicus* or the Pretty Things' *Parachute*. Unfortunately, both "By Starlight" and the album closer, "Farewell and Goodnight," are devoid of distinctive chord progressions and memorable melodies. Instead, they seem more like generic exercises in closing numbers designed to evoke a final-curtain mood through wispy acoustic strumming and feathery cooing.

Now, some might say I'm simply cherry picking bum numbers from two hours of music. But *Mellon Collie and the Infinite Sadness* is rife with drab, dull songs that might seem impressive in their sheer number and variety but don't individually stand up to close scrutiny. "Jellybelly," "Where Boys Fear to Tread," "x.y.u.," and "Bodies" are simply redundant examples of the same strident yet utterly hookless hard rock exemplified by "Fuck You (An Ode to Know One)." The far more ethereal and delicate "Take Me Down" and "Thirty-Three" are also as devoid of strong, striking melodies as "By Starlight" and "Farewell and Goodnight." And they seem similarly designed to impart a mood rather than to deliver a truly arresting hook.

I could go on and on, and, of course, that's exactly what this album does.

This is not to say that it is bereft of appealing songs; far from it. Tunes such as "1979," "To Forgive," "Stumbleine," and "In the Arms of Sleep," among several others, all ripple with warm, sonically inviting pop hooks and beguiling musicianship. Not surprisingly, they vividly embody the same tasteful qualities that made *Gish* such a satisfying listen. In fact, somewhere within the jumbled sprawl of *Mellon Collie and the Infinite Sadness,* there is the equivalent of a forty-minute collection of solid, commercially viable pop. However, Corgan was probably aware that "solid, commercially viable pop" is seldom the springboard to superstardom. In the long run, it's often the cutout bin graveyard of so many Catherine Wheels, Kitchens of Distinction, and Gin Blossoms.

273

The lavish size, scope, and funding of the album suggest that Corgan knew a grander fate awaited him, and it did. By getting so many people to buy into the notion that *Mellon Collie and the Infinite Sadness* was the first '90s album that was "great" in the same way that *Exile on Main Street* or *Quadrophenia* were great, he cinched his band's brief status as the most important commercial rock outfit of its time.

Of course, Corgan's ability to sell that idea rested on more than the stylistic scope of the songwriting or the ample breadth of the music. He also larded the album with an impressive array of clever ploys designed to reinforce the supposed significance of the music to both teenage acolytes and more grizzled rock vets. One of those involves the overall presentation of the music. Disc One is subtitled "Dawn to Dusk," while the second disc bears the rubric, "Twilight to Starlight." Corgan clearly wants to leave listeners with the impression that there's some kind of thoughtful storyline or large-scale conceptual plan. In reality, the subtitles seem to be little more than a canard, as this listener hasn't been able to detect any kind of coherent storyline or overarching thematic structure. Moreover, aside from the fairly conventional gambit of placing quiet songs at the opening and close of the album, the ordering of the tunes on each disc doesn't create any kind of impression that reflects or reinforces each disc's subtitle.

The fact of the matter is that the subtitles were pinned on this donkey simply to prop up the idea that there's a grand framework behind the music, when it's really just a loosely connected set of songs.

There are all kind of other little strategies that Corgan employs throughout the album to suggest significance and weightiness. There is the inept and seemingly gratuitous attempt at poetic Shakespearean diction in "Cupid de Locke": "Cupid hath pulled back his sweetheart's bow / To cast divine arrows into her soul / To grab her attention swift and quick / Or morrow the marrow of her bones be thick / With turpentine kisses and mistaken blows." There are also self-important song titles such as "Mellon Collie and the Infinite Sadness" and "Porcelina of the Vast Oceans," which imply grandeur and mythical dimension even though the songs are simply conventional pop tunes.

Then there's the elaborate album art, with its mythical, fairyland motif cribbed from innumerable late-'60s psychedelic masterpieces. This artwork is clearly intended to imply that the music inside is similarly cosmic and mind-blowing. (Note to Corgan: As often loopy as Roger Dean's artwork and Yes's music were, at least there was a very clear, if often impressionistic, connection between the paintings that adorned Yes' albums and the lyrical / musical content inside. Despite repeated listens to *Mellon Collie and the Infinite Sadness*, I have not been able to make any connection between the booklet's collage of rabbits playing baseball before a crowd of infants and any of the songs on the album.)

Individually, all of these little gambits might seem silly and superficial, but in the aggregate, they fulfill their mission exceedingly well, because they contribute to a veneer of substance and significance, a veneer that a large portion of the public bought wholesale. But that's not surprising, because veneer has long been Corgan's middle name.

From the carefully calculated look of his bands, to his "Zero the Hero" T-shirts, to his occasional penchant for face-painting, Corgan seems obsessed with radiating an aura of mystery, of eccentricity, of genius, of stardom. He goes to great lengths to appear cryptic and deep and gifted because that helps generate the buzz he needs to fulfill his arena-sized ambition and quell his apparent need for attention. And if there's one thing he knows how to do, it's getting media attention and cutting his losses when it fades. That's probably why he broke up the Pumpkins when their sales started to slide, and why he pulled the plug on his next band, Zwan, when it failed to ignite a commercial and critical firestorm. He often seems less committed to music than he is to publicity.

It's worth noting that rock history is littered with groups both commercially powerful (Blue Öyster Cult, Jethro Tull) and comparatively slight (Yo La Tengo, Guided By Voices) that have soldiered on through the inevitable ups and downs of a career in music because on some level they genuinely believed in the music they were making. Granted, if no one at all showed up for the next Blue Öyster Cult tour, I'm sure Buck Dharma and Eric Bloom would opt to stay home and watch the royalty checks for "Don't Fear the Reaper" roll in. But as long as those five hundred to one thousand people continue turning up each night, despite the fact that they're a fraction of the group's mid-'70s crowds, the band will still be eager to go out and give them a good show.

Not Corgan. If a band isn't capable of fueling his requisite level of media attention, he doesn't seem to want any part of it. It increasingly appears as if music isn't an end for him, it's the means to an end. And in his case, that end often looks like gossip-column blurbs, courtside tickets for the NBA, and endless speculation about his next move.

In the final analysis, *Mellon Collie and the Infinite Sadness* was a large-scale step in Corgan's plans to climb to the top of the rock celebrity heap, and it was spectacularly successful in that regard, as well as in commercial terms. But far from being a coherent rock masterpiece, it is the arena-sized dream of a club-level talent. One might look more forgivingly on it if it was simply a kind of noble failure, like Love's nineteen-minute opus, "Revelation." But loaded as it is with gratuitous grandeur and hyperbolic gestures, it often seems more like a ruse than a record for the ages.

RADIOHEAD
OK Computer
Capitol, 1997
By David Menconi

he "official" version of the saga of Radiohead's *OK Computer* is that it quietly slipped into the marketplace one day in June 1997 with little fanfare—the third album by a well-regarded but relatively obscure British band best-known to college-radio audiences—and the rest of the world went nuts. In this version, no one connected with the band or its label had anything to do with stoking the greatest-album-of-all-time hype that greeted the disc, suddenly turning Radiohead into Godhead.

This is bollocks, of course. In truth, the mythology of *OK Computer* was carefully orchestrated. Months before the album's release, Capitol Records sent out advance promotional copies on cassette tapes that had been permanently glued into portable tape players. This was an expensive promotional gimmick, but it obviously paid off. The idea emerged that *OK Computer* was a conceptual manifesto about technology-induced emptiness, alienation, and paranoia. In the process, it elicited the sort of absurdly grandiose reviews that almost no album could live up to.

OK Computer was released the same year as U2's *Pop*, another ambitious, quasi-electronic movie by a rock band, as well as *Titanic*—a movie that, for all its corniness, was nevertheless a far more effective and less pretentious rumination on futuristic dread involving transportation issues. Like *El Niño* or the identity of Biggie Smalls's murderer, the masterpiece status of *OK Computer* stands as one of 1997's most enduring and poorly understood mysteries. I spent a lot of time that year trying to figure out why I seemed to be the only person I knew who found the album to be completely unmoving. The first time I played it, I thought it was so pompous, dull, and static that I didn't even make it halfway through before giving up and filing the disc away. But after hearing friends talk it up and reading some of the rave reviews—"landmark," "the best album of 1997," "one of the greatest albums of living memory"—I concluded that I must have missed something. So I retrieved the disc from the pile, listened again, got bored again, and filed it away again. After reading still more raves, I tried again. And again. Finally, I decided I was destined never to get it, and I moved on.

Nobody else did, though. It took Bob Dylan's near-death and his best album in two decades to keep *OK Computer* from winning *The Village Voice*'s annual "Pazz & Jop" critics poll, but readers of the British rock magazine *Q* voted *OK Computer* the number-one album of all time, not just of 1997, and they've since made Radiohead the perennial winner of the magazine's annual award for "the World's Best Band." Actor Brad Pitt told *Rolling Stone* magazine that he listened to *OK Computer* for inspiration while filming the movie *Fight Club*, and he called Radiohead "the Kafka and Beckett of our generation." If that's not high-falutin' enough, jazzman Brad Mehldau and classical pianist Christopher O'Riley have given songs from *OK Computer* serious high-art cred by recording reverent covers.

Radiohead mastermind Thom Yorke and his bandmates have reacted to all this adulation with a public stance of revulsion, even as they've done little to discourage this idol worship. *Meeting People Is Easy*, the 1999 documentary drawn from the band's world tour in support of *OK Computer*, should be subtitled, *The Rock Star's Burden*. A true landmark in myth-making passed off as a cry for help, the film's central point seems to be that nothing could possibly be more soul-crushing or dehumanizing than to be in a successful rock band. Interviews are a particular chore, a point that the film beats into the ground with multiple montages of hack questions, many of them in broken English: "What is the stupidest question a journalist ever asked you during an interview?"

By now, Radiohead's critical reputation has grown to such bloated proportions that it has to be addressed in every review of the band as an important aspect of "The Meaning of Radiohead." Radiohead is also the ultimate modern-day symbol of snobby pretentiousness. Do a Google search on the phrase "I hate Radiohead," and see how many hits turn up (not as many as "I love Radiohead," but the gap is closing). Or watch lowbrow rap-rock star Kid Rock's 2002 video for "You Never Met a Motherfucker Quite Like Me," in which he uses toilet paper printed with the word "Radiohead." Or listen to the children. In September 2003, a weekly newspaper in California played a selection of Radiohead songs for a group of fifth-graders, asking the kids to draw pictures based on their impressions of the music. One youngster's drawing showed a graveyard with a dead body strung up lynching-style, surrounded by images of skulls and grim reapers, with a booth to the side advertising "Free Suicides." Another depicted an ominous hooded figure pushing people off a cliff, one of whom calls out his last words: "I hate my life."

While aficionados cite *OK Computer* as Radiohead's masterwork, it's actually not even the best album in the group's catalog. *The Bends* (1995) is still Radiohead's best overall album, a skillful merger of atmospheric production effects and solid popcraft. Radiohead's 1993 debut, *Pablo Honey*, had better (or at least more memorable) songs, led by the breakthrough anti-anthem single, "Creep." *Hail to the Thief* (2003) is also vastly overrated, but it still comes closer to masterpiece status than *OK Computer*. And *Kid A* (2000), which is intermittently unlistenable, at least has the redeeming distinction of being arguably the weirdest album ever to hit number one on *Billboard*'s Top 200 albums chart (besides which, you've got to admire anyone with the nerve to open a record with the immortal line, "Yesterday I woke up sucking a lemon").

Yet it is *OK Computer* that gets cited as Radiohead's "capital-I"

279

Important Record. Even otherwise sensible people who really should know better—meaning people who don't think the perfect Friday night is to fire up a bong and synch up a DVD of *The Wizard of Oz* and an audiophile CD of *The Dark Side of the Moon*—seem to lose all critical faculties when it comes to this album. Ask for an explanation of why it is not the narcolepsy-inducing fraud that it seems to be, and you get a lot of stammering along the likes of, "Like, wow, they're just... so... you know, AMAZING." Or, "At least they're not [insert name of critically reviled current pop star here]." Or maybe you'll hear a lot of psychobabble about technophobia and dread that doesn't really address the disc's crushing musical dullness, or an incredulous, "How could you not like it?" It's as if the magnificence of *OK Computer* is so self-evident that any attempt to explain its greatness in a coherent way would somehow diminish it.

The album does begin promisingly enough, with a metallic guitar riff and a staccato drumbeat that bubbles up from underneath the mix. But then resident genius Yorke's warbly tenor starts in with the gibberish: "In the neeeeeext world waaaaar / In a jackknifed juggernaut, I am born again." A couple of lines later, Yorke declares he is "back to save the universe," then refers to a wreck in "a fast German car" that he was "amazed" to survive, thanks to an airbag. So is this song a tribute to crafty German automobile engineers, or is it about someone with a bizarre Jesus complex? You decide.

Track number two, the single "Paranoid Android," hit the top five of the British charts and is probably the best-known song on the album. That's odd, because it has a disjointed arrangement that feels like several different songs stuck together over the length of its more than six minutes. It starts with a chiming acoustic guitar, builds up to an electric-guitar explosion two minutes later, decelerates to spacey ambience ninety seconds after that, and then speeds up again toward the end. But the parts never quite cohere, and the song itself is a lot less memorable than its grotesque, possibly "South Park"-inspired cartoon video. The lyrics don't make much more sense than the music, describing a first-person narrator stricken by "all the unborn chicken voices in my head." Meanwhile, a faintly heard robotic voice chants in the background, "I may be paranoid, but not an android." Yorke would also like us to know that, "Your opinion… is of no consequence at all," and that, "Ambition makes you look pretty ugly." And, oh yeah, "God loves his children."

"Paranoid Android" accuses, "You don't remember." The object of that declaration might be the narrator of the following song, "Subterranean Homesick Alien," who says, "I keep forgetting." This is actually one of the album's better tunes, with a space-twang guitar riff that ebbs and flows between atmospheric and driving, and twinkling keyboards evoking astral travel. The storyline is even somewhat whimsical, imagining aliens hovering overhead making films of us silly humans for a *Truman Show*-style program back home. But the narrator is afraid to say much about this for fear that he'll be locked up. "I'm just uptight, uptight," Yorke yelps over and over at the end.

Things get truly grim with "Exit Music (for a Film)," which describes running away from someone about whom the narrator can only say, "We hope that you choke" (a sentiment the group found important enough to repeat below the track list on the back cover). Spectral keyboard washes duplicate a choir of minor-key background voices wordlessly howling, giving this the feeling of soundtrack music for a pretentious, subtitled black-and-white film set in Eastern Europe during World War II.

"Let Down" is just as bleak, likening the disorientation of high-speed transportation with life in the food chain. Except Yorke doesn't just feel out of sorts, he feels "crushed like a bug in the ground." The song has no melody to speak of, just a mushy guitar riff that kinds of oozes along without going anywhere—which might be the point, although one would hope there's a less soporific way of making it.

"Karma Police" is one of several songs on *OK Computer* that employs a sing-song nursery-rhyme lilt, with a piano riff reminiscent of "Sexy Sadie" by the Beatles. The song's point seems to be that the fascist brown shirts are on the loose, and they've got a message: "This is what you get when you mess with us." The outro, on which Yorke repeats variations of "I lost myself" over and over as a guitar makes like a helicopter crashing to earth, has the unmistakable odor of something that's supposed to mean something, but unfortunately it doesn't. That's nothing compared to the following "Fitter Happier," which is presented as a sort of hyper-ironic piece of found art. The background consists of piano, computer sounds, and a repeating, faintly heard conversation ("procedure" is the only word that's clearly audible). Up front, the same mechanical voice from "Paranoid Android" chants random and banal phrases seemingly lifted from a lifestyle-advice catalog—"more productive…comfortable…not drinking too much…regular exercise at the gym three days a week"—that gradually wander toward left field. By the end, the song's subject is "no longer empty and frantic like a cat tied to a stick that's driven into frozen winter shit…a pig in a cage on antibiotics." It might qualify as, you know, DISTURBING, if there were any there there.

Fortunately, the following "Electioneering" is the best song on the album. Here Yorke's tendency toward lyrical vagueness works in his favor, because this song's evocation of zero-sum political power seems eerily prescient in light of what happened in the 2000 presidential election: "I will stop at nothing…. When I go forwards you go backwards and somewhere we will meet." It also helps that "Electioneering" has some musical get-up-and-go, with a teeth-rattling guitar riff that combines with Yorke's strangled howl to build up some actual momentum.

Alas, that's about it for the high points. "Climbing Up the Walls" is a slow, pulsing ode to paranoia that just never gets started, and feels like it goes on for about forty-five minutes. The sing-song effect returns on "No Surprises," which ruminates on depression without bringing much to the topic besides an acknowledgement that it exists—although this song is more interesting when it's seen as well as heard, thanks to a creepy video in which Yorke appears to nearly drown. Like "Paranoid Android," the penultimate song, "Lucky," feels like multiple songs stuck together. Finally, this rather dull "masterpiece" closes with "The Tourist," a drowsy tune in which a dog barks at that earlier "Subterranean Homesick Alien" as he flies by. "Hey man, slow down, slow down," Yorke croons. If this were any slower, however, it would be moving in reverse.

The very last sound on *OK Computer* is a bell that rings once. Time for tea, one supposes. Thanks, but you'd better make mine an espresso.

WILCO
Yankee Hotel Foxtrot
Nonesuch, 2003
By Allison Augustyn

I am of the new generation of rock critics, young enough that my "classic" of choice is fairly recent. I call it a classic because I've been told that it is, and I've also been told that I've had the privilege of seeing that classic "in the making." I wasn't actually there, but I was here in Chicago when it was happening, and I suppose that's enough for most people. The "you had to be there" mentality has built a verbal shrine around many an album, protecting it from critical harm. Everyone likes souvenirs, and many of these alleged classics strike me as a way for people to fondly remember pieces of their former lives. It's always hard to live in the now, no matter what you're doing, or how far you've come in life.

The times that I want to remember are well served by the Stooges' *Raw Power*, the Stones' *Let It Bleed*, or Nirvana, Björk, Pavement, and the Silver Jews, to name a few. These are bands with something wild, valid, and interesting to say. I don't get that from Wilco, and I'm surprised by how many people do. As time goes on and this album refuses to die, I have to believe there's something seriously wrong with a generation—my generation—that doesn't relate to something more substantive, or hell, more raucous, than *Yankee Hotel Foxtrot*. It's offensive to be told that Wilco represents me and mine, because I think Wilco is *boring*, and it reinforces the values of a generation I see as tranquilized and unimaginative.

It would be fine if I could turn it off and never hear it again, but I hear it, and hear about it, all the time—in bars, at coffee shops, and even at work. I have many theories about why, but primarily, I think Wilco's popularity is a reflection of people increasingly believing themselves to be accepting thanks to an extended knowledge of other people and their practices. I think the word is "tolerance."

In the process of making some important breakthroughs in becoming more tolerant of one another, we've also been asked to make sacrifices, learning to use politically correct terms and avoid off-color jokes. There's no misogyny allowed, and no women in the kitchen. Blacks, whites, Jews, Catholics, the queers who want to live normal lives, the straights who want to pervert their own exis-tences—everyone's accepted, and nothing is offensive. La-de-dah, everyone's so filled with love and understanding. Meanwhile, I've seen my generation become an inflated group of narcissistic maniacs and spineless morons, so afraid to say anything that no one has any fun anymore, because you can't make any real progress without offending *someone*. At the end of the day, my peers content themselves with settling down and mildly wondering if they'll grow a personali-ty as they crank the latest album by the White Stripes. No one makes an effort, no one gets angry, and no one is inspired.

This is a problem, because my generation has a lot to be angry about. We should be furious about how other people perceive us—as a group of solipsistic egomaniacs with cell phones and deep wallets, ripe for the financial picking as we fumble our way toward finding ourselves. Even if we aren't concerned with a lack of direction, polit-ical convictions, or standards, we should still just want to rip shit up once in a while—to cause some carnage, because, hey, we're young and you only live once.

I recently saw two girls at a club flirting with a couple of tricked-out indie boys wearing tailored jackets and Converse hightops. One of the girls wore a shirt that said "Bitch," and the other wore a top that said "Nice Girl." They must have planned it before they came to the club and started talking about how much they love rock music. But if Mick Jagger or Keith Richards had gotten their hands on either one of them, they'd have been knocked up faster than you can say "Rocks Off." If the rock 'n' roll Bitch had lived up to the promise of her shirt, she'd have taken it off and been pinned up against some guy in the bathroom with a needle sticking out of her arm. *That's* rock 'n' roll for you. There is no such thing as "nice" rock 'n' roll, because rock music isn't about "nice," or it shouldn't be. It didn't use to be. The Stones, Jimi Hendrix, Janis Joplin—they weren't about being nice. But we all know what rock bands *were*: They used to be a force to shake you out of complacency. The problem is determining what they are now.

No matter how hard you try to relate to everyone, all men (and women) are not created equal; sometimes other people are assholes. We should be angry with them, instead of making excuses for them. We should stop being complacent. But for inspiration, we need music to challenge us, not sedate us. From the riots that greeted the debut of Stravinsky's *The Rite of Spring,* to Elvis's scandalous hip-shaking, to a nation of kids in the '90s paying a powerful tribute to the late Kurt Cobain, music can be a compelling force. It can *mean something*.

Kill my idols? There aren't many left. There weren't even that many to begin with. No, I think I'll protect my idols and kill *yours*. It is your fault, after all. Which brings me back to *Yankee Hotel Foxtrot*.

This one goes out to all you rabid fans who argue that if I just listen to the album one more time, I'll finally hear what I've been missing. There's never any thought that maybe *they* are the ones who are missing something. The emphasis is always on the positive; it's easier to like something and support it than it is to hate it and have to fight off a wave of righteous indignation. I will grant that this is not the worst album of all time, but that's part of its problem: It's painful to listen to music that is so close to being solid but is ultimately doomed. To hint at the promise of something good and then pervert it is worse than something being lousy from the get-go. *Yankee Hotel Foxtrot* teases with something like real emotion, but it ultimately fails; its songs come close to being breakthroughs, but then pussy out because... well, I'm not really sure why the band made the choices it did. To be honest, I don't care, because knowing won't make it any better, and after I write this, I won't listen to this album ever again.

There are moments—entire songs even—that are really *catchy*, and there are a few good lyrics here and there. But Wilco is trying too hard to be something that it's not. The band made an album that tries to be cohesive and complete, attempting to create a balance between desperation and loss, happiness and innocence. But it tries to do too much at once, and it wrecks some of its best sounds in the process.

It starts with such promise. "I Am Trying to Break Your Heart" is a brilliant song musically; the instrumentation is heavy and gorgeous, the sound effects are eerie but oddly appealing. But Jeff Tweedy's vocals are so delicate that they sound as if they're broken—out of tune and crumbling—which immediately dispels the enchantment of the music. The vocals don't have to be flimsy to convey the obvious juxtaposition of the loss and anger of the lyrics ("This is not a joke so please stop smiling / What was I thinking when I said it didn't hurt?") with the weird, unnatural tranquillity of the music. If the point is to be purposefully, almost freakishly relaxed about losing a former lover, then there has to be more to support this weird feeling than an unconvincing, distracting voice singing meaningless lines ("I am an American aquarium drinker").

"Radio Cure" is another example of what could have been a beautiful, slow, dark song that becomes something tedious instead when it's interrupted with the simple, childlike chorus, "Distance has no way of making love understandable." In trying to offset the importance of the line, Wilco inserts a completely unrelated and lame glockenspiel and an annoying distorted sound effect. It just doesn't make sense to pull back to sounds this inconsequential after building up to something so tangibly despairing.

At times, the band tries to go in the other direction. "Heavy Metal Drummer" is so utterly unconvincing, so nostalgic and upbeat, that I want to wretch. The lyrics are hideous (except for that great line, "Unlock my body and move myself to dance"), the music so kitschy that it's hard to make it through the song without wanting to throw the stereo out the window. "I miss the innocence I've known,"

Tweedy sings. "Playing Kiss covers, beautiful and stoned." I miss the fifteen dollars I spent on the album, and I wish that I'd been stoned when I listened to it.

There are good songs like "Kamera," which comes as a clean break from the preceding endgame mess of "I'm the Man Who Loves You." It's complete, a slip of a song in a major key with a beginning, an end, and a steady beat in between, and it's imminently listenable. Tweedy is stronger here, using his soft voice more effectively to say, "No, it's not O.K." There's defiance here, instead of the wandering, warbling sound we heard at the start. Despite the ridiculous title, "War on War" is a good follow-up to "Radio Cure," and it makes effective use of more of those weird noises to accentuate the acoustic instruments. "Poor Places" is even better, striking a successful balance between being loose and being chaotic, with a great, slow build at the start. But these songs aren't enough to mark *Yankee Hotel Foxtrot* as any better than any of Wilco's previous albums, much less as a milestone for our generation.

If you still doubt that I'm right, consider the worst offense on the album, "I'm the Man Who Loves You." This far into the disc, it's so surprising to hear anything resembling excitement that the guitar intro sounds almost divinely inspired. The first time I heard it, I was ready to forgive and forget the rest of the band's sins. Finally, something different, something with balls! I should have known that the band couldn't go ten measures without fucking it up. The song is laughable as it shifts from jarring guitar to sugary, laid-back pop bullshit. It's as if the band is reverting to what it knows all those alternative-country fans want. So much for daring reinvention. Yet people love—love!—that song, and I don't know what's wrong with them: It sucks.

The rest of songs on the album are just plain boring. "Jesus, Etc." starts with some pretty nice violin, but it's quickly dragged down by its plain and uninteresting lyrics and melody. "Ashes of American Flags" has the same full sound of "I Am Trying to Break Your Heart," but once again, Tweedy sounds too reedy at the end of the choruses, croaking out weak lyrics such as, "I shake like a toothache / When I hear myself sing." You and me both. "Pot Kettle Black" is hardly worth mentioning, just like "Reservations," the last song on the album, which is so saccharine that it's vile.

That wraps it up. These songs are so bland, I can't even rip on them. There's nothing revelatory here, nothing that hasn't been done before, nothing that you couldn't find from other, better artists. The whole thing just leaves me cold.

I know that Wilco could do much better, which is another frustrating aspect to the album. I recently got my paws on a copy of the *Yankee Hotel Foxtrot* demos, which are great. I mean, really, really good. They're loud and raw and Tweedy's vocals sound much more self-assured. It evokes an emotional response that the studio version doesn't, and it begs the question: If Wilco knows the difference between right and wrong, why did it release what it did? Why did it take the album from someplace gritty and polish all the raw emotion out of it? It isn't right to peddle adult sedation in the guise of youthful gaiety, making boys out of potential men, and taking the whore out of the girls. So why are listeners so willing to embrace this balled-up kitten of an album?

People are too quick to endorse something if the artist's intent is perceived as being good-natured. Back to that happy tolerance. All rock music doesn't have to provoke, but Wilco goes too far to the other feeble extreme when it champions pets and babies wearing tiny Wilco T-shirts, available for sale on the "Kids and Pets" merchandise section of the band's Web site. Rock 'n' roll is about making noise, not making friends. You're supposed to hurt your way into this world, kicking and biting and clawing because that's the only way to get things done. You're supposed to make distinctions between what you value and what you hate. You can't get along with everyone, not everyone is worth your time, and you don't have to accept anything just because it's the easy way. If this essay has made you angry, then at least you know at some level that the music is important, and it's worth your time to think and fight about it.

It feels kind of good to be pissed off, doesn't it? There's hope for you yet.

ABOUT THE CONTRIBUTORS

LORRAINE ALI is a Los Angeles-based writer who specializes in pop music. She is the music critic for *Newsweek* magazine, and has also written about subjects ranging from Palestinian rappers to Italian Mafia music for publications such as *Rolling Stone*, *The New York Times*, and *GQ*. Her top ten albums are: 1.) Marvin Gaye, *What's Going On*; 2.) X, *Los Angeles*; 3.) No Doubt, *Rock Steady*; 4.) Lauryn Hill, *The Miseducation of Lauryn Hill*; 5.) David Bowie, *Ziggy Stardust and the Spiders from Mars*; 6.) Nirvana, *MTV Unplugged in New York*; 7.) the Pogues, *Rum, Sodomy & the Lash*; 8.) Neil Young, *Decade*; 9.) Johnny Cash, *Essential Recordings*; 10.) Fatboy Slim, *On the Floor at the Big Beat Boutique*.

💀💀💀

ALLISON AUGUSTYN writes a music review column for the *Pioneer Press* newspapers, which are distributed in the Chicago suburbs. She has also contributed to the *Chicago Sun-Times*'s *Red Streak*. Her top ten albums are: 1.) (tie) the Rolling Stones, *Exile on Main St.* and *Let It Bleed*; 2.) David Bowie, *Ziggy Stardust and the Spiders from Mars*; 3.) Echo and the Bunnymen, *Ocean Rain*; 4.) Pulp, *Different Class*; 5.) the Silver Jews, *The Natural Bridge*; 6.) Morrissey, *Vauxhall and I*; 7.) Blur, *Parklife*; 8.) the Stooges, *Raw Power*; 9.) Tom Waits, *Nighthawks at the Diner*; 10.) the Jefferson Airplane, *Surrealistic Pillow*.

💀💀💀

ADRIAN BRIJBASSI's first novel, *50 Mission Cap* (Trafford, 2001), was inspired by the music of the Tragically Hip, and he has just completed his second novel, *Gutenberg's Echo*. He is an assistant editor at *Newsday*, and his award-winning writing has appeared in *Confrontation*, *Proteus*, *Newsday*, the *Toronto Star*, *The Kitchener-Waterloo Record*, *The East Hampton Star*, and others. More of his work can be read at www.50missioncap.com. His top ten albums are: 1.) Bruce Springsteen and the E Street Band, *The Wild, the Innocent, & the E-Street Shuffle*; 2.) the Tragically Hip, *Fully, Completely*; 3.) the Doors, *L.A. Woman*; 4.) the Rolling Stones, *Exile on Main St.*; 5.) Bob Marley, *Legend*; 6.) Sarah McLachlan, *Fumbling Towards Ecstasy*; 7.) Kathleen Edwards, *Failer*; 8.) Blue Rodeo, *Five Days in July*; 9.) Terrence Trent D'Arby, *The Hardline According to Terrence Trent D'Arby*; 10.) Buddy Guy, *Feels Like Rain*.

DAVE CHAMBERLAIN's family used to love babysitting for him—push the crib next to the stereo, turn the Black Sabbath up to eleven, and baby Dave was out like a light. Apparently, Ozzy's subliminal rants did some good: He's been the author of *New City*'s weekly Chicago music column, "Raw Material," for seven years, and has garnered writing credits from *Timeout*, *Voyager*, *Gravity*, *Playboy*, *Sportsjones*, and several other publications. His top ten records are, in no order: Nirvana, *Bleach*; Slayer, *Reign in Blood*; Eric B and Rakim, *Follow the Leader*; Sizzla, *Praise Ye Jah*; Sonic Youth, *Sister*; Exploited, *Horror Epics*; Public Enemy, *Fear of a Black Planet*; the Smiths, *The Smiths*; New Bomb Turks, *Destroy Oh Boy*; Ice Cube, *Death Certificate*.

MICHAEL CORCORAN was the country music critic with *The Dallas Morning News* during the Garth Brooks craze. He was paroled in 1995 and has been the music critic and occasional gossip columnist for the *Austin American-Statesman* ever since. He really prefers sports to music. His top ten albums of all time are: 1.) Bruce Springsteen, *Nebraska*; 2.) Elvis Costello, *Get Happy!*; 3.) AC\DC, *Let There Be Rock*; 4.) Elvis Costello, *Trust*; 5.) Bob Dylan, *Highway 61 Revisited*; 6.) Patti Smith, *Horses*; 7.) Geto Boys, *Geto Boys*; 8.) Lou Reed, *Rock 'n' Roll Animal*; 9.) Jane Olivor, *Stay the Night*; 10.) Oasis, *Definitely Maybe*.

CHRISSIE DICKINSON is the former editor of *The Journal of Country Music*. In 2003, she received the Charlie Lamb Award for Excellence in Country Music Journalism, a career-achievement honor given by the International Country Music Conference. She also served as the staff pop music critic at the *St. Louis Post-Dispatch*, and has contributed to a number of publications, including the *Chicago Tribune*, the *Chicago Reader*, *Request*, *Country Music Magazine*, and *Off Our Backs*. She was also the guitarist for the all-female punk bands, the Altered Boys and Sally's Dream. She lives in Chicago, where she is at work on her first book. Her top ten albums are: 1.) the Sex Pistols, *Never Mind the Bollocks... Here's the Sex Pistols*; 2.) Merle Haggard, *A Working Man Can't Get Nowhere Today*; 3.) the original Broadway cast recording, *Sweeney Todd, The Demon Barber of Fleet Street*; 4.) Frank Sinatra, *Strangers in the Night*; 5.) the Band, *The Band*; 6.) Bob Dylan, *Blood on the Tracks*; 7.) X, *Los Angeles*; 8.) the Rolling Stones, *Beggars Banquet*; 9.) Ronnie Dawson, *Monkey Beat!*; 10.) the Pogues, *Rum, Sodomy & the Lash*.

☠ ☠ ☠

DAWN EDEN is a rock historian who has written liner notes for more than eighty CD reissues, including *Harry Nilsson: Personal Best* and many Curt Boettcher-related reissues for Sony, Sundazed, Rev-Ola, and other labels. Her articles have appeared in *Mojo*, Salon.com, the *New York Press*, and *Billboard*. She now composes punning headlines for the *New York Post* and writes about the intersection of faith and popular culture in her Weblog, The Dawn Patrol, at dawneden.com/blogger.html. Her top ten albums are: 1.) the Millennium, *Begin*; 2.) the Zombies, *Odyssey And Oracle*; 3.) Curt Boetcher, *There's An Innocent Face*; 4.) Sagittarius, *Present Tense*; 6.) Judee Sill, *Judee Sill*; 7.) Emitt Rhodes, *Emitt Rhodes*; 8.) John Carter, *Measure for Measure: The John Carter Anthology 1961-1977*; 9.) the Ivy League, *Major League*; 10.) Seymour Hayden, *J.S. Bach: Goldberg Variations*.

☠ ☠ ☠

BURL GILYARD lives and writes in his hometown of Minneapolis. His work has appeared in the *Wall Street Journal*, the *New York Times*, Slate.com, and *Rolling Stone*, but his career has been rolling steadily downhill since his promising start as the co-editor and publisher of the *Page Five* fanzine. His top ten albums are: 1.) the Replacements, *Let It Be*; 2.) Dan Penn, *Nobody's Fool*; 3.) Elvis Presley, *Elvis' Golden Records*; 4.) Willie Nelson, *Who'll Buy My Memories? The IRS Tapes*; 5.) the Beach Boys, *Pet Sounds*; 6.) the Faces, *A Nod Is as Good as a Wink… to a Blind* Horse; 7.) Mudboy & the Neutrons, *Negro Streets at Dawn*; 8.) Warren Zevon, *Warren Zevon*; 9.) Johnny Cash, *At Folsom Prison*; 10.) Big Star, *Third/Sister Lovers*.

JASON GROSS is the straw boss of the online music magazine Perfect Sound Forever (www.perfectsoundforever.com), and he is the perpetrator and instigator behind recent reissues of Kleenex/Liliput and Essential Logic on Kill Rock Stars and Oh OK on Collector's Choice, with more to come as time and sanity permits. Otherwise, when he's not freelancing, he crochets and makes his own ammo. As for his top ten, he writes: "No need for these lists anymore. Load up as many songs as you can on your computer or mp3 player, hit 'random,' and make your own radio station."

MELANIE HAUPT lives in Austin, Texas, and is a regular contributor to the *Austin Chronicle,* the *Houston Press, Denver Westword,* and *Harp* magazine. Her hobbies include drinking tea with too much sugar, pursuing frustrating male-female relationships (usually with poets), and knitting sweaters for her cats. Her top ten albums are, in no particular order: Jeff Buckley, *Grace*; Tori Amos, *Songs from the Choirgirl Hotel*; Martin Sexton, *The American*; Spoon, *Kill the Moonlight*; Tom Waits, *Mule Variations*; Rufus Wainwright, *Rufus Wainwright*; Pavement, *Wowee Zowee*; Nick Drake, *Pink Moon*; Radiohead, *OK Computer*, Modest Mouse, *The Lonesome Crowded West*.

STEVE KNOPPER is a Denver-based writer who has contributed to *Rolling Stone, Spin,* the *Chicago Tribune, Newsday, Esquire, Entertainment Weekly, Wired, New York* magazine, and many other publications. He has edited two books and co-written *The Complete Idiot's Guide to*

Starting a Band, due from Alpha/Penguin in Spring 2004. He spent much of his youth trying to reproduce Keith Moon's drum solo from "Smash the Mirror" using chairs and trash cans. His top ten (in loose order of preference) is: 1.) the Rolling Stones, *Exile on Main St.*; 2.) Public Enemy, *Fear of a Black Planet*; 3.) various artists, *The Anthology of American Folk Music*; 4.) the Beatles, *Revolver*; 5.) the Sex Pistols, *Never Mind the Bollocks... Here's the Sex Pistols*; 6.) the Modern Lovers, *The Modern Lovers*; 7.) Lucinda Williams, *Lucinda Williams*; 8.) the Who, *Sell Out*; 9.) Liz Phair, *Exile in Guyville*; 10.) Television, *Marquee Moon*.

MARCO LEAVITT is a journalist in Albany, New York. He is the author of the stage play, *Smokers*, and an aspiring filmmaker and screenwriter. His top albums are: 1.) Gang of Four, *Entertainment*; 2.) the Mekons, *Until the End of the World*; 3.) Pink Floyd, *Animals*; 4.) the Pretenders, *Pretenders*; 5.) Rancid, *Life Won't Wait*; 6.) the Shoes, *Present Tense*; 7.) Television, *Marque Moon*; 8.) Johnny Thunders, *So Alone*; 9.) the Velvet Underground, *Live 1969*; 10.) the Velvet Underground, *The Velvet Underground*.

CHRIS MARTINIANO sold his soul to the advertising industry in 1995 and is currently devising ways to make you buy stuff from his secret tower in Chicago. Before he came to this crossroads, he spent time in Detroit, cutting his teeth at the *Metro Times*, and hiding from the surging hair-metal scene. You can find him now trying to reclaim his credibility as bassist and guitarist with the punk-rock bands Vortis and Teeth. Oh, and he designed the cover for this book. His "top ten big fucking important records" are: 1.) Slint, *Spiderland*; 2.) the Stooges, *The Stooges*; 3.) Mudhoney, *Mudhoney*; 4.) the MC5, *Kick Out the Jams*; 5.) Wire, *Pink Flag*; 6.) the Cramps, *Songs the Lord Taught Us;* 7.) the Jesus Lizard, *Goat*; 8.) the Velvet Underground, *The Velvet Underground & Nico*; 9.) Run-DMC, *The Kings of Rock*; 10.) the Flaming Lips, *The Soft Bulletin*.

The product of early and frequent exposure to the oeuvres of the Faces, Raymond Chandler, and W.C. Fields, **BOB MEHR** has sacrificed his liver in service of Village Voice Media, New Times, Inc., and the *Chicago Reader*, where he currently works as a music columnist. Although his writing has appeared in numerous publications, including *Mojo*, *Spin*, and *Magnet*, he still hopes to realize a lifelong dream of being the smallest point guard to ever start for the Los Angeles Lakers. His top ten albums are: 1.) the Rolling Stones, *Exile on Main St.*; 2.) Bob Dylan, *Bootleg Series #4: The "Royal Albert Hall" Concert*; 3.) the Clash, *The Clash* (U.S. Version); 4.) Townes Van Zandt, *Live at the Old Quarter (Houston, Texas)*; 5.) (tie) Neil Young, *On the Beach*, and the Replacements, *Tim*; 6.) Rod Stewart, *Never a Dull Moment*; 7.) the Dream Syndicate, *The Days of Wine and Roses*; 8.) the Gun Club, *Fire of Love*; 9.) the Pogues, *Rum, Sodomy & the Lash*; 10.) Uncle Tupelo, *Anodyne*.

DAVID MENCONI is the music critic at *The News & Observer* in Raleigh, North Carolina. He has also written for *No Depression*, *Spin*, and *Billboard* magazines, and is the author of *Off the Record* (www.OffTheRecordBook.com), a novel set in the music business. His top ten albums are: 1.) Sly and the Family Stone, *There's A Riot Goin' On*; 2.) R.E.M., *Murmur*; 3.) the Who, *Who's Next*; 4.) the Beatles, *Rubber Soul*; 5.) Vincent Guaraldi, *A Charlie Brown Christmas*; 6.) the Replacements, *Tim*; 7.) the La's, *The La's*; 8.) various artists, *Nuggets*; 9.) Ennio Morricone, *The Legendary Italian Westerns*; 10.) Big Star, *#1 Record*.

FRED MILLS is an Asheville, North Carolina-based journalist, and, as editor of the short-lived *Biohazard Informae*, a veteran of the late-'70s punk fanzine wars. In addition to penning liner notes, he has contributed to *Stereophile*, *ICE*, *No Depression*, *Harp*, *Option*, *The Bob*, *Creative Loafing*, the *Seattle Weekly*, and *Detroit Metro Times*. He is currently the associate editor of *Magnet* magazine. His top ten albums are: 1.) Neil Young and Crazy Horse, *Everybody Knows This Is Nowhere*;

2.) the Flamin' Groovies, *Shake Some Action*; 3.) the Stooges, *Fun House*; 4.) the Who, *Sell Out*; 5.) the Clash, *Sandinista!*; 6.) the Rolling Stones, *Let It Bleed*; 7.) Patti Smith, *Horses*; 8.) the Allman Brothers, *At Fillmore East*; 9.) Bruce Springsteen, *Darkness on the Edge of Town*; 10.) Spirit, *The Twelve Dreams Of Dr. Sardonicus*.

KEITH MOERER has worked as an editor at *Request, Rolling Stone*, and Amazon.com, and he has written for *Spin, The Village Voice*, and Salon.com. He's currently writing a book about Great Falls, Montana, the strange Western town where he grew up. His "all-time top ten" changes with almost pathological frequency, but the ten albums released in 1972 that he will always enjoy more than *Exile on Main St.* are: 1.) David Bowie, *The Rise and Fall of Ziggy Stardust and the Spiders from Mars*; 2.) Nick Drake, *Pink Moon*; 3.) Randy Newman, *Sail Away*; 4.) Big Star, *#1 Record*; 5.) Dr. John, *Dr. John's Gumbo*; 6.) Curtis Mayfield, *Superfly*; 7.) Neil Young, *Harvest*; 8.) Various Artists, *Nuggets: Original Artyfacts from the First Psychedelic Era, 1965-1968*; 9.) Mott the Hoople, *All the Young Dudes*; 10.) the O'Jays, *Back Stabbers*.

Depending on who you ask, **JEFF NORDSTEDT** is either a burgeoning indie-rock star who maintains a secret life as a publishing executive, or a publishing executive who has a secret life as an indie-rock star. With his band, the Milwaukees, he has toured across the U.S., Canada, and Europe. As vice president of Barricade Books, he has been involved in the publication of hundreds of books, including William Powell's *The Anarchist Cookbook,* Andrew MacDonald's *The Turner Diaries,* Helen Gurley Brown's *Sex and the Single Girl,* and Ed Koch's *Giuliani: Nasty Man.* In his spare time, he reviews albums for *Jersey Beat.* His top ten albums are: 1.) the Clash, *London Calling*; 2.) Elvis Costello and the Attractions, *This Year's Model*; 3.) Nirvana, *In Utero*; 4.) the Beatles, *Rubber Soul*; 5.) Liz Phair, *Exile in Guyville*; 6.) Van Halen, *Fair Warning*; 7.) Thin Lizzy, *Jailbreak*; 8.) Radiohead, *OK Computer;* 9.) the Pixies, *Come On Pilgrim*; 10.) Sugar, *Copper Blue.*

ROB O'CONNOR was the editor of *Throat Culture* fanzine. He has written about socially unredeeming music for *Rolling Stone*, Launch.com, *Musician, Mojo, Entertainment Weekly, Sound & Vision*, Beer.com, and many other publications, and is currently the reviews editor for *Harp* magazine. His top ten albums are: 1.) American Music Club, *Mercury*; 2.) the Stooges, *Fun House*; 3.) Nick Drake, *Bryter Layter*; 4.) Van Morrison, *Veedon Fleece*; 5.) the Bicycle Thief, *You Come and Go Like a Pop Song*; 6.) X, *Los Angeles*; 7.) the Mountain Goats, *The Coroner's Gambit*; 8.) Elvis Costello, *Get Happy!!!*; 9.) Ron Sexsmith, *Other Songs*; 10.) Red House Painters, *Rollercoaster*. He writes, "George Jones, Webb Pierce, Damien Jurado, Richard Thompson, and many others also belong on that list."

💀💀💀

When not teaching English to the college-bound students of southwestern Louisiana, **ARSENIO ORTEZA** writes regular music columns for both *World* magazine and *The Times of Acadiana*. The number-one song in the country at the time of his birth was "Sherry" by the Four Seasons, and his top ten albums are: 1.) Various artists, *Hitsville U.S.A.: The Motown Singles Collection, 1959-1971*; 2.) the Rolling Stones, *Some Girls*; 3.) Loudon Wainwright III, *Grown Man*; 4.) the Globetrotters, *The Globetrotters*; 5.) Maria Muldaur, *Gospel Nights*; 6.) Frank Sinatra, *The September of My Years*; 7.) Quincy Jones, *Q's Jook Joint*; 8.) Queen, *Greatest Hits*; 9.) Arlo Guthrie, *Outlasting the Blues*; 10.) the Incredible String Band, *The Hangman's Beautiful Daughter*.

💀💀💀

Born in Watts and raised in Whittier, California, **TOM PHALEN** was a working musician for fifteen years. When the work and his passion for singing in bars to people who didn't listen waned, he went to work for a local newspaper in Seattle, Washington, and eventually became a music journalist. His writing has appeared in *Rolling Stone, Guitar World, Billboard, Entertainment Weekly, Us*, and *The Seattle Times*. His top ten albums are: 1.) Steely Dan, *The Royal Scam*; 2.) the Beatles, "The White Album"; 3.) Jefferson Airplane, *After Bathing At Baxter's*; 4.) Love, *Forever Changes*; 5.) Randy Newman, *Little Criminals*; 6.)

Buffalo Springfield, *Again*; 7.) Shawn Colvin, *Fat City*; 8.) Fountains of Wayne, *Utopia Parkway*; 9.) the Rolling Stones, *Let It Bleed*; 10.) the Beatles, *Rubber Soul*.

☠ ☠ ☠

LEANNE POTTS lives in Albuquerque, New Mexico, and is the pop culture writer for the *Albuquerque Journal*. She was born and raised in Alabama and got her B.A. at Auburn University. She has won several state and national writing awards. She likes indie rock, alt-country, naps, martinis, macaroni and cheese, staring into space, Mardi Gras, dogs, parrots, pop culture of no-, low-, and highbrow, her iPod, and letting the world know she still gives a rat's ass. Her top ten albums are, in no particular order: U2, *The Joshua Tree*; Nirvana, *Nevermind*; R.E.M. *Murmur*; Prince, *1999*; the B-52's, *The B-52's*; Beck, *Odelay*; Van Halen, *Van Halen*; Los Lobos, *How Will the Wolf Survive?*; X, *Los Angeles*; Run-DMC, *Run-DMC*.

☠ ☠ ☠

BOBBY REED was born in Nashville and lives in Chicago. He has contributed articles to the *Chicago Sun-Times, Country Music Today, Country Weekly, Harp, No Depression,* and *Road King*. His top ten albums are: 1.) Bob Dylan, *Blood on the Tracks*; 2.) Lucinda Williams, *Lucinda Williams*; 3.) the Clash, *London Calling*; 4.) Neil Young, *Comes a Time*; 5.) Dwight Yoakam, *Hillbilly Deluxe*; 6.) Guy Clark, *Old No. 1*; 7.) Weezer, *Weezer* (1994); 8.) the Specials, *The Singles Collection*; 9.) Ella Fitzgerald, *Ella in Rome: The Birthday Concert*; 10.) Neko Case, *Blacklisted*.

☠ ☠ ☠

RICK REGER is a freelance writer living in the Chicago suburbs and contributing primarily to the *Chicago Tribune*. His favorite albums are, in no particular order: John Cale, *Paris 1919*; Steely Dan, *Katy Lied*; PJ Harvey, *Stories from the City, Stories from the Sea*; Felt, *The Strange Idols Pattern and Other Short Stories*; Love, *Forever Changes*; Hüsker Dü, *Flip Your Wig*; the Television Personalities, *Privilege*; Todd Rundgren, *Something/Anything?*; the Bevis Frond, *New River Head*; Frank Zappa and the Mothers of Invention, *One Size Fits All*.

☠ ☠ ☠

ANDERS SMITH LINDALL lives in Chicago, where he roots for the Cubs, rails at the state of our beleaguered union, and writes about rock 'n' roll for the *Chicago Sun-Times*, *City Pages*, *Harp*, *No Depression*, and other publications. His opinions and expositions have also appeared in Salon.com, the *Chicago Reader*, Addicted to Noise.com, *Request*, and many more proponents of the printed word, most of them now defunct. His top ten albums of all time are: 1.) the Beatles, *Revolver*; 2.) Bob Dylan, *Blood on the Tracks*; 3.) the Replacements, *Let It Be*; 4.) R.E.M., *Murmur*; 5.) Uncle Tupelo, *Still Feel Gone*; 6.) Lucinda Williams, *Lucinda Williams*; 7.) Aretha Franklin, *I Never Loved A Man The Way I Love You*; 8.) Big Star, *Third/Sister Lovers*; 9.) Tom Waits, *Bone Machine*; 10.) Nick Drake, *Bryter Layter*.

DAVID SPRAGUE is a former editor of *Creem* magazine and a writer whose work has appeared in *Variety*, the *Village Voice*, the *Daily News*, the *New York Post*, *Rolling Stone*, *Billboard*, and the *Cleveland Plain Dealer*. His top ten albums are: 1.) the Dictators, *Go Girl Crazy*; 2.) John Coltrane, *A Love Supreme*; 3.) Love, *Forever Changes*; 4.) the Stooges, *Fun House*; 5.) the Ramones, *Ramones*; 6.) the Rolling Stones, *Sticky Fingers*; 7.) Television, *Marquee Moon*; 8.) Pere Ubu, *Dub Housing*; 9.) James Brown, *Live at the Apollo*; 10.) Run-DMC, *Run-DMC*.

ALLISON STEWART is a freelance writer living in New York City. She has written for the *Washington Post*, *Rolling Stone*, *No Depression*, and the *Chicago Tribune*. Her top ten albums are: 1.) the Replacements, *Tim*; 2.) Bruce Springsteen, *Tunnel of Love*; 3.) Son Volt, *Trace*; 4.) Liz Phair, *Exile in Guyville*; 5.) U2, *Rattle and Hum*; 6.) Radiohead, *The Bends*; 7.) Joe Henry, *Kindness of the World*; 8.) various artists, *The Stax Story*; 9.) Uncle Tupelo, *Anodyne*; 10.) the Verve, *Urban Hymns*.

STEVEN STOLDER is a Seattle-based freelance writer. His past experience includes stints as managing editor for Amazon.com books & music, editor of *BAM* magazine, and contributor to *Rolling Stone*, *Request*, *Pulse*, the *San Francisco Chronicle*, and *Entertainment Weekly*.

He's currently working on developing a new music and culture magazine. His top ten albums are: 1.) Bob Dylan, *John Wesley Harding*; 2.) the Replacements, *Let It Be*; 3.) Junior Wells, *Hoodoo Man Blues*; 4.) Nirvana, *MTV Unplugged in New York*; 5.) the Beach Boys, *Pet Sounds*; 6.) the Zombies, *Odessey & Oracle*; 7.) Dusty Springfield, *Dusty in Memphis*; 8.) the Flying Burrito Brothers, *Gilded Palace of Sin*; 9.) the Clash, *The Clash* (U.S.); 10.) Loudon Wainwright III, *Last Man on Earth*.

JIM TESTA is best known as the editor of *Jersey Beat*, the music fanzine that he has published continuously since 1982. As a freelancer writer, his work has appeared in publications ranging from *Rolling Stone*, *Request*, and *Guitar World*, to fanzines such as *MaximumRockNRoll*, *Punk Planet*, and *The Noise*. He takes particular pride in noting that *Jersey Beat* helped launch the rock-crit careers of Dawn Eden, Karen Schoemer, Ben Weasel, and many others, although he refuses to take the blame for Jim DeRogatis. His ten favorite albums of all time are: 1.) the Ramones, *Rocket to Russia*; 2.) the Velvet Underground, *The Velvet Underground & Nico*; 3.) the Beach Boys, *Pet Sounds*; 4.) R.E.M., *Murmur*; 5.) Patti Smith, *Horses*; 6.) the Feelies, *Crazy Rhythms*; 7.) Nirvana, *Nevermind*; 8.) Bob Dylan, *Blood on the Tracks*; 9.) Television, *Marquee Moon*; 10.) the Modern Lovers, *The Modern Lovers*.

By day, **ERIC WAGGONER** teaches American Literature and Cultural Studies at a Mid-Atlantic liberal arts college. By night, he's an itinerant music writer for *Magnet*, *Harp*, *Jazziz*, and several other magazines and alt-weeklies, thereby proving that if a man is going to be passionate about one low-paying activity, he might as well be passionate about two, if he wants to make the rent and buy gin. His top ten albums are: 1.) Tom Waits, *Swordfishtrombones*; 2.) Bob Dylan, *Bringing It All Back Home*; 3.) Captain Beefheart & His Magic Band, *Doc at the Radar Station*; 4.) the Velvet Underground, *White Light / White Heat*; 5.) John Coltrane, *A Love Supreme*; 6.) the Residents, *Third Reich and Roll*; 7.) Funkadelic, *Maggot Brain*; 8.) Patti Smith, *Horses*; 9.) Black Flag, *Damaged*; 10.) Ween, *The Pod*.

JIM WALSH is a columnist for *City Pages* in Minneapolis, a sometimes-singer-screamer-songwriter, and the former pop music critic for *The St. Paul Pioneer Press*. He has written for myriad publications, and his essay, "Baptism by Bruce," is included in the first edition of the Da Capo Best Music Writing series. A 2002-2003 John S. Knight Fellow at Stanford University, he has long been intrigued by Warren Commission minutia and Mick Jagger's fear of getting shot on stage. He lives in Minneapolis with his wife, Jean, and their children, Henry and Helen; no guns are allowed on the premises. His top ten albums are: 1.) the Clash, *The Clash*; 2.) Lucinda Williams, *Lucinda Williams*; 3.) Bruce Springsteen, *Born to Run*; 4.) the Ramones, *Ramones*; 5.) Al Green, *Greatest Hits*; 6.) the Replacements, *Let It Be*; 7.) Jackson Browne, *Late for the Sky*; 8.) Bob Dylan, *Blood on the Tracks*; 9.) the Rolling Stones, *Exile on Main St.*; 10.) the Only Ones, *Even Serpents Shine*.

💀💀💀

ANDY WANG, founder of the award-winning online magazine, Ironminds.com, is an editor at the *New York Post*. He was on the launch team of MSNBC.com and worked as the features editor at *Gear*. His criticism has appeared regularly in the *Las Vegas Weekly*, *New York Press*, and Chicago's *New City*, and his work has also been published in the *New York Times* and numerous other daily and weekly newspapers. His top ten albums are: 1.) Guns N' Roses, *Appetite for Destruction*; 2.) R.E.M., *Out of Time*; 3.) the Magnetic Fields, *69 Love Songs*; 4.) Nine Inch Nails, *Pretty Hate Machine*; 5.) Elliot Smith, *XO*; 6.) Social Distortion, *Social Distortion*; 7.) Pet Shop Boys, *Actually*; 8.) Interpol, *Turn on the Bright Lights*; 9.) Bright Eyes, *Lifted or The Story is in the Soil, Keep Your Ear to the Ground*; 10.) Jewel, *Pieces of You*.

💀💀💀

MARC WEINGARTEN is a writer in Los Angeles. His work appears in the *New York Times*, the *New York Observer*, *San Francisco* magazine, and *Entertainment Weekly*. His book, *Who's Afraid of Tom Wolfe?*, a history of New Journalism, will be published in 2005. His top ten albums are (in alphabetical order): 1.) Big Star, *#1 Record*; 2.) the Beach Boys,

About the Contributors

Pet Sounds; 3.) Black Sabbath, *Paranoid*; 4.) Todd Rundgren, *The Ballad of Todd Rundgren*; 5.) Captain Beefheart & His Magic Band, *Trout Mask Replica*; 6.) Led Zeppelin, untitled ("IV"); 7.) Love, *Forever Changes*; 8.) Neil Young, *Everybody Knows This is Nowhere*; 9.) Jimi Hendrix, *Axis / Bold as Love*; 10.) X, *Wild Gift*.

☠ ☠ ☠

ABOUT THE EDITORS

JIM DeROGATIS is the pop music critic at the *Chicago Sun-Times*, a contributor to *Spin, Guitar World, Modern Drummer, Harp*, and Playboy.com, and the co-host of *Sound Opinions*, the world's only rock 'n' roll talk show, on WXRT-FM and WTTW TV in Chicago. He has written three books: *Let It Blurt: The Life and Times of Lester Bangs, America's Greatest Rock Critic* (Broadway Books); *Turn On Your Mind: Four Decades of Great Psychedelic Rock* (Hal Leonard), and *Milk It! Collected Musings on the Alternative Music Explosion of the '90s* (Da Capo). He jokes that he is not a musician, but he *is* a drummer, and he has released two albums with the band Vortis. His top ten albums change three times daily, but at this particular moment, he's going with: 1.) Wire, *Pink Flag*; 2.) Nirvana, *In Utero*; 3.) the Flaming Lips, *Transmissions from the Satellite Heart*; 4.) My Bloody Valentine, *Loveless*; 5.) the Velvet Underground, *White Light/White Heat*; 6.) De La Soul, *3 Feet High and Rising*; 7.) X-Ray Spex, *Germfree Adolescents*, 8.) the Feelies, *Crazy Rhythms*; 9.) Brian Eno, *Here Come the Warm Jets*; 10.) the Beatles, *Revolver*.

☠ ☠ ☠

Born and raised on the South Side of Chicago, **CARMÉL CARRILLO** is a self-taught photographer and theremin player. She is an assistant editor at the *Chicago Tribune* and has worked at the *Baltimore Sun*, the *Chicago Sun-Times, Newsday*, and the *St. Louis Daily Record*. She studied classical flute for several years and therefore declined to list her top ten rock albums in order to avoid embarrassing herself and her loved ones. She is currently finishing a chapbook titled *Beyond the Gate: Childhood Poems and Portraits*.